PRAYER

and the

PRIESTHOOD OF CHRIST

in the Reformed Tradition

PRAYER

and the

PRIESTHOOD OF CHRIST

in the Reformed Tradition

GRAHAM REDDING

T & T CLARK
A Continuum imprint
LONDON • NEW YORK

T&T CLARK LTD
A Continuum imprint

59 George Street
Edinburgh EH2 2LQ
Scotland

370 Lexington Avenue
New York 10017–6503
USA

www.tandtclark.co.uk

www.continuumbooks.com

First published 2003

ISBN 0 567 08883 9

British Library Cataloguing-in-Publication Data
A catalogue record for this book is available from the British Library

Typeset by Fakenham Photosetting Ltd, Fakenham, Norfolk
Printed and bound in Great Britain by MPG Books, Bodmin

Contents

Acknowledgements

This study is the product of doctoral research and parish ministry. It is intended for liturgists and parish ministers as well as students and teachers of theology. To the people of Somervell Memorial Presbyterian Church I owe a debt of thanks, not only for being partners in prayer and ministry for nine wonderful years, during which time this research was completed, but for their willingness to grant me a one-year sabbatical, their financial support, and their encouragement to complete my doctoral studies.

To my doctoral supervisor, Professor Alan Torrance, I also owe much. It was he who first opened my eyes to the fact that theology, properly understood, is grounded in the act of worship and should never be an exercise in abstract speculation. His friendship and encouragement and, above all, his sheer enthusiasm for theology, have meant a great deal.

Professor Torrance, of course, is related to the two leading figures in this book, the Very Reverend Thomas F. Torrance and Professor James B. Torrance. It has been a privilege to meet both these gentlemen and a joy to discover that they are churchmen of immense wisdom and men of prayer, as well as theologians of considerable stature. For the very kind hospitality extended by James and Mary Torrance towards my family during our brief stay in Edinburgh, I am especially grateful.

I acknowledge with love and gratitude the support provided by my wife Jenni, especially during our year in London. It was a wonderful year in so many ways, not least in relation to our family life together.

Last, but not least, I acknowledge my mother, Colleen, who, during the course of my research, struggled with terminal cancer. I rejoice that such a difficult period saw grace and peace flourish in her life. It became a time of prayer, in which the priesthood of Christ was very evident on a personal level. It is to the memory of my mother, whose life and humanity was joined to and clothed with Christ's in the final weeks of her life, that this volume is dedicated.

Introduction

Defining the Issue and Setting the Agenda

In his book, *Worship, Community and the Triune God of Grace*, James Torrance makes the critical observation that most worship today 'is in practice unitarian, has no doctrine of the mediator or sole priesthood of Christ, is human-centred, has no proper doctrine of the Holy Spirit, is too often non-sacramental, and can engender weariness'.[1] Accordingly, worship and prayer are regarded as things that *we* do – no doubt enabled by God's grace and following Jesus' example – but still things that *we* do. 'In theological language,' says Torrance, 'this means that the only priesthood is our priesthood, the only offering our offering, the only intercessions our intercessions.'[2]

What is intriguing about this description of the unitarian nature of contemporary worship and prayer is that, to the extent that it is true, it flies in the face of a strong revival of trinitarian doctrine that has been sweeping through the Church in recent decades. R. J. Feenstra and C. Plantinga note that 'virtually every serious theological movement of recent years has sought on its own terms to state and shape trinitarian doctrine'.[3] Commenting on the same trend, Colin Gunton notes its truly ecumenical nature. Treatises on the Trinity, he says, now represent all the main traditions of Christendom: 'Roman Catholic (Kasper), Orthodox (Zizioulas), Lutheran (Jensen), Reformed (Moltmann) and Anglican (Brown)'.[4] Liberation

---

[1] J. B. Torrance, *Worship, Community and the Triune God of Grace* (Downers Grove, Illinois: InterVarsity Press, 1996), p. 20.
[2] Torrance, *Worship, Community and the Triune God of Grace*, p. 20.
[3] R. J. Feenstra and C. Plantinga, Jr, eds, *Trinity, Incarnation, and Atonement: Philosophical and Theological Essays* (Notre Dame, Indiana: University of Notre Dame Press, 1989), p. 3.
[4] C. E. Gunton, *The Promise of Trinitarian Theology* (Edinburgh: T&T Clark, 1991), p. 1.

theologians and feminist theologians have seen in the Trinity a model for the liberation and transformation of human society.[5] It is used as a basis for defining Christian ethics, promoting models of human sociality and community, articulating theologies of personhood, and developing theological anthropologies, as well as dictating the shape of more conventional doctrinal concerns, namely, the doctrine of God, soteriology and ecclesiology.

Immanuel Kant once argued that 'from the doctrine of the Trinity, taken literally, nothing whatsoever can be gained for practical purposes, even if one believed that one comprehended it – and less still if one is conscious that it surpasses all our concepts'.[6] Undergirding the contemporary revival in trinitarian thinking is a conviction that Kant and his followers were wrong. The Trinity is deemed to be highly relevant for today's world. Hence the irony of Torrance's criticism, because, to the extent that it is true, it suggests that the resurgence of trinitarian doctrine is failing to overcome and transform unitarian tendencies in Christian worship and prayer. Despite the strong impetus given by the liturgical movement to a renewed trinitarian emphasis in the theology and practice of worship, unitarian tendencies persist and, especially in non-liturgical worship within the Reformed tradition, there appears to be a gap and, indeed, a contradiction, between that which is being so strongly affirmed at a doctrinal level and that which is being embodied in the worshipping life of the Church.

In this context, and in the light of Torrance's further criticism of the lack of a doctrine of the priesthood of Christ

---

[5] Leonardo Boff, for example, describes the Trinity as good news for men and women, especially for the poor. He writes: 'Society is not ultimately set in its unjust and unequal relationships, but summoned to transform itself in the light of the open and egalitarian relationships that obtain in the communion of the Trinity, the goal of social, and historical process. If the Trinity is good news, then it is so particularly for the oppressed and those condemned to solitude' (*Trinity and Society*, trans. P. Burns (New York: Orbis, 1988), p. 158).

[6] I. Kant, *Der Streit der Fakultaten*, PhB 252, p. 34, cited by J. Moltmann, *The Trinity and the Kingdom of God*, trans. M. Kohl (London: SCM Press, 1981), p. 6.

in contemporary worship, an interesting question arises: What difference would a proper doctrine of the priesthood of Christ make to the Christian conception of worship and prayer? It is with that question, especially as it pertains to liturgical prayer, that this book is concerned. The relevance of the question is accentuated by the current resurgence in trinitarian thinking, and by an inextricable link between the doctrines of the Trinity and the priesthood of Christ. Indeed, as we shall see in Chapter One, it was as the Church responded, from the fourth century onwards, to a variety of doctrinal issues of a trinitarian and christological nature that it experienced a profound shift in both the structure of its prayers and the dynamics of its worship. The irony was that doctrinal clarity in relation to the doctrine of God heralded liturgical uncertainty in relation to the vicarious humanity and priesthood of Christ.

Ever since then, the Church has struggled to overcome this uncertainty. In the Scottish Reformed tradition, with which we are concerned in this book, the struggle is particularly evident. On the one hand, as we shall see in Chapter Two, John Calvin and those who introduced his doctrine to Scotland, including John Knox and John Craig, articulated the Reformed principle of *sola gratia* in a thoroughly trinitarian way, both doctrinally and liturgically. Moreover, they saw that trinitarian thinking is inconceivable without a proper appreciation of the mediatorial role of Christ, certainly in relation to the atonement, but also in relation to prayer and worship. On the other hand, the Westminster tradition's attempt similarly to impart a trinitarian doctrine of God and proclaim *sola gratia* was undermined by its failure to grasp the nature and extent of Christ's vicarious humanity and priesthood. We shall consider the reasons for this, and its effects, in Chapter Three.

Although the federal Calvinism of the Westminster tradition largely defined Reformed doctrine and worship for nearly two hundred years, the struggle was not over. In Chapter Four, we shall focus on John McLeod Campbell who, in his teaching on the atonement and prayer, challenged the doctrinal presuppositions of federal

Calvinism, gave renewed emphasis to the human priesthood of Christ, and provided the theological basis for subsequent liturgical reform. We shall consider, albeit briefly, some of the main features of that nineteenth-century reform and its leading contributors.

In Chapter Five, in and through a comparative study of eucharistic liturgies dating from the Genevan Reformation through to the current day in the Church of Scotland, we shall consider the extent to which the Reformed tradition's struggle to see the significance of the priesthood of Christ for prayer has manifested itself in the worshipping life of the Church.

Finally, in the Conclusion to this book, we shall seek to identify the distinguishing features of a doctrine of prayer that gives full recognition to the vicarious humanity and priesthood of Christ, and, indeed, to explore the extent to which a recovery of interest in the doctrine of the Trinity requires a parallel recovery of interest in the priesthood of Christ.

A Word on Scope

In focusing primarily on the Scottish Reformed tradition it is clear that our intention in this book is not to provide a comprehensive historical survey of the relationship between the priesthood of Christ and prayer in Christian doctrine. Rather, it is to discuss the importance of the issue with reference to a particular tradition. In attending to the works of T. F. and J. B. Torrance on this subject, both of whom are ordained ministers within the Church of Scotland, we will, to a certain extent, be following their lead, and concentrating on those areas on which they themselves have written extensively. As such the book will serve, in part, as a critical evaluation of their analysis of a central weakness in the Christian tradition, and their attempts constructively to address this. It will also, in the Conclusion, probe the significance of these issues for contemporary theological and ecumenical debates. In other words, our historical analysis serves a deeper theological agenda, which will become apparent as the book proceeds.

A Preliminary Comment on Atonement, Worship and the Priesthood of Christ in Scripture

Although this book focuses primarily on theological and liturgical issues, many of these issues have their origin in scripture. For this reason, the following summary of biblical teaching, as it pertains to our subject area, is offered.

The interrelation of atonement and worship

In the cultic life of ancient Israel, which we see in the Old Testament, atonement and worship were interrelated. As Trevor Hart observes in his aptly titled article, 'Atonement and Worship', a substantial part of Israel's worship 'was concerned precisely with the mode of atonement for sin prescribed by God'.[7] Reconciliation with God was a liturgical act.

The same interrelation between atonement and worship is carried over into the New Testament, where Jesus is presented both as the One who atones for sin, once and for all, and as the One whose human life glorifies the Father and in whom the Father is well pleased. In him there is perfect atonement and perfect *koinonia* between God and humankind.

It is important to bear this interrelation in mind as the book proceeds, because virtually all of the issues that we will be considering in relation to prayer and worship are bound up with issues that pertain to the atonement. As Hart succinctly sums it up, 'the logic of atonement and worship are basically the same'.[8]

The high priest and the sacrificial cult

At the heart of Israel's religious cult and sacrificial system stood the person of the high priest, who, through his

---

[7] T. Hart, 'Atonement and Worship', *Anvil* 11.3 (1994), p. 208.
[8] Hart, 'Atonement and Worship', p. 203.

vicarious ritual of sacrifice and prayer mediated at-one-ment between God and the people of Israel. While the cult required the services of many priests, it was the high priest alone who entered into the presence of God on the Day of Atonement, embodying in his own person the continuance of the covenant relationship, and making an atonement for the whole nation. The covenant between God and Israel was concentrated as it were in the person of the high priest.

For the purposes of this book, two aspects of that annual cultic ritual need to be highlighted. The first of these concerns the twofold representative role of the high priest. When he entered into the holy presence of God in the sanctuary that he might present all Israel in his person to God, *all Israel entered in his person*. Conversely, when he vicariously confessed their sins and interceded for them before God, God accepted them and forgave them *in the person of the high priest*.[9]

The vicarious role of the high priest is of crucial importance, for it establishes the twofold fact that the covenant was maintained and renewed at the hands of a mediator, and that mediator, though divinely appointed and anointed for the task, was truly of the people – he was bone of their bone and flesh of their flesh. In the context of the cultic ritual his humanity was no longer the humanity of a solitary individual – it was a vicarious humanity. Accordingly, the act of atonement was never regarded as some kind of divine action that was external to the life and humanity of the people. It occurred in their midst. They were fully involved in it, through the person of the high priest. This is important to bear in mind when we come to consider the role of Christ as High Priest.

The second point worthy of being highlighted concerns the nature of sacrifice, as conveyed in the ritual shedding of blood associated with the sin- and guilt-offerings. As Nugent Hicks puts it, 'the fundamental feature in the sin-

[9] J. B. Torrance, 'The Vicarious Humanity and Priesthood of Christ in the Theology of John Calvin', in *Calvinus Ecclesiae Doctor*, ed. W. H. Neuser, (Kampen, Netherlands: Uitgeversmaatschappij J. H. Koh, n.d.), pp. 69–84, at pp. 75–6.

and guilt-offerings is undoubtedly the use of the blood. It is not the death that atones, but the life (Lev. 17). The death is vital to the sacrifice, because it sets free the blood, which is the life.'[10] The fact that it is not the death that atones, but life, establishes the fact that sacrifices were not desperate, crude attempts to appease an angry deity through the means of ritual slaughter. Rather, they were the means by which God, in a sovereign act of mercy, graciously approached the people of God, covered their sin, overcame their guilt and maintained the holiness of the community. At its best – although it seldom reached this level, according to the prophets – sacrifice was a 'sacrament', a visible means of grace.

In Deutero-Isaiah's portrait of the Suffering Servant the theology of sacrifice attains its highest expression in the Old Testament. The Servant is led like a lamb to the sacrificial slaughter, but his sacrifice has a far greater power than any animal sacrifice. It is a willing self-sacrifice, made for others. The Servant is not a mere scapegoat upon whom people can cast their sins; rather, he is the agent through whom God overcomes broken relations and draws the world into a reconciling embrace.

The connection between the prophetic and priestly traditions

The Old Testament depicts an integral connection between the sacrificial cult, represented by Aaron, and the word and law of God, represented by Moses. Over time, however, a conflict appears to have arisen between the two traditions, which grew into a long tension between priest and prophet and eventually led, in post-exilic times, to the existence of a self-sufficient and independent sacrificial cult that proved incapable of bringing about the true at-one-ment with God that the covenant relationship promised and demanded. The scribe took the place of the prophet, and the Torah

[10] F. C. N. Hicks, *The Fullness of Sacrifice: An Essay in Reconciliation* (London: Macmillan, 1930), p. 18.

took the place of the raw, intervening, independent, eschatological, prophetic word. Devoid of this word, the best the cult could do was point forward to a future time when that which was promised would be fulfilled and the prophetic anticipation of a new covenant would be realised.

Christ: Mediator of a new covenant

It is the New Testament conviction that in Christ the prophetic promise of a new covenant has been established. In his person the prophetic and priestly functions of Moses and Aaron, for so long in tension with one another, have been thoroughly integrated: he is both God's Word and High Priest. As the Word, he is the One who comes with the manifest *exousia* (power) of God as revealed in his life-giving word of forgiveness and healing of the sick. He has authority over the sabbath and over the temple itself, and even over the law. He thus calls both scribe and priest to account.

As High Priest, he is the One in whom and through whom the old sacrificial cult has at last been fulfilled, both in his work and in his very own person, resulting in true and complete at-one-ment between God and humankind. He is the One by whose faithful obedience the new and everlasting covenant is secured, through whose self-offering and sacrifice on the cross the sins of the world are expiated,[11] by whose faith the unrighteous are justified or declared righteous, in whose perfect humanity our fallen humanity is sanctified or made holy, and by whose intercessions the people of God are upheld. As High Priest, Christ stands personally at the centre of the Christian understanding both of the atonement and of worship.

Christ the High Priest and the book of Hebrews

Most interpreters of the epistle to the Hebrews recognise the centrality of the idea of Christ's high priesthood and, at

---

[11] Christ the High Priest is also the Lamb of God. He is both Offerer and Offering.

the same time, its connection to the notion of covenant.[12] Jesus is portrayed as the new and better Moses (3:3), the mediator of a new (9:15; 12:24) and better (8:6) covenant, a priest forever after the order of Melchizedek (7:17).[13] A strong analogy is drawn between the work of Jesus and the role of the high priest on the Day of Atonement. For all the corresponding features[14] that constitute that analogy, there are a number of contrasting features, which Susanne Lehne summarises in the following schematic form:[15]

Cult under Old Covenant	*Cult under New Covenant*
Many mortal priests with genealogy	One high priest lives forever
Appointment by fleshly commandment/law, in weakness	By word of oath perfected forever
Offer for their own sins	Sinless, blameless
Daily earthly ministry	Superior heavenly ministry
Patterns of the heavenly things	The very heavenly things
Holy places made with hands	Heaven itself
Figures of the 'real'	God's presence
Many offerings	One eternal offering
Many (annual) entries	One entry
Continual services	Climax of ages
Limited access; barriers	Access to the 'real'
No final purgation	Sins definitively removed
Sacrifice of animals	Sacrifice of himself
Animal blood	Christ's own blood

---

[12] Cf. S. Lehne, *The New Covenant in Hebrews*, JSNT Supplementary Series 44 (Sheffield: JSOT Press, 1990), p. 94; M. E. Isaacs, *Sacred Space: An Approach to the Theology of the Epistle to the Hebrews*, JSNT Supplementary Series 73 (Sheffield: JSOT Press, 1992), p. 15; and D. J. MacLeod, 'The Doctrinal Center of the Book of Hebrews', *Bibliotheca Sacra* 146 (1989), pp. 291–300.
[13] The book of Hebrews looks behind Aaron to Abraham's day, to Melchizedek, to a prior and personal priesthood before the institutional priesthood of the Levitical law.
[14] Cf. Lehne, *New Covenant in Hebrews*, p. 98.
[15] Lehne, *New Covenant in Hebrews*, pp. 98–9.

The above table highlights the superiority of the new cult, Christ's priesthood, and the new covenant which it mediates.

In interpreting the high priesthood of Christ for the purposes of this book, we may say that the author of the epistle draws attention to at least four interrelated areas, each of which embraces a twofold affirmation. He directs the reader:

(a) To both the *divinity* and *humanity* of Christ, or, in theological terms, the hypostatic union. Redemption is not a divine action that remains external to the human condition but is something that in Christ penetrates to the deepest level of human existence and is worked out from within the limitations and fallenness of that condition.[16]

(b) To both the *work* and the *person* of Christ. What Christ accomplishes is utterly bound up with who he is; he does not act in a way that is contrary to his nature.[17]

(c) To both the *substitutionary* and *representative* aspects of the atonement. The sacrificial death of the One on behalf of the many is utterly bound up with the life of faithful obedience of the One on behalf of the many.[18]

(d) To both that which has *already been accomplished* on our behalf at Calvary and that which *continues to be*

---

[16] Cf. Heb. 5:7–9, which holds together the divinity and humanity of Christ, and portrays salvation as being worked out from within, not apart from, the depths of his humanity.

[17] Throughout the epistle, Christ's sacrificing high priesthood is grounded in who he is in his eternal sonship. It is the unity of person and work, of Priest and Sacrifice in Christ, that means the final end of all sacrificing (Heb. 9:12, 25).

[18] That Jesus is regarded as both substitute and representative is evident from the epistle's references to him as 'a forerunner *on our behalf*' (6:20), as the One who appears 'in the presence of God *on our behalf*' (9:24), and as the One who has opened up a new and living way for us (10:20) – italics mine. We enter the presence of God not with our own confession but with Christ's confession, because he is our forerunner, accomplishing in our stead and on our behalf that which we cannot accomplish on our own. Cf. D. J. MacLeod, 'The Present Work of Christ in Hebrews', *Bibliotheca Sacra* 148 (1991), pp. 184–200, at pp. 188–93.

accomplished on our behalf and through us in worship and prayer.[19]

With this biblical background in mind, we are now in a position to consider the implications of the priesthood of Christ for a Christian doctrine of prayer.

---

[19] The reconciliation wrought by Christ, though complete, is given a counterpart in the worship, adoration and confession of the Church, which renders its offering in, through and with the One whose perfect, atoning, eternal offering of himself alone constitutes an acceptable and pleasing sacrifice to the Father. As Trevor Hart sums it up, 'It is the Church's hallowing of the Father's name which does not and cannot take place apart from the presence in its midst of the one whom the writer to the Hebrews calls our *Archiereus*, our High Priest, who offers to the Father an atoning liturgy in his life and death in our place and on our behalf (See Heb. 4:14–5:10; 7:23–25)' ('Atonement and Worship', p. 212).

1
The Impact of Arianism and Apollinarianism on Liturgical Development, and its Legacy in the Christian West: The Jungmann–Torrance Thesis

While the primary context of this book is the Reformed tradition, and in particular the Church of Scotland, it is important to acknowledge that the debates waged within that tradition often have their conceptual origins in the debates of the early Church. This is so in relation to the doctrine of the priesthood of Christ, at the centre of which stand two fundamental questions: (1) What is the nature and significance of the hypostatic union between God and humankind in the person of Christ?; and (2) What is the nature of Christ's mediatorial or priestly activity in relation to (a) the atonement, and (b) worship and prayer? If the second question focuses mainly on the *work* of Christ, it cannot be answered without addressing the first, and indeed primary, question of *who* Christ is.

It was this first question which occupied the attention of the Church Fathers at the Council of Nicea in AD 325 as they sought to settle the issue of whether the Son was truly *homoousios to patri*, of one being with the Father, in whose very own person God and creation were clasped together in a reconciling union, or whether he was but a created intermediary, a kind of bridging figure between an eternal God and a transient created order who is neither fully God nor fully human. Both doctrinal positions employed biblical texts in support of their respective arguments, and both recognised in Christ a mediatorial function, but they understood that function in contrasting ways, reflecting not only different soteriologies at work, but also conflicting epistemologies and world-views, one Hebraic (unitive) the other Greek (dualistic).

Much more was at stake in this debate than the definition of orthodoxy at a doctrinal level. Also at stake was the way in which worship, prayer and the Christian life were being conceived. It is for this reason that we must acquaint ourselves with some of the key doctrinal debates of the fourth century and the patterns of worship that emerged in their wake. We do so, not attempting to break new ground in the field of patristic studies, but merely to show that the issues, which will be discussed later in this book in relation to the Reformed tradition, are but variations on ancient themes of a truly catholic nature.

Arianism and the Liturgy: The Jungmann Thesis

In 1925, Josef Andreas Jungmann published *The Place of Jesus Christ in Liturgical Prayer*, a book that over time has come to be regarded as one of the classic studies in liturgiology. Through an extensive examination of liturgies in the early Church, ranging from ancient Church Orders, such as the *Didache* (end of the first century) and the *Church Order of Hippolytus* (circa AD 220), to Egyptian, Syrian, Byzantine, Gallic and Roman liturgies, Jungmann detected a distinct shift in liturgical prayer, with regard to its form of address. While from apostolic times private prayers addressed to Christ were customary, and while the tradition of trinitarian formulae in public prayer informs us that Christ was worshipped equally with the Father and the Holy Spirit, the Church mostly kept to the rule of addressing God the Father *through* Christ the High Priest in public prayers of praise and thanksgiving, especially in the Eucharist. As Catherine LaCugna confirms, virtually all extant texts of the pre-Nicene Church, including the *Didache* and the *Church Order of Hippolytus*, are characterised by a mediatory pattern of prayer, especially in the *anaphoras* and doxologies. 'In general,' she notes, 'the thanksgiving of the Eucharistic prayer was offered to God because of what God has done *through* Christ, and the praise giving of the doxological prayer is offered up to God *through* Christ.'[1]

---

[1] C. LaCugna, *God for Us: The Trinity and Christian Life* (San Francisco: Harper, 1991), p. 114.

Origen reflected the practice of his day by instructing that all prayers end 'by praising the Father of all *through* Jesus Christ *in* the Holy Spirit'.[2]

However, by the end of the fourth century, especially in the East, this situation had changed. Liturgical prayers, which once had been addressed to the Father through Christ, were just as likely now to be addressed to the Son alone, or to the Father *and* the Son, or to the Father *and* the Son *and* the Holy Spirit.

The substitution of 'Son' for 'Christ' and the more explicit use of formal trinitarian formulae reveals a distinct move in the Church towards emphasising the *deity* of Christ and highlighting his grandeur within the triune Godhead. Through an examination of the Church's councils, creeds and liturgies Jungmann argues that this was in large part due to the Church's reaction to Arianism.[3] This explains why the changes are evident more in the Eastern Church than in the West, for Arianism initially was a much stronger phenomenon in the East.

Arianism had its strongest ecclesiastical presence and theological influence in the two cities of Antioch and Caesarea. In Caesarea in particular there was a direct confrontation between St Basil the Great, who was bishop, and his Arian opponents. We note Maurice Wiles' argument that Arianism was a much more diverse phenomenon than often has been acknowledged,[4] but we conclude that for all the diversity there was nevertheless a common core of thinking which Wiles himself concedes,[5] namely, an assumed division between the uncreated (eternal and changeless) God and the created (temporal and transient) order, and a stress on the

---

[2] Origen, *De Oratione* 33 (PG 11, 561), cited by LaCugna, *God for Us*, p. 115.

[3] By taking up and extending the train of thought of Origen and of Lucian of Samosata, Arius concluded that the Son is less than the Father. Although possessing divine dignity he is not from all eternity. He is a creature of the Father, made in time, hence subordinate to the Father. Cf. J. Jungmann, *The Early Liturgy: To the Time of Gregory the Great*, trans. F. A. Brunner (London: Darton, Longman and Todd, 1959), pp. 188f.

[4] Cf. M. Wiles, *Archetypal Heresy: Arianism through the Centuries* (Oxford: Clarendon Press, 1996).

[5] Wiles, *Archetypal Heresy*, p. 25.

unchanging transcendence of the Father whose Word, rather than his essential self, was the creative and immanent power of our universe.

The weakness with Wiles' thesis appears to be that, in desiring a fresh appreciation of the insights that Arianism may have to offer the Church, he fails to acknowledge the fundamental contradictions between Arianism and Nicene orthodoxy – for example, in relation to the divinity of Christ. On some matters we cannot afford the luxury of affirming valid insights from both sides of a debate – we simply have to make a choice between two mutually exclusive world-views or theological positions that take us down two quite different paths of doctrinal formulation. That is what the Church did at Nicea, where nothing less was at stake than the very heart of the Christian doctrines of God and salvation.

Doctrinal clarity, liturgical confusion

The influence of Arianism on liturgical developments in the fourth century at first glance is surprising because, at a formal doctrinal level, Arianism had been soundly defeated at Nicea in AD 325. In direct refutation of the Arian claim that Jesus was merely a created intermediary and was not fully divine, the Council of Nicea, under the guidance of Athanasius, stipulated in the Creed that the Son was *of the same substance* (*homoousios*) as the Father. That is to say, he was fully divine, as well as being fully human.

However, while Arianism had been condemned, it was not subdued; the whole century came to be filled with this dispute and even in the following centuries the argument was carried on in one form or another. Indeed, the real influence of Arianism proved to be felt not over the Creeds but over worship, for, as Jungmann argues, it raised fundamental questions about the structure of prayer, and liturgical prayer in particular: May the Son be honoured and adored just like the Father? What position was Christ to occupy in prayer?[6]

---

[6] Jungmann, *Early Liturgy*, p. 189.

Wiles' assertion that people 'do not normally feel so deeply over matters of formal doctrinal statement unless those matters are felt to bear upon the practice of their piety'[7] proved to be precisely the case with Arianism. Its adherents searched the scriptures, collecting all texts in which a 'humbling' was attributed to Christ, and which suggested a subordination of Christ to the Father.[8] They singled out those texts that referred to Jesus praying to the Father. At the same time, they latched on to those prayers and doxologies in the liturgy that were addressed to God the Father through Christ. Jungmann notes that this mode of prayer is found in all the remnants of the liturgy preserved from the era of the primitive Church, including the New Testament itself. The prayers of the *Didache*, for example, end with the doxology, 'For thine is the glory and the power *through* Jesus Christ forever.'[9] The Arians interpreted all prayers that expressed the mediatorial role of Christ as furnishing evidence of the Son's subordination to the Father. Scripture and tradition seemed to bear joint witness to the fact that the Son exists in some sort of intermediary stage below the Father.

Such views were strongly refuted. Certainly there are numerous passages in the Bible that depict Jesus as standing in some manner below the Father. But that is precisely the significance of the incarnation, through which the Son, as a human being, subordinated himself to the Father's will, praying, suffering and dying as a human being so that in his very Person the humanity which he assumed – *our* humanity – might be reconciled to God. Thus understood, the *per Christum* or the *per Filium* of the Catholic liturgy was deemed entirely appropriate: as One who is fully human, Christ is our Saviour and High Priest; as One who is fully human, he is now our Mediator with the Father.

However, while this might have been clear at a doctrinal level – and the Council of Nicea made it unambiguously

---

[7] M. Wiles, *The Making of Christian Doctrine* (Cambridge: Cambridge University Press, 1967), p. 62, cited by LaCugna, *God For Us*, p. 111.

[8] J. Jungmann, *The Place of Christ in Liturgical Prayer*, second English edn, trans. A. Peeler (London: Geoffrey Chapman, 1989), p. 172.

[9] Jungmann, *Early Liturgy*, p. 190.

clear – at a popular level there was considerable uncertainty. The Church set about removing this ambiguity by rewording liturgical prayers and doxologies in such a way that the Arians would find nothing to support their subordinationist claims. As Jungmann observes, the Catholics 'began dropping the old doxology, not because it was erroneous, but because it could be misunderstood and, as a matter of fact, was misunderstood. Therefore as a rule they no longer prayed (if we may reduce the various formulas into one scheme): *Gloria Patri* per *Filium* in *Spiritu Sancto*, but *Gloria Patri* et *Filio* et *Spiritui Sancto*.'[10]

Distinctions within economy of salvation, not subordinationism within doctrine of God

As we have already noted, the dispute was particularly fierce in the Eastern Church. St Basil, the Bishop of Caesarea, caused considerable controversy when he decided to use the old doxology '*through* the Son *in* the Holy Spirit' alongside the new anti-Arian one, '*with* the Son *together with* the Holy Spirit'. Such was the controversy that ensued, that he wrote a treatise, *De Spiritu Sancto*, in which he outlined the rationale behind this practice. Whereas the old formula gave prominence to the voluntary abasement by which the Son became our Saviour and Shepherd, the new formula expressed the adoration we owe equally to the Father and to the Son and to the Holy Spirit and, in so doing, is in harmony with the words with which we are baptised, 'in the name of the Father and of the Son and of the Holy Spirit'.[11]

As far as Basil was concerned, the apparent subordinationism of some doxologies merely reflects the economy of salvation; no inequality is implied at an ontological level between Father, Son and Spirit. To say that Christ is the way to the Father does not mean that Christ is subordinate or inferior to the Father; to say that the Spirit is the way to Christ does not mean that the Spirit is less than Christ and

---

[10] Jungmann, *Early Liturgy*, p. 193.
[11] Cf. Jungmann, *Early Liturgy*, pp. 193–4.

also less than the Father. In the liturgical context a distinction needs to be drawn between the order of salvation (*oikonomia*) and the order of God's eternal being (*theologia*), a distinction which the Arians failed to make.[12] Basil's support for both old and new doxologies did not in itself represent the victory of orthodoxy. Other bishops were uncertain as to where they stood on the issue. Jungmann gives the example of Bishop Leontius of Antioch, who, being quite open about his uncertainty on the matter, is alleged to have resolved his indecision by pronouncing the words of the doxology so softly and indistinctly that even those standing next to him could not ascertain which one was being used.[13]

By the end of the fourth century, the dispute in the East had been settled at dogmatic and liturgical levels. No longer enjoying the protection previously awarded by the Byzantine emperors, Arian bishops were obliged to retire. There was now no resistance to the restructuring of prayers and doxologies to eliminate all ambiguity concerning the Arian heresy.

Of the anti-Arian doxology employed by the Church in the East, Jungmann has identified three different forms. The first form, which became dominant in the region of Antioch, offered glory 'to the Father with Christ together with the Holy Spirit'. The second form, which sought to combine the old and the new and which prevailed in Alexandria, gave glory to 'our Lord Jesus Christ, through whom and with whom be to Thee glory together with the Holy Spirit'. The third form, which arose in the Orient and was in wide usage around Byzantium, was modelled after the words of baptism derived from Matthew 28:19, in which glory is offered 'to the Father and to the Son and to the Holy Spirit'. Jungmann notes that this third formula, which became connected with the psalmody, was employed by the Western Church, where it still prevails: *Gloria Patri et Filio et Spiritui Sancto*.[14]

---

[12] Cf. LaCugna, *God for Us*, p. 120.
[13] Jungmann, *Early Liturgy*, p. 194.
[14] Jungmann, *Early Liturgy*, pp. 194–5.

Effects of liturgical changes on worship, Eucharist and prayer

While these liturgical changes were perfectly understandable under the circumstances, they had a most unfortunate and unforeseen effect. Jungmann points out that, as the mediatorship and humanity of Christ faded into the background and Christ was thrust up into the majesty and grandeur of the Godhead, a gap emerged and came to yawn large in Christian thinking between the eternal God and sinful humanity. The worshipper was confronted immediately with the overwhelming majesty of the triune God. 'Stress was now placed not on what unites us to God (Christ as one of us in his human nature, Christ as our brother), but on what separates us from God (God's infinite majesty).'[15]

This had the added effect of dramatically changing the inner dynamic of the Eucharist, insofar as that which had always been regarded as a sacrament of divine grace and favour (in and through Christ) took on characteristics of fear.[16] Jungmann detects a subtle but significant change in liturgical language around this time, calculated to inspire awe and fear in the recipient. A chapter in Basil's *Shorter Rule*, for example, is captioned, 'With what fear ... we ought to receive the Body and Blood of Christ.'[17] And John Chrysostom speaks about 'the terrible sacrifice', about the 'shuddering hour' when the mysteries are accomplished, and about the 'terrible and awful table'.[18] The impact of this injection of fear into the eucharistic liturgy is to be seen in the sharp drop in the reception of communion during the fourth century. Of this decline, Jungmann asks: 'Is it any wonder that the ordinary faithful, conscious of the pressures of their daily occupations, conscious too of their unworthiness before the divine majesty, lost courage?'[19]

---

[15] Jungmann, *Early Liturgy*, p. 195.
[16] Jungmann, *Place of Christ*, pp. 246f.
[17] Basil, *Reg. Brev. Tract.* 172 (PG 31, 1195), cited in Jungmann, *Early Liturgy*, p. 197.
[18] Jungmann, *Early Liturgy*, p. 196.
[19] Jungmann, *Early Liturgy*, p. 197; cf. also LaCugna, *God for Us*, p. 127.

At the same time as the Eucharist was undergoing significant change, the vacuum created by Christ's displacement from the mediatorial role in Christian thinking was increasingly filled by the veneration of the saints, to whom intercessory powers were attributed in the belief that they could provide the necessary bridge between mortal human beings and God.[20] The rise in the veneration of the saints in the fourth and fifth centuries coincided with the rise of Mariology, which, Jungmann argues, is largely attributable to the Church's struggle against Nestorianism in the fifth century.[21] The net effect of all this, he concludes, was that the Church's struggle with heresy, though ultimately victorious, led at many points to losses, especially with regard to the shaping of liturgical prayer, which became largely monophysite in structure. The Monophysites were the antithesis of the Arians, insofar as they denied the human nature in Christ and recognised only the divine. 'Now it is precisely the Monophysites,' says Jungmann, 'who in their liturgy give the greatest expression to those sentiments of fear and awe towards the sacrament. The Thanksgiving should be begun in fear, in fear one should bow before the Lord, and for communion the rubric reads: Draw near in fear and partake in holiness.'[22]

The Monophysites had considerable influence in the non-Chalcedonian regions, where it is noticeable that in the address of the eucharistic prayers there was little differentiation between Christ and the Father. Jungmann gives the example of the fifth-century Syrian *Testament of Our Lord*, in which prayer to Christ appears within the Mass; similarly, the Gregorian *anaphora* addresses Christ throughout.[23] He concludes that by the end of the fifth century there was no room for the mediatory priesthood of Christ. Rather, there was 'liturgical prayer to Christ alone, in every shape, and even at the heart of the Mass, in the

---

[20] Cf. Jungmann, *Place of Christ*, p. 268; LaCugna, *God for Us*, p. 127.
[21] Jungmann, *Early Liturgy*, p. 196.
[22] Jungmann, *Early Liturgy*, p. 198.
[23] Jungmann, *Place of Christ*, pp. 14, 20–1; cf. also, LaCugna, *God for Us*, p. 126.

anamnesis, and with deliberate alteration of an existing model.'[24]

LaCugna, concurring with Jungmann's thesis on the changing structure of liturgical prayers and doxologies under the impact of Arianism in the fourth century, notes the transition from glorifying God through Christ in the Holy Spirit, according to the pattern of the economy, to glorifying the Trinity. This in turn reflected a changed understanding of the mediatorial role of Christ in prayer and worship. In pre-Nicene liturgies Christ 'reaches up into heaven' and mediates our worship *to God*. In the post-Nicene anti-Arian era, Christ 'reaches down from heaven' and mediates God's blessings *to us*. As LaCugna points out, the shift in emphasis here is dramatic:

> Christ's human mediation has become divine intervention; the adopted Son has become incarnate God. The praise of God through the only-begotten Son has become the praise of God the Son. Likewise, the Spirit who makes possible the praise of God becomes an object of praise, worshipped and glorified together with the Father and the Son.[25]

Critique of Jungmann's thesis

While LaCugna and Torrance generally accept Jungmann's thesis, it should be noted that some aspects of it have been challenged from within liturgiological circles. These criticisms are gathered together by Albert Gerhards in his 1982 article, 'Zu Wem Beten?' ('To Whom Do we Pray?').[26] It is claimed that while Jungmann's thesis is generally true in relation to the Church in the West, it tends to overgeneralise in relation to the Church

---

[24] Jungmann, *Place of Christ*, p. 225.
[25] LaCugna, *God for Us*, p. 127.
[26] A. Gerhards, 'Zu Wem Beten?' ('To Whom Do we Pray?) *Liturgisches Jahrbuch* 32 (1982), pp. 219–30.

in the East. In particular, we note the following specific criticisms.

First, Jungmann's strong reliance on the *Church Order of Hippolytus* for drawing conclusions about the early Church liturgy is challenged on the grounds that it may not have been as representative and influential as he assumes. There is now known to be a greater diversity of liturgies from that period.

Second, while Jungmann's thesis is generally correct in relation to prayers made at the altar by the priest, it is not true in relation to prayers made elsewhere in the liturgy, including the hymns, where Christ was often regarded as the one to whom prayers should be directed.

Third, it is not clear that the liturgical development to which Jungmann refers was as clear-cut as he maintains, especially in the East. Whereas he posits a sixth-century dating of the Coptic *anaphora* of Gregory of Nazianzus (which is entirely addressed to Christ) to support his claim of a change in the form of address, recent studies now posit an earlier date, possibly as early as the fourth century. If true, this would suggest that the tradition of addressing Christ directly has an earlier origin than that proposed by him. Indeed, it is argued that, as far as the Eastern Church was concerned, there was always a tradition of addressing prayers to Christ. This tradition, it is alleged, was built upon a (high) Johannine Christology.[27] It existed alongside the *per Christum* prayers, and was merely regarded as a variation on the one theme of praying to God.

Thus Gerhards asks, 'Is Jungmann really right when he says that the address to Christ in the Eucharistic prayer cannot be shown until the fourth century?'[28] He concludes by suggesting that Jungmann's thesis needs to be modified to give greater recognition to the fact that prayers

---

[27] This (high) Johannine Christology, Gerhards argues, is to be distinguished from the (low) Antiochene Christology which was stronger in the West, and which gave greater emphasis to the mediatorial role of Christ in prayer.

[28] Gerhards, 'Zu Wem Beten?', p. 227.

addressed to Christ in public worship belonged to the earliest stratum of Church liturgies and hence were not a post-fourth-century development in response to the Arian threat. Arianism did not provide the impetus for a wholly new liturgical development, namely making Christ the object of prayer. Rather, it provided the impetus for giving greater weight to one existing liturgical tradition over another.

For the purposes of this book, we can draw two conclusions from the debate thus described. First, the main challenge to Jungmann's thesis focuses on his portrayal of the liturgical developments in the *East*, whereas our main concern is with the Church in the *West*, for it is from within that tradition that the Reformed tradition emerged. Second, it is important to note that Gerhards does not reject Jungmann's thesis. Rather, he calls for it to be modified in the light of more recent research. With these comments in mind we are now in a position to consider T. F. Torrance's thesis concerning the impact of Apollinarianism on liturgical developments in the post-Nicene Church.

Apollinarianism and the Liturgy: The Torrance Thesis

If Arianism proved to have considerable influence on Church liturgies in the fourth century and beyond, albeit in a secondary way through the reactions that it generated, so too did Apollinarianism. This is a point made by T. F. Torrance in his incisive essay, 'The Mind of Christ in Worship: The Problem of Apollinarianism in the Liturgy'.[29] While he expresses profound admiration for Jungmann's thesis, he says that, because his historical analysis is restricted to the examination of liturgical texts, and not the underlying theology, he has not seen the force of Apollinarianism which 'seeped into the liturgy like

---

[29] T. F. Torrance, *Theology in Reconciliation: Essays Towards Evangelical and Catholic Unity in East and West* (Grand Rapids, Michigan: Eerdmans, 1975), pp. 139–214.

smoke', and was much more subtle than Arianism in the way it affected the understanding of Christian worship.

Apollinarianism and the hypostatic union

The central issue in Athanasius' refutation of Apollinarianism was the nature of the hypostatic union in Christ. Apollinaris interpreted the hypostatic union in terms of an incarnation of the Logos in which the human mind was set aside and replaced by a divine mind or soul, which the Logos himself is as divine Spirit. In positing this thesis, Torrance observes, Apollinaris was seeking to overcome a twofold difficulty: While the mind is the governing or directing principle through which the flesh, which cannot determine itself, is controlled, it is also sinful and prey to evil thoughts.[30]

This twofold difficulty presupposes a theological anthropology shaped by the prevailing Greek world-view, which assumed a sharp disjunction not only between the divine and creaturely realms, but also between body and soul. Arianism took this dualistic world-view for granted too. But whereas it served the dualism by denying the deity of Christ altogether, Apollinarianism projected the dualism into the being of Christ, denying his deity only in part by arguing that in him there was a fusion between a creaturely body and a divine Logos or mind. Christ was not fully human but only *like* a human being, insofar as he was not *homoousios* with humankind in the supreme governing principle of human existence.

Thus Apollinaris affirmed the doctrine of the incarnation, but only in part, and in a distorted form. Against Apollinaris, says Torrance, Athanasius insisted that the fullness of Christ's humanity included his having a human mind, for otherwise the soteriological work of Christ 'for our sakes', 'on our behalf' and 'in our place' was meaningless. For Athanasius, nothing less was at stake here than the doctrine of salvation. This is because it is in

---

[30] Torrance, *Theology in Reconciliation*, p. 146.

the mind, not just in the flesh, that sin is entrenched. But, suggests Torrance, 'whereas this led Apollinaris to put forward a notion of incarnation in which the human mind was not assumed, Athanasius found it all the more important to stress that it is in our very mind that we need to be redeemed, otherwise redemption would be empty of saving significance or relevance for us'.[31]

Maurice Wiles, who argues that Athanasius was himself uneasy about the notion of Christ having a human soul, does not share Torrance's interpretation of Athanasius on this point. To understand the basis of Wiles' claim here we need to acquaint ourselves a little more fully with the patristic backdrop against which Athanasius and Apollinaris articulated their views.

Christ's soul in patristic thought[32]

The issues at stake in Apollinarianism, especially those pertaining to the humanity of Christ, have their origins in Gnosticism, which provided the backdrop against which second-century figures like Irenaeus and Tertullian defined their understanding of Christ's humanity.[33] In refuting the gnostic denial of the full humanity of Christ, both of these early Christian theologians affirmed the wholeness of Christ's humanity, a wholeness which included both body and soul. The purpose of this affirmation was not merely to secure a satisfactory description of Christ's person, but rather to safeguard the Christian doctrine of salvation. This soteriological motive underpins Irenaeus' famous principle, expressed in Book V of his

[31] T. F. Torrance, *The Trinitarian Faith* (Edinburgh: T&T Clark, 1988), p. 165.
[32] In this section I am indebted to C. C. Twombly's excellent summary of the debate between Aloys Grillmeier and T. F. Torrance in his article, 'The Nature of Christ's Humanity: A Study in Athanasius', *Patristic and Byzantine Review* 8.3 (1989), pp. 227–41.
[33] For a thorough exposition of the significance of Christ's humanity for Irenaeus' soteriology, see Trevor Hart's 'Irenaeus, Recapitulation and Physical Redemption', in *Christ in our Place: The Humanity of God in Christ for the Reconciliation of the World*, eds T. A. Hart and D. P. Thimell (Exeter: Paternoster Press, 1989), pp. 152–81.

work against the heresies, that Christ 'became what we are in order that he might bring us to be even what he is himself'.[34] Tertullian echoes the same theme. Wiles argues, however, that in both of these cases the accent was placed on the flesh, rather than the soul, not because the soul was deemed to be less important, but because, in the docetic atmosphere of Gnosticism, it was the body that was the issue. It is for this reason, he says, that Tertullian asserted, 'The salvation of the soul I believe needs no discussion; for almost all heretics, in whatever way they accept it, at least do not deny it.'[35] Wiles detects in Tertullian's thinking here the anti-Apollinarian principle of Gregory of Nazianzus: 'What is not assumed is not healed.'[36]

In the East, Wiles continues, Origen seems to have shared Tertullian's soteriological concern. In his *Dialogue with Herakleides*, he posited that 'the whole man would not have been saved unless he had taken upon himself the whole man'.[37] However, as we shall see, Origen, who shared the Greek belief in the pre-existence of the human soul, and therefore attributed a pre-existent human soul to Christ as well, went on to affirm the complete perfection of Christ's soul, as distinct from the fallenness of other souls, and saw for it a mediating role linking the divine Logos and human flesh in a union which otherwise would have been impossible. For Origen, the soul of Christ played a vital mediating role in effecting the incarnation, by bridging the disjunction that ordinarily exists between God and human flesh.

While Origen attributed a human (albeit pre-existent) soul to Christ, Wiles notes that subsequent Origenists, such as Malchion and Pamphilus, became increasingly uneasy with the notion of a human soul, because its presence appeared to compromise the unity of the person of Christ.

---

[34] *Adversus Haereses*, V.I.1, cited by Maurice Wiles, 'The Nature of the Early Debate About Christ's Human Soul', *Journal of Ecclesiastical History* 16 (1965), p. 140.
[35] *De Res. Carn.*, ii; Wiles, 'Nature of Early Debate', p. 141.
[36] Wiles, 'Nature of Early Debate', p. 141.
[37] Cited by Wiles, 'Nature of Early Debate', p. 142.

And yet, because the notion was embedded in the language of scripture, it could not be openly repudiated, so it tended just to be ignored.

It was this general uneasiness with the notion of Christ having a human soul that, according to Wiles, prepared a *common ground* upon which such fierce opponents as the Arians and Athanasius stood. When Arius wished to show the creatureliness of the Logos, he did not have first to demolish the belief that Christ possessed a human soul, because the majority of his first opponents, as well as of his first supporters, held no such belief. 'For the same reason,' Wiles suggests, 'no surprise ought to be felt when it is shown that Athanasius did not make use of the concept of Christ's human soul as a way of countering the teaching of Arius. The approach of Athanasius needs to be understood in the light of the immediately preceding teaching of the late third century, not in the light of the subsequent teaching of Apollinarius.'[38]

In presuming a common ground between Athanasius and Arius – namely, a shared belief that Christ did not have a human soul – Wiles is representing the views of one school of thought in a debate,[39] the origins of which can be dated to around the beginning of the twentieth century. Building upon the work of F. C. Baur, two studies appeared in 1899 by K. Hoss and A. Stulcken arguing that in Athanasius' Christology there is no prominent place for the human soul of Christ. Though G. Voisin (1900) argued against this view, it enjoyed subsequent support from M. Richard (1947), Johannes Quasten (1960), Aloys Grillmeier (1965) and R. P. C. Hanson (1988). While Richard argued that Athanasius shared the Arian notion that Christ's humanity was somehow other than ours, Grillmeier sees the possibility of an evolution in Athanasius' thought by which he came to acknowledge a human soul in Christ but never found any theological

---

[38] Wiles, 'Nature of Early Debate', p. 145.
[39] Cf. J. Quasten, *Patrology* (Vol. III): *The Golden Age of Greek Patristic Literature from the Council of Nicaea to the Council of Chalcedon* (Antwerp: Spectrum Publishers, 1960), pp. 72–6.

function for it.[40] The essential argument put forward by this school of thought, then, is that the human soul in Christ, for Athanasius, is either non-existent or of negligible significance. The opposing line of thought is represented by T. F. Torrance, who argues that it is of crucial significance for Athanasius, especially in relation to his development of the Irenaean (and even Origenist) understanding of salvation as the redemption 'of the *whole man*'.[41]

A passive human soul or a vicarious humanity?

In his major work, *Christ in Christian Tradition*, Grillmeier uses two frameworks, *Logos-sarx* and *Logos-anthropos*, to delineate the various christological positions of the patristic period. It is the first of these frameworks that is of interest here, because he includes within it Arius, Athanasius, Apollinaris and the Alexandrians generally.

Grillmeier claims that Athanasius' understanding of the Logos is derived from the Stoic-Alexandrian Logos doctrinal tradition, which regarded the Logos as 'the force from which all life and all movement comes'.[42] Within this framework of understanding, Grillmeier cites *Contra Gentes* 30–34 to suggest that for Athanasius the human soul is a microcosmic logos, doing for the human body what the Logos does for the world as a whole. He interprets Athanasius as referring to the human, rational soul as 'the most perfect copy of the Logos within the earthly, corporeal creation. It fulfils in the body the function which

---

[40] A. Grillmeier, *Christ in Christian Tradition* (Vol. 1): *From the Apostolic Age to Chalcedon (AD 451)*, second edn, trans. J. Bowden (London: Mowbrays, 1975), pp. 308, 310.

[41] Torrance, *Theology in Reconciliation*, p. 225.

[42] Grillmeier, *Christ in Christian Tradition*, p. 311. Grillmeier cites *Contra Gentes* 44 in support of this definition, the relevant part of which reads: 'For as by his own providence bodies grow and the rational soul moves, and possesses life and thought ... so again the same Word of God with one simple nod by his own power moves and holds together both the visible universe and the invisible powers, allotting to each its proper function'.

the Logos has in the cosmos. It is a Logos in microcosm, and therefore also a way to him and to the Father.'[43]

If the human soul is, in a real sense, a copy of the greater Logos, a critical christological question arises: In the incarnation, did the Logos completely overwhelm, if not entirely replace, the human soul in Christ? In reply, Grillmeier conjectures, 'Athanasius' view might be put in these words: where the original itself appears with all its power, the copy, with its secondary and derived power, must at least surrender its function, even if it does not give place altogether.'[44] In other words, the human soul in Christ is subordinated to, not obliterated by, the divine Logos. The subordination is so complete, however, that, according to Grillmeier, Athanasius 'completely forgets about the human soul of Christ. Indeed he seems to have no place for it.'[45] Accordingly, it is the divine Logos, not the human soul, which is the real, physical source – the 'sole motivating principle' – of all the actions of Christ's life.

If this is the case, though, what are we to make of the sufferings of Christ? In his passion was the impassible, immutable divine Logos subject to the same physical and emotional sufferings to which ordinary human beings, consisting of body and soul, are subject? In addressing this question Grillmeier identifies a reluctance in Athanasius to attack the heretical presuppositions of the Arians on the subject of Christ's human suffering. The Arians took the various signs of Christ's humanity (suffering, ignorance, hunger, etc.) as signs of his basic creatureliness, leaving themselves vulnerable to a counter-claim that these very manifestations of finitude merely underwrite the fullness of his human nature. But Athanasius fails to drive this point home, leading Grillmeier to interpret his silence in the following terms:

---

[43] Grillmeier, *Christ in Christian Tradition*, p. 311. Indeed, Athanasius does argue in *Contra Gentes* 33 that the human soul is immortal, and seeks to prove it by reference to: (1) its being distinct from the body; (2) its being the source of motion; and (3) its power to go beyond the human body in imagination and thought.

[44] Grillmeier, *Christ in Christian Tradition*, p. 311.

[45] Grillmeier, *Christ in Christian Tradition*, p. 312.

Athanasius displays a general tendency to weaken the character of certain of Christ's inner experiences which might be attributed to a human soul so as to dissociate the Logos from them from the start. Thus Christ's anguish was only 'feigned', and not real anguish; his ignorance was no real ignorance, but only an *ignorantia de jure*, which was proper to the human nature from the start. Not only does such a qualification relieve the pressure on the Logos itself, but it also raises the possibility of representing the human *sarx* of Christ as the subject of such affections as we should properly ascribe to the soul. As a result, we have Athanasius' remarkable procedure of making the 'flesh' of Christ the physical subject of experiences which normally have their place in the soul. He can speak of an 'ignorance of the flesh' in which the term 'sarx' clearly begs the whole question. From the whole of his explanation of the ignorance of Christ it follows that the thought of a human knowledge, a limited human consciousness in Christ, has not occurred to him.[46]

If the *Logos-sarx* framework can be used to interpret Athanasius' understanding of the incarnation and suffering of Christ, so too, suggests Grillmeier, can it be used to interpret his understanding of Christ's death,[47] which, he says, is described by him in terms of a separation not of the (human) soul from the body but rather of the (divine) Logos from the body. It is the Logos, too, who descends into the underworld.

Grillmeier cites Athanasius' exegesis of John 10:18 and 12:27 in support of his theory.[48] Both texts refer to Christ's soul. In John 10:18, Christ refers to his power to lay his soul down and to take it up again, which Athanasius says set him apart from ordinary human beings: 'For man dies ... by necessity of nature and against his will; but the Lord,

---

[46] Grillmeier, *Christ in Christian Tradition*, p. 315.
[47] Grillmeier, *Christ in Christian Tradition*, pp. 315–16.
[48] *Contra Arianos* 3.57, cited in Grillmeier, *Christ in Christian Tradition*, p. 316.

being himself immortal, had *power as God to become separate from the body* and to take it up again when he would.'

If Athanasius' commentary on John 10:18 seems to fit Grillmeier's *Logos-sarx* framework rather neatly, his commentary on John 12:27 is a little more problematic, for in this text Christ says that his soul is *troubled*, an experience that is more befitting a human soul than the divine Logos. Indeed, Athanasius says as much when he comments that for Christ's soul *to be troubled was proper to the flesh*. Grillmeier notes, significantly, that Athanasius understands the biblical word, 'soul', in this context, to mean merely 'life'. With this done, he points out how nicely the separation of God from the body fits into the *Logos-sarx* framework.

However, as Charles Twombly says of Grillmeier at this point, he makes nothing of what Athanasius himself says on the matter. Moreover, Twombly asks, 'is a mere body capable of being troubled? Do we have here "another" instance of Athanasius attributing to the flesh what is ordinarily attributed to the soul? Or does Athanasius' understanding of "flesh" include some notion of soul as well?'[49]

Twombly aside, other patristic scholars tend to assume the correctness of Grillmeier's *Logos-sarx* framework. Quasten, for example, claims that Athanasius' failure to speak of the soul leaving the body at the moment of Christ's death 'proves that Christ's soul does not really figure in his concept of the Saviour's death and descent'.[50] Similarly, Hanson asserts that until the year 362 it never crossed Athanasius' mind 'that there was any point in maintaining that Jesus had a human soul or mind'.[51] And Wiles says of Athanasius that he 'never seems to have taken the idea of Christ's human soul over into his own theological thinking. It is true and significant that we do find him in a later writing repeating the soteriological

[49] Twombly, 'Nature of Christ's Humanity', pp. 233–4.
[50] Quasten, *Patrology*, p. 75.
[51] R. P. C. Hanson, *The Search for the Christian Doctrine of God: The Arian Controversy 318–81* (Edinburgh: T&T Clarke, 1988), p. 451.

argument that Christ's incarnation was a full and real incarnation, and that it needed to be such for him to save the whole man, soul and body.'[52] But even in that context he does not find it necessary himself to assert Christ's assumption of a specific human soul as an explicit element in that full incarnation.[53]

Like Grillmeier, Wiles seems to read a lot into the fact that, with the exception of one passage, Athanasius appears not to affirm directly or at length the human nature of Christ's soul, concluding that it is therefore not important to his soteriology. Grillmeier goes so far as to say, 'the debate with the Arians was of such a character that silence over the soul of Christ was tantamount to a denial'.[54] The exception is a passage from Athanasius' *Tomus ad Antiochenos*, 7, to which Quasten, Grillmeier and Wiles all refer,[55] and to which we must therefore devote some attention.

The *Tomus* was written as a summation of the deliberations of the synod of Alexandria, which Athanasius convened in 362, in order to mediate between, and hopefully draw together, two factions. Subtitled, 'The human Nature of Christ complete, not Body only', the passage states that 'the Saviour had not a body without a soul, nor without sense or intelligence; for it was not possible, when the Lord had become man for us, that His body should be without intelligence: nor was the salvation effected in the Word Himself a salvation of body only, but of soul also'.[56]

At first glance, this appears to be a clear endorsement of the presence and importance of a human soul in Christ, as

---

[52] Wiles cites *Ad Epictetum* 7 here, the relevant section of which reads: 'but the Saviour having in very truth become Man, the salvation of the whole man was brought about. For if the Word were in the Body putatively, as they say, and by putative it meant imaginary, it follows that both the salvation and the resurrection of man is apparent only . . . But truly our salvation is not merely apparent, nor does it extend to the body only, but the *whole man, body and soul alike*, has truly obtained salvation in the Word Himself' (italics mine).

[53] Wiles, 'Nature of Early Debate', pp. 147–8.

[54] Grillmeier, *Christ in Christian Tradition*, p. 325.

[55] Quasten, *Patrology*, pp. 73–4; Grillmeier, *Christ in Christian Tradition*, pp. 318–26; Wiles, 'Nature of Early Debate', pp. 146–8.

[56] *Tomus ad Antiochenos*, 7.

Grillmeier himself concedes.[57] But, he says, the crucial phrase, 'not a body without a soul' can also be translated, 'not a lifeless body', which radically alters the meaning of the passage as a whole. This alternative translation, he claims, 'stems from the "Alexandrianism" of the *Logos-sarx* christology'.[58]

What is striking about this statement is that the only justification being offered by Grillmeier for the revised translation is that, in consequence, it enables the passage as a whole to fit his theory concerning the *Logos-sarx* Christology. Charles Twombly gets to the heart of the problem here when he says of Grillmeier generally: 'Perhaps he represents the danger of someone who forces a rather rigid (and perhaps alien) scheme on another's thought without letting that thought suggest the categories by which it might best be understood.'[59]

Athanasius and the Alexandrian School

Grillmeier's assumption concerning the degree of Alexandrian influence on Athanasius' Christology is by no means accepted by all patristic scholars. It is true that there was a tendency among the theologians of the early Church to divide into two camps – those of the Antiochian school who stressed the historical humanity of Jesus, and those of the Alexandrian school who stressed the eternal nature of Christ as divine Logos.[60] As we have seen, Grillmeier places Athanasius in the second of these two schools. Torrance, however, argues that 'there was a third "school", running from Irenaeus to Athanasius. This school stressed the vicarious humanity of Jesus along with its stress upon the Deity and Lordship of Christ.'[61]

[57] Grillmeier, *Christ in Christian Tradition*, p. 321.
[58] Grillmeier, *Christ in Christian Tradition*, p. 323.
[59] Twombly, 'Nature of Christ's Humanity', p. 241.
[60] Cf. R. V. Sellers, *Two Ancient Christologies: A Study in the Christological Thought of the Schools of Alexandria and Antioch in the Early History of Christian Doctrine* (London: SPCK, 1954).
[61] T. F. Torrance, 'The Place of the Humanity of Christ in the Sacramental Life of the Church', *Church Service Society Annual* 26 (1956), pp. 3–10 at p. 4.

In assessing this claim we need to understand a little more about the Alexandrian catechetical tradition to which Athanasius is usually assigned. The intellectual climate was dominated by a collision between Hebraic-Christian and Hellenistic thought-forms. Whereas the Greek world-view was controlled by a cosmological and epistemological dualism, the biblical world-view was inherently unitive, or non-dualistic: The infinite and eternal God is not utterly removed from the world of finite beings, as a dualistic world-view presupposes, but rather is the living and personal Creator who himself draws near to his creation and is intimately involved in it, working towards its redemption. The challenge facing the likes of Clement and Origen in Alexandria and Nestorius and Theodore in Antioch was how to communicate the biblical doctrine of God within the culture and philosophy of the Graeco-Roman world.

In Alexandria, Clement, who was intent upon attracting the educated Greeks to the Christian message, sought a synthesis of thought-forms by positing a single historical process of human knowledge beginning with the law of Moses, continuing with the philosophy of the Greeks, and coming to completion through 'him from whom all instruction comes', the Logos made man, that through him humankind might possess that perfect knowledge, the attainment of which spells salvation.[62] Here the primary function of the Logos was deemed to be 'the Revealer of the Divine: as the Power, the Wisdom, the Knowledge, and the Truth of the Father ... the Logos has ever been the Instructor in the divine mysteries, and, to give men the fulness of light, has in these last days himself become flesh'.[63] Human beings are so constituted that they are able to partake of the divine nature through their own rationality, which is in the image of the divine Logos. 'Man,' says Clement, 'alone of all the other living creatures, was in his creation endowed with an understanding of God',[64] 'born

---

[62] *Paed.* i. 8; *Protrept.* xi, cited by Sellers, *Two Ancient Christologies*, p. 4.
[63] *Strom.* vii. 2; iv. 25; vi. 8, Sellers, *Two Ancient Christologies*, p. 10.
[64] *Strom.* vii. 2, Sellers, *Two Ancient Christologies*, p. 11.

for the contemplation of heaven'.[65] While the human outlook is perverted through ignorance of the true Reason, people can rise above such a state as, passions quelled, they devote themselves to the contemplation of the Divine, which has been manifested in Christ.[66]

Even though Clement sought to give priority to the person of Christ in his reflections on the divine Logos, his Christology was ultimately controlled by an Aristotelian-Stoic epistemology that gave priority to 'gnosis', or reason, over faith: 'Faith . . . is essential, but only as the first step which a man must take towards understanding the divine mysteries – it is "gnosis" which effects the soul's transformation to the better.'[67]

One of the decisive contributions of Origen was his reversal of the Aristotelian-Stoic relation of the human reason to God through his emphasis upon the transcendence of God above all things. However, as T. F. Torrance points out, because he 'still worked with the Philonic and Neoplatonic dichotomy between the *kosmos noetos* and the *kosmos aisthetos*, he was forced to speak of God as finally beyond being and knowing and so lapsed into the old Platonic doctrine of God'.[68] This in turn forced him to look for the reality of Christ and his redemption 'beyond history'.[69] As Sellers expresses it, for Origen (as for Clement), Christ was regarded as the Illuminator whose life was the pattern-life, rather than the Healer of a fallen humanity.[70]

At the same time as Origen assumed a cosmological and epistemological disjunction between Creator and creation, on an *ontological* level he assumed a necessary and logical link between them: for God to be Creator or *Pantocrator* meant the eternal co-existence of the creation, at least in the

---

[65] *Protrept.* x, Sellers, *Two Ancient Christologies*, p. 11.

[66] *Paed.* i. 13; *Strom.* ii. 15, Sellers, *Two Ancient Christologies*, p. 13.

[67] Cf. *Strom.* vii. 10, Sellers, *Two Ancient Christologies*, p. 13.

[68] Plato, *Republic* VI. 509b; cf. Origen, *Contra Celsum*, VII:38, cited by Torrance, *Theology in Reconciliation*, p. 218.

[69] *In Evangelium Ioannis*, I:8, 25–6, cited by Torrance, *Theology in Reconciliation*, p. 93.

[70] Sellers, *Two Ancient Christologies*, pp. 14, 27.

mind of God. Thus there is no distinction to be made ontologically between the eternal generation of the Son and the creation of the world, for both are located timelessly and eternally within the being or *ousia* of God. It is this failure by Origen to distinguish between the cosmological and ontological dimensions, and between eternal generation and creation that constitutes one of the fundamental problems with his thought.[71]

No such problem can be found, though, with Athanasius. He makes a sharp distinction between generation and creation, the former taking place timelessly and eternally within the being or *ousia* of God, and the latter taking place by a free act of divine will, in bringing into existence out of nothing something beyond and outside the being of God, yet wholly and contingently dependent upon the being of God.[72] As Torrance correctly observes, in making this distinction, Athanasius is not succumbing to 'the old cosmological dualism between God and the world, for God is held to be unceasingly present in the universe, maintaining its existence by grace, granting it its created order and function, and thus continuously interacting with what he has made'.[73]

While Athanasius is at one with his Alexandrian predecessors in upholding the notion that human beings are rational beings, who, made in the image of the Logos, are capable of knowing God, he also draws on the teaching of Irenaeus to point out that those same beings are *fallen* beings. The human soul, the seat of rationality, is fundamentally abased,[74] and the human race as a whole has descended 'into a hopeless depth of delusion and superstition'.[75] Given this fact of sin, Christ as Redeemer is not the One in whom there is found illumination or perfect

---

[71] Cf. G. Florovsky, 'The Concept of Creation in Saint Athanasius', *Studia Patristica* VI (1962), cited by Torrance, *Theology in Reconciliation*, p. 220.

[72] 'For God has not only made us out of nothing; but he gave us freely, by the Grace of the Word, a life in correspondence with God' (*De Incarnatione* 5; cf. also *De Incarnatione* 2, 3, 17, 42). On the important distinction between generation and creation, cf. *Contra Arianos* 2.22.

[73] Torrance, *Theology in Reconciliation*, pp. 221–2.

[74] *Contra Gentes* 4.

[75] *Contra Gentes* 8.

Reason, but the Second Adam, the root of a new creation, the One in whom and through whom our abased and deluded human condition has been healed and sanctified.

Of fundamental importance here is Athanasius' understanding of the hypostatic union in Christ, which provided the grounds both of redemption and of humanity's knowledge of God. This in turn is of crucial importance for grasping his understanding of the Logos. As we noted above, Grillmeier quotes *Contra Gentes* 44 to substantiate his claim that Athanasius is dependent on the Stoic-Alexandrian doctrine for his understanding of the Logos as 'the force from which all life and movement comes' – that is to say, 'the Logos acts as life-giving principle towards the world',[76] is the 'sole motivating principle in Christ',[77] and is 'the spiritual principle which effected the real act of redemption'.[78] But if we understand aright the nature of the hypostatic union as expounded by Athanasius then Grillmeier's interpretation of the Logos as a mere cosmological principle immanent in the universe is exceedingly difficult to sustain.

It is this same failure to understand the nature of the hypostatic union in Christ, and the tendency therefore to interpret the incarnation in static, dualistic categories, which seems to characterise Hanson's exposition of Athanasius' doctrine of the incarnation. Hanson describes Athanasius' doctrine rather crudely as a 'space-suit Christology':

> Just as the astronaut, in order to operate in a part of universe where there is no air and where he has no experience of weightlessness, puts on an elaborate space-suit which enables him to live and act in this new, unfamiliar environment, so the *Logos* put on a body which enabled him to behave as a human being among human beings.[79]

76 Grillmeier, *Christ in Christian Tradition*, p. 311.
77 Grillmeier, *Christ in Christian Tradition*, p. 313.
78 Grillmeier, *Christ in Christian Tradition*, p. 314.
79 Hanson, *Search*, p. 448.

As we have seen, this tendency to interpret Athanasius' thought within a docetic framework has massive implications, for it demands a perception of the divine Logos in terms of something which is ultimately untouched by Christ's human suffering, ignorance and fear. In an article entitled 'Did Athanasius Deny Christ's Fear?',[80] Alvyn Pettersen argues convincingly that as far as Athanasius is concerned, while the Logos as some kind of self-contained entity would not have experienced these things, the *incarnate* Logos most certainly did.[81] It is of the very essence of both the incarnation and the atonement that the Logos became fully human in truth and not merely in appearance. In the same vein, Ian Wallis argues that 'Athanasius does not maintain that the incarnate Son is only a human being; rather, he is the eternal Son or Logos incarnated in order that through his solidarity with humanity he might redeem it.'[82]

It is increasingly apparent that by placing Athanasius in the Alexandrian catechetical tradition Grillmeier tends to assume a continuity of thought from Clement and Origen to Athanasius himself that does not bear closer scrutiny. Our brief survey of the key features of the three Alexandrians' works seems to confirm Torrance's observation that 'Alexandrian Christianity never really expelled the Gnostics, and never offered the sharp critical front to the tradition of Basileides and Valentinus which we find in the teaching of Irenaeus.'[83]

Torrance's argument here finds solid support from Trevor Hart, who says that in 'stark contrast to some of the apologetic theologies of the early Alexandrian tradition in which the adoption of dualistic structures of thought made it difficult to do proper justice to the idea of an incarnation of the Son of God, Irenaeus insists upon maintaining the integrity of both the humanity and the deity of the Saviour

---

[80] A. Pettersen, 'Did Athanasius Deny Christ's Fear?', *Scottish Journal of Theology* 39 (1986), pp. 327–40.
[81] Cf. *Contra Arianos* 3.55.2–21.
[82] I. Wallis, *The Faith of Jesus Christ in Early Christian Traditions* (Cambridge: Cambridge University Press, 1995), p. 208.
[83] Torrance, *Theology in Reconciliation*, p. 215.

in the history and person of Christ, for he realises that it is precisely the *becoming* of God within this history that saves mankind. God *becomes* a man. This is what the Greek mind cannot tolerate, and what Irenaeus knows must be proclaimed, for it is in this *becoming* that the redemption is wrought.'[84]

If, as the evidence suggests, Athanasius' Christology is grounded in an Irenaean rather than Alexandrian tradition, then Grillmeier's rendering of an alternative translation of Athanasius' reference to the human nature of Christ's soul in the *Tomus ad Antiochenos*, on the basis that it 'stems from the "Alexandrianism" of the *Logos-sarx* christology', is difficult to justify.

Ecclesiastical strategy or theological conviction?

Rather than uphold Grillmeier's alternative translation of that key passage in the *Tomus ad Antiochenos*, Wiles takes a slightly different line. He stresses the mediatorial and pastoral role of Athanasius at the synod: To the Eustathian faction that was unhappy about the ascription of a human soul to Christ because it seems to destroy the uniqueness of the incarnation and set it on a level with the inspiration of the saints, Athanasius offers reassurance in the first half of the passage quoted – the Word *became* flesh, and did not merely enter the flesh. And to the Paulinian faction that was concerned about the soteriological importance of Christ's human soul, Athanasius offers the assurance that the salvation effected in the Word himself was not a salvation of body only but of soul also. In so doing he reintroduces a concept that since the time of Tertullian and Origen had largely fallen into disuse because of the misgivings that were held over its implications for an understanding of the unity of Christ's person.

The important thing to note here is that, as far as Wiles is concerned, Athanasius' reintroduction of the concept serves an ecclesiastical and pastoral strategy rather than

---

[84] Hart, 'Irenaeus, Recapitulation and Physical Redemption', p. 178.

personal theological conviction. He concludes that 'the
soteriological line of argument was successful in
persuading Athanasius that the Paulinians were brothers
to be embraced in Christian fellowship. He himself never
seems to have taken the idea of Christ's human soul over
into his own theological thinking.' Thus, for Wiles, the
significance of the *Tomus ad Antiochenos*, 'is that it reveals
the resurrection of the original soteriological argument as
the one way in which the main body of the Eastern Church
was enabled to feel at all at home with the idea of Christ's
human soul. From that point on the argument dominates
the scene and sweeps all before it, including above all
Apollinarius.'[85]

One must ask, however, whether Wiles' hypothesis
relies rather too much on his ability to discern the true
intention of Athanasius and identify a subordination of
theological truth to ecclesiastical sensitivities. Is it not more
plausible that the reason for Athanasius' general silence on
the issue of Christ having a human soul is not that he did
not hold personally to the belief, but rather that the nature
of the hypostatic union in Christ compelled him to reject
the traditional body–soul dualism of Greek thought and
develop a doctrine of the incarnation that employed a
different conceptuality derived from a non-dualistic
cosmology and epistemology?

Following this line of thinking, T. F. Torrance mounts
the following argument:

> Athanasius' consistent rejection of cosmological and
> epistemological dualism in his doctrine of Christ as
> well as in his doctrine of God enabled him to develop
> the Irenaean (and even Origenist) understanding of
> salvation as the redemption of the whole man, which
> rather makes irrelevant the distorting distinction
> between a *Logos-sarx* and a *Logos-anthropos* approach
> which some scholars have employed as a framework
> for the interpretation of Patristic Christology.[86]

[85] Wiles, 'Nature of Early Debate', pp. 147–8.
[86] Torrance, *Theology in Reconciliation*, pp. 225–6.

Torrance accuses Grillmeier and other advocates of a *Logos-sarx* interpretive framework of interpreting Athanasius' works with dualistic categories that Athanasius himself had abandoned. By way of contrast, he advocates an approach that seeks to penetrate beneath the surface meanings of various passages to the underlying theological reasoning that connects them and gives them their full meaning.

This contrast of methods is summed up by Twombly, who observes that by focusing narrowly on the issue of a human soul in Athanasius' thinking Grillmeier 'seems to miss the fruitful implications arising out of the larger theme'.[87] It is because of the rigidity of his framework, Twombly points out, that he

> ... stumbles over phrases like 'ignorance of the flesh'. Rather than re-working his conceptual scheme, Grillmeier attributes some kind of confusion to Athanasius. Torrance, on the other hand, sees in the attribution of various mental and emotional qualities to the 'flesh' a basis for affirming that Athanasius frequently uses 'flesh,' in a manner reminiscent of the Bible, to mean full humanity, body and soul.[88]

According to Torrance, beneath the surface of Athanasius' use of the term 'flesh' – which includes body and soul – are his understandings of the unique hypostatic union that exists in Christ and the soterio-logical purposes of God which were being worked out in and through that hypostatic union. These are the 'larger themes' which Grillmeier seems to miss in his rather narrow focus on the issue of a human soul in Christ. That is to say, Christ as the One who is both fully God *and fully human* had an important role to perform on our behalf and as our representative.

In a decisive passage, Torrance says that 'Athanasius piled up the various Greek prepositions, to make clear the fullness and depth of the *vicarious humanity* of Jesus Christ,

---

[87] Twombly, 'Nature of Christ's Humanity', p. 241.
[88] Twombly, 'Nature of Christ's Humanity', p. 236.

and so insist that in the incarnation the Son of God *minis-tered not only of the things of God to man but ministered of the things of man to God.*'[89] For Athanasius, then, 'the human priesthood and the saving mediatorship of Jesus Christ in and through human kinship with us' was of fundamental significance. It was, says Torrance, 'certainly one of the major emphases of Athanasius in the *Contra Arianos*, as well as in other writings where he expounds the doctrine of the saving humanity of Christ in terms of his obedient life and self-sanctification on our behalf, and yet it is so often completely omitted by patristic scholars, as in the recent work of A. Grillmeier, *Christ in Christian Tradition*'.[90] It is precisely this omission, Torrance continues, that seriously distorts Athanasius' doctrine of Christ and imports into it 'false problems for which false solutions are then sought'.[91]

The important point here, is that implied in Grillmeier's position is a separation between Christ – who does not have a human soul – and the rest of humanity, so that 'the doctrine of redemption tends to be expounded in terms of external relations between Christ and a sinful human race, and so the judicial element assumes a role of predominant significance'.[92] Indeed, says Torrance, this is precisely what has transpired in the Western Church, owing partly to the reintroduction of a dualistic framework of thinking into theology through Augustine, and partly to the anthro-pocentric and forensic frame of mind inherited from Tertullian. It is particularly pronounced in the Protestant tradition, as evidenced by all the monographs produced on the atonement, which presume to deal with the subject in isolation from the incarnation. That sort of thing, he says, did not, and could not, occur in Greek patristic theology because in its non-dualistic framework of thinking incar-nation and redemption are inseparably one:

> For Athanasius, it is everywhere apparent, the incar-national assumption of our fallen Adamic humanity

[89] Torrance, *Theology in Reconciliation*, pp. 228–9.
[90] Torrance, *Theology in Reconciliation*, p. 229.
[91] Torrance, *Theology in Reconciliation*, p. 229.
[92] Torrance, *Theology in Reconciliation*, p. 230.

from the Virgin Mary was essentially a sanctifying and redeeming event, for what Christ took up into himself, the whole man, he healed and renewed through his own holy life of obedient Sonship in the flesh, and his vicarious death and resurrection.[93]

By way of conclusion in relation to this debate, the evidence seems to support Torrance's interpretation of Athanasius, rather than Grillmeier's and Wiles'. Athanasius refuted the dualistic categories of Origen and Clement in the Alexandrian school and, following Irenaeus, gave full emphasis to the humanity of Christ, body and soul. His soteriology hinged on the fact of Christ's assumption of the human condition rather than the displacement of the soul by the divine Logos. Christ's growth as a man, therefore, was not the progressive unveiling of the incarnate Logos to humankind but rather the progressive deification of human nature in the person of the Mediator.[94] Similarly, Christ's 'ignorance' was not 'feigned' as Grillmeier and Hanson assert – rather, it was voluntarily assumed as part of his truly human nature.[95] It seems that at almost every point in Athanasius' writings we are met with the vicarious nature of Christ's humanity through his assumption of human flesh and limitation.

The exception of faith

The only exception to this assumption of human flesh and its consequent limitation, it would seem, is Jesus' *faith* – a

[93] Torrance, *Theology in Reconciliation*, p. 230.
[94] Cf. *Contra Arianos* 3.53, which reads: 'And as we said that he suffered in the flesh, and hungered in the flesh, and was fatigued in the flesh, so also reasonably may he be said to have *advanced in the flesh* ... but the *manhood advanced* in Wisdom, transcending by degrees human nature, and being deified' (italics mine).
[95] Cf. *Contra Arianos* 2.76, which reads: 'he made this (declaration of ignorance) as man by reason of the flesh. For this as before is not the Word's deficiency, but *of that human nature whose property it is to be ignorant* ... for since he was made man, he is not ashamed, because of the flesh which is ignorant, to say "I know not," that he may show that knowing as God, he is but ignorant according to the flesh.'

point made by Ian Wallis, who observes Athanasius' reluctance to attribute faith to the human nature of the incarnate Son.[96] This is especially puzzling, he comments, considering Athanasius' otherwise strong emphasis on Jesus' human limitations. If he was prepared to maintain that such things as weeping and fear and 'other signs of human frailty were indicative of the incarnate Son, why did he not also include faith as a characteristic of that dispensation? Further, if he recognised the salvific necessity for the Son to enter fully through his incarnate life into humanity so that he might redeem all and bear all to the Father, surely the Son would need to share the human response of faith?'[97]

On face value, Wallis declares, it appears that Athanasius not only 'declined a golden opportunity to underline the completeness of the incarnation',[98] but his silence on the matter is even consistent with a *Logos-sarx* Christology.[99] However, Wallis warns against reaching this conclusion too quickly, without taking into consideration the polemical context in which Athanasius wrote.[100] Athanasius, he says, was addressing the issue of Jesus' faith in the context of his refutation of Arianism, and was therefore concerned to establish the fact that the Son was not a mere creature. As far as he was concerned, it was impossible for the incarnate Son to have faith in God and, in this way, to share in the human predicament, for this would imply the Son's creatureliness and thus a diminishing of his divinity. Wallis notes that 'as Athanasius maintained that the incarnate Son is also the eternal Son, his relationship to God must be intrinsic, eternal and consubstantial. In consequence, faith cannot be considered an appropriate disposition within such a dynamic and cannot, therefore, have been embraced at the incarnation.'[101]

Wallis goes on to conjecture that Athanasius might have viewed the issue of Christ's faith differently had he

[96] Wallis, *Faith of Jesus Christ*, p. 206.
[97] Wallis, *Faith of Jesus Christ*, p. 206.
[98] Wallis, *Faith of Jesus Christ*, p. 206.
[99] Wallis, *Faith of Jesus Christ*, p. 207.
[100] Wallis, *Faith of Jesus Christ*, p. 207.
[101] Wallis, *Faith of Jesus Christ*, pp. 208–9.

addressed it in a less polemical context, but also concedes that this is by no means certain. While one of Athanasius' contemporaries, Hilary of Poitiers, did attribute faith to the human nature of Christ, many of those who followed Athanasius did not, including Gregory of Nazianzus, Gregory of Nyssa and Augustine.[102]

It thus appears that Athanasius' inconsistency on the matter of attributing faith to Christ's humanity is an inconsistency shared by other Church Fathers, reflecting the polemical context in which they wrote and their need to emphasise the divinity of Christ in refutation of the Arian position. It does not in itself overturn Torrance's thesis and lend support to the notion of a *Logos-sarx* Christology.

Consequences of Apollinarianism for theology and worship

Having acquainted ourselves with the debate over Athanasius' understanding of Christ's soul and ventured an opinion on the validity of Torrance's interpretation, we are now in a position to consider his essay, 'The Mind of Christ in Worship: The Problem of Apollinarianism in the Liturgy'. Our intention here is to follow the logic of his argument before looking at the picture of worship and prayer that emerges in relation to the Church as it moved from the patristic period to the Middle Ages.

In tracing the implications of Apollinarianism, T. F. Torrance identifies four major consequences. First, in attributing to Jesus a divine mind, which by definition is immutable, unchangeable and sinless, the humanity of Jesus is severely undermined. It disqualifies him from being a priest joined to us by our frailties and infirmities at every level (including the mind), and so cuts away the ground from his mediatorial activity on behalf of and from humankind towards the Father.[103] With Jesus' representative

---

[102] Wallis, *Faith of Jesus Christ*, pp. 209–12. Wallis notes, for example, that in Gregory of Nazianzus' defence of Christ's complete identification with humanity, he alludes to almost every human attribute of Jesus *apart from faith* (*Orationes* XXIX.18, cited in *Faith of Jesus Christ*, p. 210).

[103] Torrance, *Theology in Reconciliation*, p. 148.

capacity before God thus destroyed, he argues, it follows that worship of God cannot be *through Christ* but at best only *for Christ's sake*.[104]

Second, by teaching that Jesus was not really *homoousios* with us in the wholeness of our human being, sharing with us our mind (or rational soul) as well as our body, Apollinarianism damages the 'complete economy' of salvation, insofar as the gap between God and our human situation has not really been bridged in Christ after all.[105] If Jesus did not really have a human mind then his death was merely his own death on a purely physical level, and not our death made his own by his vicarious action as the Son of God become human.[106]

Third, in denying Christ a human mind in all its primal corruptness and propensity for evil, the Apollinarian gospel is unable to cope with original sin or the root of sin at its deepest level. It thereby misses the point that it was precisely in and through the assumption of *every* aspect of our human condition by Christ (including our mind) that our corrupt human nature was at the same time healed, sanctified and renewed in him.[107] Moreover, writes Torrance, this has 'the effect of divorcing worship of God from redemption of the human soul where it is so deeply in need of salvation within the depth of its struggle with sin'.[108]

Fourth, Apollinarianism's acknowledgement of Christ's creatureliness in terms of his body, but not of his rational soul, not only implies a disjunction between our physical being (which has been assumed by Christ) and our intellectual nature (unassumed), it also undermines the totality of the reconciling exchange which has taken place in Christ, and implies a rather 'instrumentalist' view of salvation, as something which affects the outer body but not the innermost constitution of the human person. This also has consequences for worship, argues Torrance, for if

[104] Torrance, *Theology in Reconciliation*, p. 148.
[105] Torrance, *Theology in Reconciliation*, p. 148.
[106] Torrance, *Theology in Reconciliation*, p. 148.
[107] Torrance, *Theology in Reconciliation*, p. 149.
[108] Torrance, *Theology in Reconciliation*, p. 149.

there is no real relation between God and the human soul,
or between the divine will and the human will in and
through the rational soul and will of Christ, because the
Son of God has not assumed a human mind, then worship
cannot be thought of taking place *with* Christ any more
than through or in him.[109]

Torrance concludes his discussion of the implications of
Apollinarianism for worship by saying that

> ... in allowing no room for the mental and moral life of
> Jesus as a man and in denying to him authentic human
> agency in his saving work, it left no place for the
> vicarious role of the human soul and mind and will of
> Jesus in the reconciling 'exchange' of like for like in the
> redemption of man. And, by destroying his represen-
> tative capacity, it had no place for his priesthood or
> human mediation in our worship of the Father, and by
> the same token it took away the ground for any worship
> of God with our human minds. A mutilated humanity
> in Christ could not but result in a mutilated Christian
> worship of God.[110]

Athanasius and the Cappadocians

The groundwork for the orthodox refutation of
Apollinarianism, says Torrance, was laid by Athanasius,
built upon by the Cappadocians, in particular Gregory of
Nazianzus, and made complete by Cyril of Alexandria. He
notes the continuum of theological argument: In the course
of his defence of the Nicene faith, first against the Arians
and then against the Apollinarians, Athanasius laid great
emphasis on the vicarious humanity of Christ the High
Priest, thereby rejecting any instrumentalist notions of the
atonement by which salvation was said to be effected
without the human condition having been fully assumed
by God in Christ. For Athanasius, the act of assuming our

[109] Torrance, *Theology in Reconciliation*, p. 150.
[110] Torrance, *Theology in Reconciliation*, p. 150.

flesh of sin and corruption was at the same time a healing and sanctifying of our human nature in Christ, which has direct implications for the way in which we conceive of the act of worship:

> It was by his purity in our impure flesh that our impurity was overcome, by his obedience to the Father in our disobedient humanity that we are restored to sonship, by his sanctifying of our flesh of sin which he assumed that our sins are done away, so that by participating in his self-consecration on our behalf and sharing in his Spirit, we may draw near to God through, with and in Jesus Christ, who prays to the Father for us, while taking on himself what is ours and imparting to us what he received, and thus worship the God and Father of Jesus Christ as our God and Father.[111]

Torrance suggests that the Cappadocian theologian, Gregory of Nazianzus, strengthened Athanasius' position in two respects.[112] First, he made clear that what 'Christ has not assumed he has not healed' and went on to note that by taking our sin and curse upon himself in the incarnation Christ was not transformed into either of these; rather, in him our sins and iniquities have been taken away. Second, Gregory pointed out that when we think of the divine and human wills being joined in Christ we must not think in physical terms, as in the case of two physical objects which cannot be accommodated in the same space. Rather, it is of the nature of intellectual existents, which can combine with one another differently, that two 'wholes' can be united without excluding one another.[113] In other words, as Torrance observes, Gregory was thinking about the incarnation in *relational* terms.[114]

---

[111] *Contra Arianos* 4.6–7, cited Torrance, *Theology in Reconciliation*, p. 154.
[112] Torrance, *Theology in Reconciliation*, p. 154.
[113] In making this point, Gregory was refuting the Apollinarian argument that there could not be two minds or two wills in the one incarnate Son. Cf. Torrance, *Theology in Reconciliation*, p. 155.
[114] Torrance, *Theology in Reconciliation*, p. 155.

Cyril of Alexandria

Cyril of Alexandria took this line of thinking still further, says Torrance. He put into developed theological terms the twofold emphasis found in both John's Gospel and the book of Hebrews on the divinity and the humanity of Christ. The incarnate Son is one divine-human subject or reality in which neither his divinity nor his humanity is compromised, contaminated or deprecated in any way by virtue of this union.

In expounding the nature of the incarnation, Torrance points out, Cyril gave considerable prominence to the Pauline concept of *kenosis*, or self-abasement.[115] If *kenosis* was only partial, if there was no condescension or lowering of the Son to be on our level in every respect, including that of our minds and wills, then our corrupt human condition has not really been redeemed and sanctified after all. It is of the very order of the incarnation that God become human means that God as human being acts within the limits, principles, measures and laws of what is essentially and properly human, not only in a physical sense, but also in relation to the soul or mind, indeed to the whole human nature which the Son united hypostatically to himself.[116] This was one of Cyril's central themes, and he constantly returned to Paul's teaching in Romans 8:3–4, to which, notes Torrance, he gives careful exposition in referring to the healing and sanctification of our sinful flesh in the flesh of the incarnate Son.[117]

For Cyril, then, there is an inextricable link between the doctrines of salvation and the incarnation, between justification and the economic condescension of the Son, and between Christ's vicarious priesthood and his incarnate sonship. Behind Christ's vicarious priestly self-offering to the Father, writes Torrance, paraphrasing Cyril's stance, 'lies his continuous and perfect obedience in our human nature, for it is the whole life of filial obedience which is

---

[115] Torrance, *Theology in Reconciliation*, p. 161.
[116] Torrance, *Theology in Reconciliation*, pp. 163–4.
[117] Cyril, *Scholia*, MPG LXXV, 1390C–1391A, cited Torrance, *Theology in Reconciliation*, p. 169.

offered to the Father on our behalf and once for all, and which remains for ever the oblation of a sweet odour to the Father'.[118] It was in and through the incarnate Son's life of continuous and perfect obedience in our human nature which was offered to the Father on our behalf and in our place that our abject human condition has been truly healed.

On this matter of a sanctifying union between the divine and the human in the incarnation, John McGuckin, citing *Scholia* 9, draws attention to Cyril's use of the analogy of a stick that has just caught alight from the fire: 'In that moment, the wood of the material reality is perfectly preserved, and yet the fire has become at one with it. Likewise the divinity plays through the flesh of Christ like a lancing flame to deify his own body in a most natural and intimate way, and yet also fires out from this source to restore and heal his contemporaries in Galilee, and thence to the redemption of the whole human race.'[119]

Torrance recognises in Cyril's writings not only a strong christological focus, but a pneumatological one as well:

> It is in pneumatological terms that Cyril understands the intimate union between us and Christ: the presence of the Mind of Christ in us and his offering of our mind to the Father, for the Spirit, he reminds us, is the Mind of Christ, and it is in the same Spirit that our mind is sanctified and lifted up through Christ into God.[120]

Torrance goes on to note the way in which Cyril's Christology and pneumatology combine to provide a profound theology of worship and prayer. In the Spirit, Torrance writes, representing Cyril's views

> ... our prayer and worship participate in ways beyond our understanding in the prayer and worship of the

---

[118] Torrance, *Theology in Reconciliation*, pp. 170–1.
[119] J. A. McGuckin, *St Cyril of Alexandria: The Christological Controversy* (Leiden: E. J. Brill, 1994), p. 187.
[120] Torrance, *Theology in Reconciliation*, p. 182.

glorified Christ. As High Priest of our souls Jesus Christ presides through the Spirit in all our liturgical acts in his name, in such a way that while he is offered by us in prayer to the Father, in reality it is he who offers us to the Father in the identity of himself as Offerer and Offering.[121]

In sum, Cyril's theology of worship and prayer is deeply trinitarian.

Torrance acclaims Cyril's *Commentary on the Gospel According to John* as one of the great patristic works on the theology of worship[122] and notes four main features worthy of our attention. First, and very important, because of the link between the priesthood of Christ and his incarnate sonship, we are bound to note that Christian worship is not merely something that is done in and through him, but something that is done *with* him who has become bone of our bone and flesh of our flesh. In becoming a human being, the Son of God worshipped as a human being. Having said that, Cyril objected to the idea that the worship which Christ offers is some superior kind of worship, even though he is a superior worshipper, for in the incarnation he accommodated himself to the limits and particularity of our creatureliness.[123] The renewal of worship comes not by Christ offering a superior kind of worship than we are able to offer, but by him taking what is ours and through his life making it whole.

Second, this worship offered by Christ is essentially 'spiritual', by which Cyril means worship which is appropriate to the nature of God who is Spirit, and which directs all the Church's worship to the *leitourgia* and *latreia* which Christ has already fulfilled on its behalf, rather than to institutional substitutes for worship of God in spirit and in truth.[124]

---

[121] Torrance, *Theology in Reconciliation*, p. 184. Torrance cites by way of footnote *Glaphyra in Leviticum* and numerous other passages from Cyril's writings.
[122] Torrance, *Theology in Reconciliation*, p. 177.
[123] Torrance, *Theology in Reconciliation*, p. 178.
[124] Torrance, *Theology in Reconciliation*, p. 179.

Third, worship involves a mental union with Christ, so that Christian worship is offered in and through *the Mind of Christ*,[125] recalling of course that the Mind of Christ is not the Divine Mind of Apollinarian doctrine, but rather the human mind healed and sanctified in and through the Son's self-presentation to the Father. As the Christian mind is united with his so the Church's acts of worship come to their full expression and reality in, through and with his vicarious worship of the Father.

Fourth, in keeping with what we have already noted about Cyril's pneumatology, it is through the activity of the Spirit that all these things take place. It is in the Spirit that the human mind is sanctified and lifted up through Christ into God; it is in and through the Spirit that persons are united to the Son and through him to the Father; and it is because the Spirit of the risen and ascended Christ dwells in his people as Advocate and Intercessor, to help them in the supplications they endeavour to offer to God, that they are enabled and empowered to pray in a way beyond what they are capable of in their own nature.[126]

By way of summary, Cyril's view of worship, as it is described by Torrance, is distinctive for the major place which it gives to the priesthood of the incarnate Son, and to the consequent importance of praying to the Father not only through, but also *with*, the Son. This does not rule out the appropriateness of also praying to Christ himself, for as Origen had long ago argued, since Christ is the propitiation for the sins of the world, the Church offer prayers to him first, that as High Priest he may bring their prayers and sacrifices and intercessions to the God who is over all. Origen, says Torrance, also demanded that prayer be sealed with the traditional doxology in which Christ is glorified together with the Father and the Holy Spirit is hymned together with him.[127] Thus in the liturgical development of the Church there was a combination of the mediation of the Son with the worship of the undivided

---

[125] Torrance, *Theology in Reconciliation*, p. 180.
[126] Torrance, *Theology in Reconciliation*, pp. 183–4.
[127] Torrance, *Theology in Reconciliation*, p. 186.

Trinity. 'Athanasius' conclusion to the *De incarnatione*', says Torrance, 'was typical of the underlying theological structure: "... Jesus Christ our Lord, *through* whom and *with* whom, to the Father *with* the Son Himself in the Holy Spirit ..., be honour and power and glory for ever and ever. Amen."[128] Variations upon this combination of the mediatorial and doxological formulae in which care is taken to retain a *mediatorial "with"* alongside of a *mediatorial "through"* and a *doxological "with"* are found throughout all the works of Cyril.'[129]

Historical consequences of Apollinarianism in the worship and liturgy of the Church

The Eastern Church

While the Athanasian–Cyrilian understanding of worship reached its high point in the fourth century, especially in the Alexandrian liturgical tradition, Torrance notes that the changes identified by Jungmann had already begun to set in.[130] In its reaction to Arianism the Church went to considerable lengths liturgically to emphasise the divine nature of Christ, but, as we have seen, at the unfortunate expense of the mediatorial and priestly role of Christ. The more he was glorified in the Trinity, the more his vicarious humanity faded into the background. And even when the mediatorship of Christ continued to be acknowledged, it tended to be in a manner that focused on his work as High Priest, not on his vicarious humanity, as evidenced in the growing tendency to pray 'for Christ's sake' rather than 'through Christ'.[131]

While Jungmann attributes this change almost entirely to the Cappadocian reaction to Arianism, Torrance argues that we must also acknowledge the effects of the Church's

---

[128] Athanasius, *De Incarnatione* 57, cited Torrance, *Theology in Reconciliation*, p. 187.
[129] Torrance, *Theology in Reconciliation*, pp. 186–7.
[130] Torrance, *Theology in Reconciliation*, p. 188.
[131] Torrance, *Theology in Reconciliation*, p. 189.

... comparatively undeveloped understanding of the vicarious role of the incarnate Son along the line that runs from Athanasius to Cyril, together with a further development of the doctrine of the Trinity as three *hypostaseis* in one *ousia* in respect of the coequality of the Son and Spirit with the Father, which resulted in an over-shadowing of the mediatorial aspect of prayer by the doxological.[132]

In support of this claim, Torrance refers to Basil's discussion of the problem in *De Spiritu Sancto*, in connection with his use of the doxological formulae '*with* the Son *together with* the Holy Spirit' and '*through* the Son *in* the Holy Spirit'.[133] He points out that while Basil uses 'with' and 'together with' doxologically to argue for the equality and deity of the Son, he does not seem to be aware of the mediatorial 'with' in the liturgy. In contrast to Cyril, therefore, Torrance says that Basil does not

... have anything to say about Christ praying with us or our praying with Christ and so through him to the Father, although he does speak of the Spirit as speaking on our behalf and crying 'Abba Father' in our hearts, and does use the preposition 'through' of the Spirit, in his association with the Son in mediating gifts from God.[134]

Torrance goes on to say:

When we compare Basil with Cyril it becomes apparent that when the mediatorial 'with' drops out, the mediatorial 'through' suffers a change, for its reference tends to be restricted to the saving work of Christ on our behalf which provides the

---

[132] Torrance, *Theology in Reconciliation*, pp. 189–90.
[133] Basil, *De Spiritu Sancto*, I:3, cited by Torrance, *Theology in Reconciliation*, p. 190.
[134] *De Spiritu Sancto*, XVI:38–9, cited by Torrance, *Theology in Reconciliation*, p. 190; cf. also C. Cocksworth, 'The Cross, our Worship and our Living', in *Atonement Today* (London: SPCK, 1995), pp. 113–16 for a useful summary of Basil's liturgical innovations and the reasons behind them.

ground for our approach to God and the reason for our thanksgiving.[135]

Whereas Torrance identifies in Basil's writings a clear departure from Cyril's position here, Jungmann – as we noted earlier in this chapter – merely detects an ambiguity as Basil seeks to combine the old doxology with the new. Ambiguity or not, the fact remains that the new 'non-mediatorial' doxology was becoming established in the Church, and in due course would become the predominant one. For example, notes Torrance, the works of one of Basil's friends, John Chrysostom, are characterised by a lack of conception of Christ praying with us and on our behalf, and of our worship and prayer being a participation in the worship and prayer of the incarnate Son to the Father. Accordingly, there is not any trace of a mediatorial 'with' in Chrysostom's doxologies.[136] While in the Byzantine Liturgy of St Chrysostom the mediation of Christ is duly acknowledged in terms of Christ being the kind of meeting ground of the divine and the human, thereby mediating blessings from God, notably absent is any reference to the presence of Christ with humankind in the fullness of his humanity, and of the Church's continuing participation in his worshipping and praying as a human being towards the Father.[137]

Torrance concludes that it was this failure to follow through the Athanasian theology of worship, as it was later developed by Cyril of Alexandria over against Apollinarianism (and Nestorianism for that matter), which left its mark upon the Byzantine doctrine of worship and priesthood just as much as the Church's reaction against Arianism.[138] This is borne out, he suggests, by a study of the fourteenth-century *Commentary on the Divine Liturgy* by Nicholas Cabasilas, which restricts the mediation of Christ to his creative activity as God, mediating blessings to

[135] Torrance, *Theology in Reconciliation*, p. 191.
[136] Torrance, *Theology in Reconciliation*, p. 191.
[137] Torrance, *Theology in Reconciliation*, p. 193.
[138] Torrance, *Theology in Reconciliation*, p. 193.

people through himself, while the human priesthood of Christ fades away to be replaced by the words and actions of the priest conducting worship. This is especially evident at the Eucharist, where it is the priest who offers the bread and wine as gifts, and it is the Lord who receives them, sanctifies them and turns them into his own Body and Blood. Worshippers are thereby directed by the liturgy on earth to Christ's divine priesthood, as the offerings they make by way of thanksgiving and supplication are exchanged for divine blessings mediated through Christ as God. While the classical pattern of the liturgical movement, *to the Father through the Son and in the Spirit* correlated to the movement *from the Father through the Son and in the Spirit*, is preserved in the Byzantine liturgy and understanding of worship, the neglect of the *human* priesthood of Christ has the effect of thrusting him up into the majesty of the Godhead in such a way that he is regarded as too exalted to be associated with the prayers of the liturgy which are 'couched in language befitting servants'.[139]

The net effect of all this, posits Torrance, is that the reaction to Arianism of which Jungmann has written so convincingly, namely the emphasis on the divine majesty of Christ, may well have provided orthodox cover in the Byzantine East for a similar error to creep in from Apollinarian presuppositions, namely, the neglect of the human priesthood of Christ (in the form of a servant) in favour of a divine priesthood in which Christ fulfils his mediatorship only as God.[140]

The Western Church

If that was the situation in the East, in the Latin West formulae of mediation through the Son continued to retain their place in the liturgy. Conciliar decisions at Hippo in 393 and Carthage in 397, formulated to counter apparent Gnostic and Sabellian tendencies, insisted that prayers at the altar should be addressed to the Father through the Son.

[139] Torrance, *Theology in Reconciliation*, p. 195.
[140] Torrance, *Theology in Reconciliation*, p. 196.

Over time, though, the liturgical changes in the East filtered through to the West, especially as Arianism made its presence felt there too, forcing a reaction. Predictably, the reaction was the same as that of the Church in the East, with the same result that the human priesthood and mediation of Christ were pushed further into the background in worship.[141] Torrance makes the following observation:

> After the sixth century, and right on through the Middle Ages, prayers to Christ everywhere came to occupy a more central place in the celebration of the Eucharist, so that even when the formula of mediation *per Dominum Jesum Christum* was used, it was the majesty and Godhead of the Mediator and High Priest that were brought forward throwing the manhood of Christ and therefore his human priesthood deep into the shade. The ground of prayer became the goodness and mercy and omnipotence of Christ as the exalted Son of God.[142]

The effect on the Latin Eucharist was similar to that of the Byzantine and Coptic liturgies, namely, the erection of a great barrier of mystery, awe and dread between the supplicant and Christ, who is actively present in the eucharistic sacrifice only in terms of the terrible majesty and omnipotence of sheer deity. In fact, in the medieval liturgies of the West, this effect of fear and trembling was even more pronounced than in the East, because the Latin Mass 'was not relieved as in the East by an exultant doxology in the risen Christ running throughout the whole celebration, or by an understanding of the eucharistic sacrifice as absorbed in the once and for all ascension and self-presentation of Christ to the Father'.[143]

---

[141] Torrance, *Theology in Reconciliation*, p. 199. Cf. also, J. A. Jungmann *Public Worship*, trans. C. Howell (London: Challoner Publications, 1957), pp. 26f. for a very useful summary of the sequence of historical events impacting upon the Roman liturgy.
[142] Torrance, *Theology in Reconciliation*, pp. 199–200.
[143] Torrance, *Theology in Reconciliation*, p. 200. Cf. also, Franks, 'Christian Worship in the Middle Ages', *Christian Worship: Studies in its History and Meaning*, ed. N. Micklem (Oxford: Clarendon Press, 1936), p. 112.

The changing face of Christian worship

Looking back over the history of worship in the early Church Torrance concludes that the widespread failure to give full place to the saving humanity of Christ led to serious consequences in the liturgical practice of the Church:

> Although it was not often perceived, the really fatal elements derived from an Apollinarian orientation in Christology and soteriology, namely, failure to appreciate the principle that what Christ has not taken up into himself from us has not been saved, together with failure to appreciate the fact that if Christ did not have a human mind or a rational soul, the Son of God did not really become incarnate in human being, and his love stopped short of union with us in our actual condition. Such a movement of thought could only undermine the whole economy of redemption and damage the basic Christian understanding of God.[144]

While Jungmann's historical analysis of the place of Christ in liturgical prayer is thoroughly convincing, Torrance argues that he fails to recognise that the real crux of the matter has to do, not with what might be called *liturgical monophysitism*, but with

> ... the mediation of salvation through the unimpaired humanity of Christ, in which the activity of his human mind and soul in vicarious faith, worship and thanksgiving are essential ingredients. This implies a doctrine of the incarnation of the Son of God understood, not as the coming of God into man, but as God becoming man, coming among us as man, and therefore of God as man doing for us in a human way what we are unable to do for ourselves, and bringing us in and through himself as the incarnate Son, in his inseparable union of God and man, to participate in the blessed life and communion of the Father, Son and Holy Spirit.[145]

---

[144] Torrance, *Theology in Reconciliation*, p. 201.
[145] Torrance, *Theology in Reconciliation*, p. 201.

Torrance's point here is that Jungmann focuses too exclusively on the orthodox reaction to Arianism which took the liturgy in a monophysitical direction. While he is indeed correct in pointing out that it was the Monophysites who, in their liturgy, gave the greatest expression to those feelings of fear and awe towards the sacrament, he has failed to detect more subtle influences, namely, the presuppositions of Apollinarianism concerning the human mediation of Christ.

Torrance goes on to outline several historical consequences of these developments for worship in the Church, four of which are relevant for this book and which we will consider in turn:

The Eucharist as an epiphany of the triune God and the mediator of saving and sanctifying grace

As the human mediatorship of Christ faded into the background and Christ was thrust up into the grandeur of the Godhead, the inner dynamics of worship and the sacrament of the Eucharist began to change. Torrance notes that it came to be regarded 'not so much as a participation through and with Christ in the worship which he offers to God on behalf of all humankind, but as the regular means whereby the faithful receive divine grace and are "deified" through union with Christ in his divine nature'.[146]

The perceived remoteness of Christ in worship and prayer carried with it a changed understanding of divine grace – from the personal presence of Christ through which we are brought into union and communion with the Father to a kind of supernatural power which is the source and nourishment of the spiritual life of the soul, and which is contained in the sacraments and imparted, dispensed or infused by them and through them. As Alasdair Heron points out, grace in the medieval Church was 'thought of as coming from God and set in action by him, but as nevertheless distinct from God himself'.[147]

---

[146] Torrance, *Theology in Reconciliation*, p. 202.
[147] A. Heron, *Table and Tradition: Towards an Ecumenical Understanding of the Eucharist* (Edinburgh: Handsel Press, 1983), p. 90.

This understanding of grace gave rise to the medieval notion of *ex opere operato* in relation to the sacraments. The sacraments came to be regarded as objective rites in themselves, through the right performance or administration of which grace could be dispensed.

The Eucharist accompanied by awe and dread

As we have already noted in relation to Jungmann's thesis, in response to the Arian heresy emphasis was increasingly placed upon the divinity rather than the humanity of Christ. The effect of this emphasis has been well articulated by Heron, who says of Christ:

> He came very often to be seen and depicted as a remote figure of unutterable majesty, the *Christos Pantocrator* of so many Byzantine mosaics, armed with the book of judgement and the authority to condemn, rather than as the one who has identified himself with us in our human existence, who has taken our weakness upon himself, and who has gone before us as our pioneer, representative and advocate with the Father. Particularly at the level of popular piety, a terrifying gulf opened up between him and us, a gulf which demanded to be bridged. What then tended to fill it was the church, the system of sacraments by which grace was dispensed, and the merits of the saints.[148]

Torrance observes that 'in the West contemplation of the bitter passion of God on the Cross together with fear and trembling before the majesty of God predominated in the celebration of the Mass'.[149] In conjunction with this emphasis on the passion of Christ and his death on the cross, Torrance also notes that the eschatological emphasis upon the resurrection and ascension of Christ gradually disappeared from the Eucharist, 'so that the Mass or the Lord's Supper tended to be truncated at the point of

---

[148] Heron, *Table and Tradition*, pp. 81f.
[149] Torrance, *Theology in Reconciliation*, pp. 202–3.

communion with Christ in his body and blood'.[150] This in turn laid the foundation for a rather instrumentalist understanding of the atoning work of Christ, as something which took place for us on the cross, rather than something which also involves the reconstitution of our humanity in the humanity of the incarnate One, who continues to represent us in his ascended glory.

One final change needs to be noted too. Heron points out that the Church's increasing emphasis upon the divinity of Christ in worship had a deeper and more insidious consequence, namely, the loss of awareness that it is in, through and with Jesus Christ that we are able to worship God. He writes that as the mediatorial role of Christ faded from view, 'prayer and worship came more and more to be seen as *our* action, rather than as *his*. We worship, the *church* worships, and he is the object of worship rather than its leader.'[151] In other words, worship and prayer were increasingly cast in a Pelagian mould.

The Mass as a substitute for Christ

As the human priesthood and mediatorial function of Christ fell away in the Eucharist, and as the meaning of grace changed in the Church, so, suggests Torrance, the Eucharist itself became a 'substitute' for Christ as the centre of actual devotion in the worship of the Church.[152] That this was so, is evident from two developments. First, as Nicholas Wolterstorff notes, by the Middle Ages almost all the emphasis of the liturgy had shifted over to its eucharistic component. The first half of the liturgy was understood merely as preparation for the Eucharist. Aquinas, for example, said that 'the celebration of this mystery' of the Eucharist is preceded by a certain preparation 'in order that we may perform worthily that which follows after'.[153]

[150] Torrance, *Theology in Reconciliation*, p. 202.
[151] Heron, *Table and Tradition*, p. 82.
[152] Torrance, *Theology in Reconciliation*, p. 203.
[153] *Summa Theologica* III, Q.83, art.4, resp. – cited by N. Wolterstorff in 'The Reformed Liturgy', in *Major Themes in the Reformed Tradition*, ed. D. K. McKim (Grand Rapids: Eerdmans, 1992), p. 281.

The second development was increasing significance attributed to the elevation of the sacred Host after the consecration of the eucharistic elements. Jungmann says of the medieval liturgy in this regard:

> Because the faithful no longer wanted to communicate or dared to (the clergy did not encourage frequent reception, to put it mildly), they wanted to see the sacred Host. From gazing at the sacred Species, they hoped for blessing and help in their earthly needs as well as salvation for their souls. ... We can therefore attribute a certain pious movement to the late Middle Ages. But its goal was not *celebrating* the Eucharist, or communicating more frequently, but looking at the Blessed Sacrament and venerating it.[154]

Thus, as Torrance notes, 'the Mass absorbed into itself the interest which Christ himself has for us in the Gospel'.[155] This can be seen, for example, in the way in which the language of 'sacrifice' was increasingly applied to the Mass.

In general terms, whereas the Eucharist as sacrament emphasised the movement (of grace) from God to humankind, the Eucharist as sacrifice emphasised an answering movement from humankind to God. As sacrament the Eucharist was *received*; as sacrifice it was to be *offered*.[156] This was made clear in the language of the Roman liturgy. As Wolterstorff points out, in the eucharistic liturgy approved by the Council of Trent, the priest prayed that God will 'accept this unblemished sacrificial offering which I, thy unworthy servant, make to thee, living and true God, for my countless sins, offences and neglects, and on behalf of all who are present here'.[157]

---

[154] J. A. Jungmann, 'Liturgy on the Eve of the Reformation', *Worship* 33 (1959), pp. 510–11.
[155] Torrance, *Theology in Reconciliation*, p. 203.
[156] Aquinas, *Summa Theologica* II/1, quaestiones 109–14, cited in Heron, *Table and Tradition*, p. 102.
[157] Translation from *Liturgies of the Western Church*, ed. B. Thompson (Cleveland: World Publishing, 1965), cited by Wolterstorff, 'Reformed Liturgy', p. 285.

Shortly after this he prayed that 'our sacrifice be so offered in thy sight this day that it may please thee', and invoked blessing upon 'these sacrificial gifts'.

These brief excerpts from the liturgy serve to substantiate Wolterstorff's point that 'the language of the Eucharist was overwhelmingly the language of sacrifice'.[158] While many medieval theologians, including Aquinas, were emphatic in their denial of the notion that at the hands of the priest Christ was sacrificed again for our sins in the Eucharist, they did want to maintain the idea that some kind of propitiatory sacrifice was taking place, that the Eucharist was more than just a memorial meal. This was confirmed by the Council of Trent, which went so far as to stipulate that 'by this sacrificial offering the Lord is indeed appeased, concedes the grace and gift of repentance, forgives great faults and even heinous sins'.[159]

Of course, there was nothing new about the language of sacrifice in relation to the Eucharist. Indeed, until the time of the Reformation it was taken for granted, and there was little need to mount a coordinated theological defence of the notion. While from the twelfth century a succession of theologians had taught specifically on the sacrificial nature of the Eucharist, it was generally on an ad hoc basis, reflecting a rather diverse system of thought in a stage of gradual refinement and development. In the twelfth century Peter Lombard, drawing on the teaching of John Chrysostom, described the Eucharist in terms of a memorial and representation in sacramental form of the real sacrifice that was Christ's.[160] According to this understanding, the Eucharist is neither an addition to, nor repetition of, Christ's sacrifice, which has been completed once and for all upon the cross. Rather, it constitutes a sacramental sharing in that sacrifice.

In itself there is nothing in Lombard's view of eucharistic sacrifice that contradicts the subsequent Reformed emphasis

[158] Wolterstorff, 'Reformed Liturgy', p. 285.
[159] Council of Trent: Session 22, chapter 2, cited by J. F. McHugh, 'The Sacrifice of the Mass at the Council of Trent', in *Sacriface and Redemption: Durham Essays in Theology*, ed. S. W. Sykes (Cambridge University Press, 1991), p. 177.
[160] *Sent.* 4, 12, 7, cited by K. Stevenson, *Eucharist and Offering* (New York: Pueblo Publishing Co., 1986), p. 118.

on 'participation' as a category for describing the Christian life. However, in medieval Roman thought, the *sacrifice* motif was closely bound up with the motif of *presence*, which was defined by the doctrine of transubstantiation in terms of Christ being present in the sacrament under the species of the consecrated bread and wine. In accordance with this fusion of sacrifice and presence, Aquinas said that the Eucharist 'is called a sacrifice insofar as it represents the passion itself of Christ; and it is called a victim insofar as *it contains Christ himself* who is the saving Victim'.[161] The Eucharist is thus 'at once a sacrifice *and* a sacrament'.[162]

As Alasdair Heron observes, this view of the Eucharist as sacrifice carried with it a belief that 'the priest on earth acts *in persona Christi*, as Christ's representative, through whom Christ himself works'.[163] While Aquinas was at pains to point out that Christ is not crucified in the Mass – the Mass is the presence of the One who suffered, not of the suffering of Christ – in fact, it is only a short step to believing that the officiating priest, as Christ's represen- tative in the Eucharist, actually offers the body and blood of Christ to God himself – a view in fact taught openly by Gabriel Biel in the fifteenth century.[164]

While Aquinas did not go as far as Biel, he did say that the eucharistic sacrifice does have the power to make satis- faction for sin, and so obtain forgiveness, in proportion to the faith and devotion of the person who offers the sacrifice, or those for whom it is offered.[165] Raymond Moloney comments that the key to Aquinas' approach here 'is the sacramental principle: sacraments bring about that which they signify. If the Eucharist is the sacramental sign of the sacrifice of the cross, then it must in some sense contain that sacrifice and bring its effects about in our own time.'[166]

---

[161] *Summa Theologica* II, 85, 1ff., cited by Stevenson, *Eucharist and Offering*, p. 118 (italics mine).
[162] *Summa Theologica* IIIa, 79, 5, cited by Stevenson, *Eucharist and Offering*, p. 129 (italics mine).
[163] Heron, *Table and Tradition*, p. 104. Heron cites Aquinas, *Summa Theologica* III, 83, 1.
[164] Cf. Stevenson, *Eucharist and Offering*, p. 119.
[165] *Summa Theologica* III, 79, 5, cited by Heron, *Table and Tradition*, p. 105.
[166] R. Moloney, *The Eucharist* (London: Geoffrey Chapman, 1995), p. 141.

Thus, although the Mass commemorates the unique sacrifice of Christ and does not multiply it, it nevertheless has a truly propitiatory function.

Tied to this belief in the propitiatory function of the Mass was a belief, expressed by Aquinas, that 'in several Masses the oblation of the sacrifice is multiplied; and therefore the effects of the sacrifice and the sacrament are multiplied'.[167] In practice this encouraged the saying of the Mass as often as possible in order that the maximum benefit be obtained both for the living and also for the dead, who could also be helped by it, provided that they were not in hell, but undergoing purification in purgatory.[168] The private Mass, celebrated by a priest without a congregation to receive communion – in order to secure some benefit, which might include atonement for sin, for persons either present or not communicating, including the dead – was commonplace in the medieval Church.[169]

It becomes clear from the above discussion that deeply embedded in the language of sacrifice and the corresponding belief in the propitiatory function of the Mass was a focus in medieval eucharistic theology on the death rather than the life of Christ. Whereas in the East eucharistic sacrifice was understood mainly in terms of being united with the self-offering of Christ, in the Latin West it was associated with his death: Christ's atoning, sacrificial death is effectively re-presented in the Mass. It is sacramentally present.

In this regard, Nugent Hicks, in his influential work *The Fullness of Sacrifice*, has argued that medieval theology went astray in singling out Christ's death as the essential event of his atoning sacrifice and in relating the Eucharist primarily to that death:[170]

---

[167] *Summa Theologica* III, 79, 7, cited Heron, *Table and Tradition*, p. 106.
[168] Cf. Session 22, chapter 9, canon 3 of *The Canons and Decrees of the Council of Trent*, p. 149.
[169] Cf. McHugh, 'Sacrifice of the Mass', p. 162.
[170] In the later medieval period, Hicks says, the equation 'sacrifice = death' was universally accepted in the Latin West (*Fullness of Sacrifice*, pp. 311–12).

As the scope of the sacrifice became narrowed to the 'representation' of Christ's death, and the altar became, however mystically, the counterpart not of the altar in heaven but of the altar of the Cross, it became inevitable that the conception of the Presence should adapt itself to this new point of view. If the sacrifice was thought of as in some sense an 'immolation', then, however insensibly, it was bound to follow that the Body and Blood should be thought of as the Body and Blood of Christ as slain. The path was open, to popular faith, for visions of bleeding hosts, and to popular interpretations of the Presence, which can only be called materialistic.[171]

Hicks goes on to argue that because sacrifice was equated with death, and the Mass was deemed to be a sacrifice, that medieval eucharistic theology assumed that Christ must in some way be put to death in the Mass. There was, he says, a widespread belief that the death of Christ was repeated in every Mass.[172]

Francis Clark, however, disagrees with Hicks on this point. He says that while 'it is certainly true that the pre-Reformation theologians often said that the Mass is an immolation, that in it Christ is immolated daily, and used other mystical expressions', at the same time they insisted 'that the Mass is a mystical and unbloody sacrifice, that in it Christ cannot die or suffer anew in any way, and that it is a memorial of his past death'.

In support of this counter-assertion Clark cites a number of medieval theologians, including Alger of Liège in the twelfth century, who said that 'the immolation of Christ at the altar is so called not because Christ is again killed, but because his true immolation therein represented works the same effects now at the altar that it worked then on the cross'.[173] Central to this issue is the meaning of the

---

[171] Hicks, *Fullness of Sacrifice*, p. 314.
[172] Hicks, *Fullness of Sacrifice*, p. 308.
[173] *De sacramentis*, lib. I, cap. 16; *P.L.* CLXXX, col. 786, cited by F. Clark, *Eucharistic Sacrifice and the Reformation*, second edn (Oxford: Basil Blackwell, 1967), pp. 405–6.

word 'immolation'. Citing St Albert the Great in the thirteenth century, Clark points out that *immolatio* 'was named after the rite of placing a victim for sacrifice on a large stone altar. That is to say, 'the term refers to the rite of offering up the victim, not the killing'.[174] Thus while the Church is always immolating and always sacrificing, the same cannot be said of crucifying. Of that there can be no reiteration.

Be that as it may, the key point to note for the purposes of this book is that the notion of eucharistic sacrifice, especially in relation to its propitiatory function, clearly had the effect of undermining the human priesthood and mediatorial function of Christ in the Eucharist, thereby substantiating T. F. Torrance's assertion that the Eucharist itself became a 'substitute' for Christ as the centre of actual devotion in the worship of the medieval Church.

The Church's priesthood as a substitute for Christ's priesthood

In conjunction with all the above changes, the understanding of priesthood underwent fundamental change, both with respect to Christ and with respect to the priesthood of the Church. Torrance notes that Christ came to be regarded more as a mediator of divine gifts and benefits than a bridge between humankind and God, as reflected in the change in language from *pontifex* to *sacerdos*. As a result, the Church was thrown back upon itself to provide a priesthood which could take his place, and even mediate between the sinner and Christ, dispensing his grace through the sacraments.

While the Roman doctrine of *ex opere operato* pointed to the objective reality of the sacrament rather than the personal quality of the celebrant, it nevertheless relied upon the proper office and status of the celebrant and therefore presumed a properly ordained priesthood.

In conjunction with the rise of the priesthood in the Roman Church, a sharp division arose between clergy and

---

[174] Clark, *Eucharistic Sacrifice and the Reformation*, p. 407.

the people, with the people's role being largely reduced to that of spectator. This role was accentuated by the fact that the Mass was conducted in Latin. While the liturgy was *available* to the people in one way or another, the *performance* of the liturgy was assigned to the clergy. From the sixth century there developed the practice of private Masses, said by the priest alone.

As we have already noted, with reference to LaCugna, from as early as the fourth century there developed the habit of people attending the Eucharist but not of regularly partaking of the elements. This custom of non-participation in communion grew more and more common, until in 1215 the Fourth Lateran Council found it necessary to insist that the faithful should communicate at least once a year. That this instruction was necessary was indicative, Heron suggests, 'of how far the laity had come to feel that the Eucharist was essentially a sacerdotal matter'.[175] Indeed, as Jungmann says generally of this period, 'the people were religious and they came to the services. Even when they were present, however, the liturgy was for the clergy ... The role of the laity was to all intents and purposes that of a spectator.'[176]

Finally, and as we have already noted in our discussion of Jungmann's thesis, as the human priesthood of Christ receded into the background, mediatorial functions were assigned not only to the clergy, but also to the Virgin Mary and to the saints. As Torrance concludes, this development simply reflects 'the demand for other functionaries exercising a mediatorial ministry, to make up for the human priesthood of Christ'.[177]

Prayer as a meritorious activity

The above analysis indicates that as the human priesthood of Christ was diminished in ecclesiastical doctrine the Church was thrown back upon itself to provide its own priesthood,

---

[175] Heron, *Table and Tradition*, p. 86.
[176] Jungmann, 'Liturgy on the Eve of the Reformation', p. 508.
[177] Torrance, *Theology in Reconciliation*, p. 203.

its own institutional means of dispensing grace and representing the people to God, and even its own institutional order of salvation (*ordo salutis*). This was accomplished in and through the Eucharist, the end result being that to all intents and purposes the liturgical event was detached from the objective reality with which it was integrated.

If the erosion of the doctrine of the priesthood of Christ, in combination with other influences such as the casuistic understanding of grace, affected the shape of liturgical prayer and worship, so too did it affect the inner dynamics of private or personal prayer. In particular, prayer too became a very 'Pelagian' activity. Wilhelm Niesel argues that the medieval Church regarded prayer as one of the good works by which a person acquires merit and a consequent increase in grace.[178] As such, it was not just the *content of prayer* that mattered, but the *number of prayers* as well. Hence the priority given to the Rosary prayer.[179] Moreover, some forms of prayer were regarded as more valuable than others. This is clear from the system of indulgences in use in the medieval Church, which determined the exact value of the various prayers. Of course, one element that undergirded every prayer, as in every good work, was *bono intentio*, the 'intention' with which it was prayed. It was not enough just to recite prayers thoughtlessly, though one was not expected to think of the 'intention' of every single prayer. One could also pray 'in the intention' of some other person, of a bishop or of the pope for example, and by doing so, further one's intercessions.[180]

Conclusion

We began this chapter by suggesting that the Church's understanding of Christ's mediatorial work in relation to

---

[178] W. Niesel, *Reformed Symbolics: A Comparison of Catholicism, Orthodoxy, and Protestantism*, trans. D. Lewis (Edinburgh: Oliver and Boyd, 1962), p. 67.
[179] Cf. Niesel, *Reformed Symbolics*, p. 68, for a useful account of the origin of the Rosary.
[180] Niesel, *Reformed Symbolics*, p. 68.

both the atonement and worship is grounded in a prior conception of *who* Christ is. The truth of this statement has been borne out by the above discussion of the impact of Arianism and Apollinarianism on the doctrinal and liturgical life of the early Church. On a doctrinal level, the dualistic habits of thought which lay behind both these ancient heresies had the effect of disrupting the unitary approach of Nicene orthodoxy to understanding the person of Christ and the nature of the atonement. The flow-on effect of this disruption on the liturgical life of the Church was dramatic.

In the first instance, as the Church responded to the threat posed by the Arian denial of the deity of Christ, liturgical prayers and doxologies were increasingly directed to the Son as well as to the Father. While a trinitarian formula was retained in public prayer, as Jungmann's thesis makes clear, it had in fact undergone a subtle yet profound change. For while directing prayers *to* rather than *through* Christ ensured that liturgical recognition was given to his divinity, it had the effect of eroding the Church's appreciation both of his vicarious humanity and of his mediatorial role in prayer. As he was thrust up into the majesty of the Godhead, he was increasingly perceived not as the one who prays *with* his people (as their Brother in prayer) and *for* them (as their Intercessor and Advocate), but as the One *to* whom prayer is directed.

If there is a weakness in Jungmann's thesis it is to be found in his concentrated focus on the impact of Arianism on the liturgical development of the fourth-century Church while the more subtle theological influence of Apollinarianism goes undetected. His thesis is thus well complemented by that of T. F. Torrance, who has identified several consequences of the Church's general failure to uphold the Athanasian and Cyrilian view of worship and its accompanying rejection of the Apollinarian teaching that the divine Logos became flesh without assuming a human mind. Not only did the Apollinarian position produce a mutilated view both of Christ's humanity and the economy of salvation, insofar as it ignored the atoning significance of his assumption of our humanity – which includes a human mind – it also generated a mutilated view of worship and prayer, insofar as Christ's priesthood was increasingly defined in divine rather than human categories. He came to be regarded as the mediator of divine blessings rather than the mediator of prayer and worship. As his vicarious humanity faded into the background and he was thrust up into the grandeur of the Godhead, so the mediatorial aspect of prayer was increasingly overshadowed by the doxological, and the dynamics of worship began to change. Once regarded in terms of participation through and with Christ in the worship which he offers to God on behalf of all humankind, the Eucharist or Mass came to be regarded as the regular means whereby the faithful receive divine grace and are 'deified' through union with Christ in his divine nature. Moreover, prayer was no longer seen as being mediated through Christ himself but through the priesthood of the Church, through the Virgin Mary, and through the saints. Thus while prayer might well have been uttered 'for Christ's sake' and be motivated by him, because it was no longer regarded as something which is done *with him*, and *in him*, people did not perceive themselves as having access *through him* into the immediate presence of God. They had no boldness before the throne of grace but only fear and trembling before the consuming fire of God's holiness and majesty, a sentiment that was reinforced by the medieval Latin Mass.

In sum, while the liturgical emphasis on the deity of Christ from the fourth century onwards enabled the Church to fend off the heretical influence of Arianism (Jungmann's thesis), inadvertently it had the further effect of providing a liturgical foothold for the Apollinarian denial of the full humanity of Christ (Torrance's thesis). This radically undermined the mediatorial role of Christ in prayer and altered the whole dynamic of Christian worship, which remained trinitarian in its outer form but not in its innermost content.

2
The Significance of the Doctrine of the Priesthood of Christ for John Calvin and the Early Scottish Reformed Tradition

John Calvin

The hypostatic union, the priesthood of Christ and the wonderful exchange

One of the distinctive features of the Reformation was the renewed emphasis given to the priesthood of Christ, an emphasis that, as we noted in the previous chapter, had been steadily eroded since the fourth century through the Church's confrontation with Arianism and the subtle influence of Apollinarianism, with poignant consequences for medieval doctrine and liturgical development, especially in the Latin West. While there was considerable diversity of opinion among the Reformers themselves, as fierce debates over such matters as sacrifice and real presence demonstrate, there was nevertheless a unifying conviction that the liturgy is the work not of priests on the people's behalf, but of the whole people of God under the sole priesthood of Christ. This conviction was more than an ecclesiastical reaction against the excesses and distortions of medieval clericalism. It was theologically driven, and these theological convictions provided the impetus for liturgical reform, even if the reform itself was carried out without detailed knowledge of the origins and principles of worship.[1]

Of particular interest to us in this chapter is the contribution of John Calvin to the Reformed theological emphasis upon the priesthood of Christ, for it is only by understanding his doctrinal position that we will be able to assess the extent to which federal Calvinism maintained

---

[1] Cf. W. D. Maxwell, *An Outline of Christian Worship: Its Development and Forms* (London: Oxford University Press, 1936), pp. 72–3.

that position and how well the Westminster tradition in Scotland, from the seventeenth century through to the current day, has managed to embody the doctrine of the priesthood of Christ in its understanding of worship and prayer.

The twelfth chapter of the second book of the *Institutio*, where Calvin begins to develop his Christology, opens with the sentence: 'Now it was of the greatest importance for us that he who was to be our Mediator be both true God and true man.'[2] Calvin thus begins with a reference to the hypostatic union of God and humankind in Christ. What is the purpose of this union? The answer, for Calvin, is clear. It is not because of a natural gap that exists between the Creator and creation, and the necessity or desirability of bridging that gap – rather, it is because of the gap that exists between the Creator and a *fallen* creation, and the *merciful decree* of the Father to bridge that gap so that an estranged rebellious humanity might be *restored* to God's grace and brought into a filial relationship.[3] In other words, the purpose of the hypostatic union is that the filial resolve of the Father might be fulfilled.

Only One who was both fully God and fully human could effect proper reconciliation, because only One who stands fully and simultaneously on both sides of the Creator–creation divide is, on the one hand, able to impart God's righteousness to the godless and, on the other hand, to take upon himself their estranged human condition, so that in his life of faith and obedience it might be truly healed and sanctified on their behalf. This is the 'wonderful exchange' (*mirifica commutatio*) to which Calvin is referring when he concludes: 'Ungrudgingly he [Christ] took our nature upon himself to impart to us what was his, and to become both Son of God and Son of man in common with us.'[4]

Calvin's doctrine of the hypostatic union compels him to affirm the vicarious humanity and priesthood of Christ,

---

[2] *Institutes of the Christian Religion*, Geneva, 1559, ed. J. T. McNeill, trans. F. L. Battles (Philadelphia: Westminster Press, 1960), II.12.1.

[3] Cf. *In.* II.12.1 and II.12.2.

[4] *In.* II.12.2. As we shall see, Calvin emphasises the same point in his discourse on the Lord's Supper – cf. *In.* IV.17.2.

through which he sees that a wondrous exchange has taken place. This affirmation lies at the heart of both his doctrine of justification and his understanding of the Christian life: Christians are accepted by God, not because of anything *they* are able to do, but freely by God's grace received in faith. For Calvin, as for Athanasius and the Nicene theologians, the hypostatic union belongs to the inner heart of the atonement.

Justification and sanctification

To appreciate the significance of Calvin's doctrine of justi-fication we need to compare it briefly with the medieval Roman view[5] with which he engaged and which was later enshrined in dogma at the Council of Trent.

Closely associated with the Tridentine doctrine of justi-fication was a theological anthropology which viewed the human person in its natural state of body and soul as having a 'natural' holiness, righteousness and orientation toward God which are perfected or completed by grace. To human nature, consisting of body and soul, another gift has been added by God, which is called the 'image of God'. Grace perfects nature. Even after the Fall this is still the case. Human nature has become worse not in itself but only in comparison with its original state, for human beings still possess a natural capacity to know God, and their freedom of will, though 'attenuated and bent down in its powers', is 'by no means extinguished'.[6]

This is the case because, as Hans Küng, expounding the Council's logic, explains, 'man remains man because the mercy and grace of God spared him and in patience

---

[5] In referring to 'the medieval Roman view', rather than being unmindful of the considerable diversity of theological opinion represented at the Council of Trent, we are simply referring to the general consensus of opinion that emerged during the course of the Council's deliberations and which came to be reflected in its decrees as it sought to draw a line of demarcation between Catholic dogma and Protestant teaching.

[6] Session 6, chapter 1, *The Canons and Decrees of the Council of Trent*, trans. T. A. Buckley (London: George Routledge and Co., 1851), p. 30.

preserved him for justification, that is, through the merciful power of Jesus Christ which already had in creation a preventative and inhibiting effect'.[7] Human beings, under the influence of prevenient grace and by utilising their free will, can actually prepare themselves for justification.[8] Alister McGrath sums up the Council's teaching on this point: 'Man is called through prevenient grace, without reference to his merits, to dispose himself towards justification. As a consequence of man's assenting to and cooperating with this call, God touches man's heart through the illumination of his Holy Spirit.'[9]

Armed with this theological anthropology, the Council of Trent defined justification as 'a translation from that state in which man is born a child of the first Adam, into the state of grace, and of the adoption of the sons of God, through the Second Adam, Jesus Christ'.[10] According to this definition, justification is not merely the forgiveness of sins. Nor is it a divine act by which people are declared just and receive a promise of salvation. Rather, it is an event whereby a change begins in persons, so that they become just. It is the event through which original sin has been overcome or forgiven, leaving in the human person only 'inordinate desire (*concupiscentia*), an impulse which is not evil in itself, and which serves to test the justified man in his life-long struggle'.[11] It is a process of ongoing healing.

An essential element of this divine act of justification is 'the *sanctification and renewal* of the inward man, through the voluntary reception of the grace and gifts, whereby man from unjust becomes just, and from an enemy a friend'.[12] Alongside the *justifying* (or actual) *grace* which sets aside original guilt there is the *sanctifying* (or habitual)

[7] H. Küng, *Justification: The Doctrine of Karl Barth and a Catholic Reflection* (London: Burns and Oates, 1964), p. 167.
[8] Cf. O. Weber, *Foundations of Dogmatics*, Vol. 2, trans. D. L. Guder (Michigan: Eerdmans, 1983), p. 299, who notes that this is one issue which is always at stake between Catholic and Reformed theology.
[9] A. McGrath, *Iustitia Dei: Studies in Personhood and the Church* (London: Darton, Longman and Todd, 1985), p. 82.
[10] Session 6, chapter 4, *Council of Trent*, p. 31.
[11] Niesel, *Reformed Symbolics*, p. 61
[12] Session 6, chapter 7, *Council of Trent*, p. 33.

grace with which people are infused at baptism,[13] thereby destroying sin, sanctifying them, conferring upon them the adoption of sonship and the hope of heavenly inheritance, and enabling them to keep the commandments of God and of the Church. While the justified can still commit sins – Trent does not teach perfectionism – as Otto Weber observes, the sins committed by the justified person are regarded as 'venial sins'.[14] Thus 'the Lutheran concept of "sinner and righteous at the same time" is rejected sharply'.[15]

Thus understood, sanctification carries with it a particular view of divine grace as a kind of supernatural quality or energy with which the faithful are infused. T. F. Torrance argues that this understanding is one which the medieval Church inherited from Augustine who, because of his underlying belief in a radical disjunction between the realms of the *mundus intelligibilis* and the *mundus sensibilis*, was forced to cast the notion of divine grace in impersonal categories of causality and containment – that is, in terms of the means by which these two realms are bridged.[16] It is reflected in the medieval view of the sacraments as the means by which divine grace is dispensed or imparted. Grace is, as it were, 'contained' in the sacraments, and 'dispensed' at the hands of the officiating priests.

Since in Tridentine theology justification means that grace, understood in terms of a supernatural energy, is infused into the recipient, it follows that there must be a possibility of increasing one's level of justification. The Council of Trent affirmed precisely this possibility: 'They [the justified], through the observance of the commandments

---

[13] Thus baptism is described at the Council of Trent in terms of the 'instrumental cause' of justification. The 'instrumental cause' is to be distinguished from the 'formal cause' (the righteousness of God), the 'meritorious cause' (the passion of Christ), the 'efficient cause' (the mercy of God) and the 'final cause' (the glory of God and eternal life) – cf. Session 6, chapter 7, *Council of Trent*, pp. 33–4.

[14] Venial sins are those sins that can be erased by an act of contrition. By way of contrast, mortal sins are the more serious breaches of divine law.

[15] Weber, *Foundations of Dogmatics*, Vol. 2, p. 300.

[16] Cf. T. F. Torrance, *Theology in Reconstruction* (London: SCM Press, 1965), pp. 173–80.

of God and of the Church, faith cooperating with good works, increase in the justice received through the grace of Christ, and are still more justified.'[17] 'Because of indwelling grace', comments Niesel, 'real progress in sanctification takes place and so an increase in justifying grace itself.'[18] Thus described, justification is both an event and a process. 'Only at the end of the process', Peter Toon comments, 'will the believer truly know that he is justified. His constant duty is to cooperate with the grace of God given to him.'[19]

This notion of faith cooperating with good works introduces the concept of *merit*. Medieval Roman theology made a distinction between two types of merit:[20] (a) 'deserved merit' (*meritum de condigno*), which is earned by those who, existing in a 'state of grace', perform the works required by God's commandments and the Church's commandments; and (b) 'equitable or congruous merit' (*meritum de congruo*), which is earned by those who, though they are not in a state of grace, nevertheless voluntarily perform morally good acts. The Council of Trent, Niesel comments, taught that three things are won by the works of a justified person: an increase in sanctifying grace, a right to eternal life and an increase in eternal glory.[21] As we noted towards the end of the previous chapter, one of the good works, by which one is deemed to acquire merit and a consequent increase in grace, is prayer.

Of course the flip side to the belief that one's justification may be increased, is the belief that it may decrease and even be lost altogether. Hence the Roman notion of *mortal sin*, so named because it deprives one of sanctifying grace and makes one liable to eternal death. Moreover, the possibility of falling out of grace and losing one's justification

---

[17] Session 6, chapter 10, *Council of Trent*, p. 36.

[18] Niesel, *Reformed Symbolics*, p. 63.

[19] P. Toon, *Justification and Sanctification* (London: Marshall, Morgan and Scott, 1983), p. 71.

[20] Cf. Niesel, *Reformed Symbolics*, pp. 64–5.

[21] According to the Council of Trent the justified person 'merits increase of grace, eternal life, and, if he departs this life in grace, the attainment of eternal life, and also an increase of glory' (Session 6, canon 32, *Council of Trent*, p. 46, cited in Niesel, *Reformed Symbolics*, p. 65).

has the effect of generating considerable uncertainty about one's state of grace. Not that this necessarily leads to despair, for as B. Bartmann points out, the Council of Trent taught 'a middle way between assurance of faith and doubt, namely, a moral certainty which banishes all anxiety and despair'.[22] What we end up with, therefore, despite all the categories of grace which pervade Tridentine theology, is a 'semi-Pelagianism'[23] – the sense that, at least in part, people have the power to secure their own assurance of salvation through moral acts.

While Calvin shared the Tridentine emphasis on grace, and also maintained an integral relation between justification and sanctification, he did so in a radically different way. Along with other Reformers he rejected the notion of grace as something that exists in and of itself as some kind of supernatural energy, which can be contained in certain objects and imparted through them. He also rejected both the notion of grace perfecting nature and the theological anthropology that was presumed in it. The human person, he taught, has been corrupted by sin through and through.[24] No part has been left untouched. Human nature, therefore, is in need not of being perfected but of being reconstituted, renewed, re-created. In this context, grace is not something that is imparted; it is that which re-creates. It is intensely personal. It is the personal self-giving of God to people in Christ. As such, it is totally bound up with the hypostatic union, for in the humanity of the Son the corrupt human nature which all people share has been fully assumed, healed and sanctified, giving rise to nothing less than a new humanity, a new creation. It is also bound up with one's own personal union with Christ as one is brought by the Spirit to partake of his new humanity, to be a participant in the new creation. That is to say, one's salvation is not only *per Christum* but also *in Christo*.

So important is this notion of being in union with Christ

---

[22] B. Bartmann, *Lehrbuch der Dogmatik*, eighth edn, 1932, Vol. 1, p. 5, cited by Niesel, *Reformed Symbolics*, p. 67.
[23] Cf. Torrance, *Theology in Reconstruction*, p. 176.
[24] Cf. *In*. I.15.4.

to Calvin's doctrine that it lies behind all his teaching on justification and sanctification. As Niesel points out, the distinctive feature of his teaching on the subject 'is that he first of all lays the foundation, by speaking of our union with Christ, next he deals with the gift of sanctification, and only then develops his doctrine of justification'.[25] This ordering is important, not because sanctification precedes justification, but because it highlights the fact that both gifts are received simultaneously and together. As Calvin himself writes:

> Christ justifies no one whom he does not at the same time sanctify. These benefits are joined together by an everlasting and indissoluble bond, so that those whom he illumines by his wisdom, he redeems; those whom he redeems, he justifies; those whom he justifies, he sanctifies.[26]

Having said that, care must be taken not to collapse the distinction between justification and sanctification. Of the former, Calvin says that 'justified by faith is he who, excluded from the righteousness of works, grasps the righteousness of Christ through faith, and clothed in it, appears in God's sight not as a sinner but as a righteous man. Therefore, we explain justification simply as the acceptance with which God receives us into his favour as righteous men. And we say that it consists in the remission of sins and the imputation of Christ's righteousness.'[27]

Justification, then, is about the ungodly being clothed in Christ's righteousness. It is about being judged and acquitted, condemned and vindicated, exposed as guilty and made righteous, in and through Jesus Christ. It is not a process whereby one becomes just (the Roman view), but a truth declared and completed in Christ the Mediator. As such, it can neither be added to nor taken away by anything that people do or fail to do.

---

[25] Niesel, *Reformed Symbolics*, p. 192.
[26] *In.* III.16.1.
[27] *In.* III.11.2.

At the same time, we must understand that for Calvin 'the remission of sins and the imputation of Christ's right-eousness' is not an external act or a declaration from afar. It takes place within our humanity, as Christ the Mediator and High Priest assumes the human nature that all people share, reconstitutes it from within, and by his Spirit unites people to himself so that his humanity becomes theirs. This is what sanctification refers to. So it is that Calvin says, 'we or our prayers have no access to God unless Christ, as our High Priest, having washed away our sins, *sanctifies us* and obtains for us that grace from which the uncleanness of our transgressions and vices debars us'.[28]

For Calvin, sanctification is grounded in the hypostatic union, in and through which the unholy human nature that all people share has been brought into a sanctifying union with the Son's holy nature. He insists that this applies to the whole life of Jesus, in which our conception, birth, childhood, youth, adulthood and death have all been sanctified.[29] In becoming one with humankind in the incar-nation Christ laid hold upon the rebellious human will and condition that characterises human existence, made it his own, and bent it back into obedience to, and in oneness with, the will of God. As T. F. Torrance observes, Calvin's teaching here is consistent with that found in John's Gospel, where, 'in his great high-priestly prayer, Jesus spoke of sanctifying himself that we also may be sanctified in him, and prayed that we may be consecrated in one with him as he and the Father are one'.[30]

The priesthood of Christ: retrospective and prospective

Having identified the deeply woven links in Calvin's theology between the priesthood of Christ, the hypostatic union, the wondrous exchange, justification and sanctifi-cation, we must now go on to explore more fully the nature and implications of Christ's priesthood. Taking his lead

---

[28] *In*. II.15.6 (italics mine).
[29] *In*. II.16.19.
[30] Torrance, *Theology in Reconstruction*, p. 157.

from the book of Hebrews, Calvin makes it clear that the priestly office of Christ refers not only to what he *accomplished* at Calvary, where, by the sacrifice of his death he blotted out the guilt of humankind and made satisfaction for their sins (the High Priest was also the sacrifice), but also to what he *continues to do* as an everlasting Intercessor, through whose pleading people obtain favour and in whose company they may freely enter the heavenly sanctuary so that the sacrifices of prayers and praise that they bring may be acceptable and sweet-smelling before God.[31]

The priesthood of Christ and worship

All that has been said thus far concerning the hypostatic union, justification and the priesthood of Christ has implications for the Christian understanding of worship. For Calvin, the activity of worship stems from people being in union with Christ, and is regarded as an act of participation in the worship that he offers to the Father in their name and on their behalf. As Calvin himself says, 'Christ leads our songs and is the chief composer of our hymns.'[32]

Implied in this understanding of Christ's priestly role in worship is the representative character of priesthood carried over from ancient Israel. Noting Calvin's emphasis on the priesthood of Christ in worship, J. B. Torrance says that 'true worship ... is not in the first instance what *we* do in our strength out of our own resources, it is rather that which Christ has done and is doing for us as our great High Priest, the One True *Leitourgos* of the sanctuary (Heb. 8:2), and in which we are given to participate through the Spirit'.[33]

An important consequence of this, as Calvin puts it, is that 'we who are defiled in ourselves, *yet are priests in him*', and on these grounds alone are we able to, 'offer ourselves

---

[31] *In.* II.15.6.
[32] Comm. on Heb. 2:12, CO 55, 29, cited by Torrance, 'Vicarious Humanity', p. 70.
[33] Torrance, 'Vicarious Humanity', p. 70.

and our all to God, and freely enter the heavenly sanctuary that the sacrifices of prayers and praise that we bring may be acceptable and sweet-smelling before God'.[34]

The priesthood of Christ and prayer

That which has been said in relation to Calvin's view of the priesthood of Christ and worship lies behind his teaching on the subject of prayer, about which he writes in Book III, chapter 20 of the *Institutio*. The chapter opens with a brief section on the nature and value of prayer,[35] and then proceeds to outline four rules of prayer:[36] reverence; praying from a sincere sense of want, and with penitence; yielding all confidence in oneself and humbly pleading for pardon; and praying with confident hope. Commenting upon these rules, Duncan Watson writes:

> These 'rules' are more like general comments rather than rules or a method, but basically what Calvin affirms in them is this: we abandon all self-glory, acknowledge in humility our insufficiency, and with full heart and mind pray with utter confidence and hope to the One to whom we are to give glory and in whom we shall indeed find help, knowing with assurance that we shall be answered.[37]

Conscious of people's profound inability to pray in such a way, Calvin refers immediately to the intercession of Christ.[38] Because *Christ* the High Priest intercedes for his

---

[34] *In.* II.15.6 (italics mine).
[35] *In.* III.20.1–3. Calvin here describes prayer as the chief exercise of faith by which we daily receive God's benefits. Elsewhere it is eloquently described as 'an expanding of our heart in the presence of God' (*Corpus Reformatorum* – Calvin's Works, eds Baum, Cunitz, and Reuss, Vols 1–59, (Brunswick, 1863–1900), 37, 402, cited by W. Niesel, *The Theology of Calvin*, trans. H. Knight (London: Lutterworth Press, 1956), p. 153).
[36] *In.* III.20.4–16.
[37] D. S. Watson, 'In Union with Christ: Calvin', in *Open to God: Discovering New Ways to Pray*, ed. R. Pryor (Melbourne: Uniting Church Press, 1991), p. 103.
[38] *In.* III.20.17–20.

people, the prayers which they bring before God are not in vain.[39] Their own praying is nothing other than being united through the activity of the Spirit with the prayer of Christ; and they have no hope of being heard unless he precedes them with his prayer.[40]

In what ways do people benefit from this intercession of the Son, how do they participate in his life on their behalf? Still the initiative is not theirs; again it is all of grace. By the gracious working of the Holy Spirit people are brought into union with Christ.[41] It is from this union with him in his human nature that all things flow; more precisely, that people are both justified and sanctified as they are united to him by the Spirit of the Father. Even faith, therefore, is the work of the Spirit.[42] Hence, as Niesel rightly asserts, when Calvin comes to indicate the subjective presuppositions of prayer he emphasises the work of the Holy Spirit rather than the power of faith.[43] 'Before people can utter a prayer they must have received the first-fruits of the Spirit. For he alone is the proper teacher of the art of prayer. He not only inspires in his people the words but guides the movement of their hearts.'[44]

This suggests a sharp contrast between Calvin's view of prayer and that of the medieval Roman Church. Calvin's trinitarian doctrine of prayer is thoroughly christological and pneumatological. Not only does he give full weight to the mediatorial role of Christ in both atonement and worship, but he also gives full weight to the activity of the Holy Spirit, thereby refuting the medieval tendency to view prayer as a 'good work' by which people may earn divine grace and merit. Not surprisingly, therefore, immediately following his section on the intercession of Christ, Calvin attacks the Roman doctrine of the intercessions of saints.[45] All this doctrine does, he says, is

[39] *In.* III.20.18.
[40] *Corpus Reformatorum* 37, 402, cited by Niesel, *Theology of Calvin*, p. 154.
[41] *In.* III.1.1, then III.20.5.
[42] *In.* III.1.4.
[43] Niesel, *Theology of Calvin*, p. 155.
[44] *Corpus Reformatorum* 48, 16; *In.* III.20.5, cited by Niesel, *Theology of Calvin*, p. 155.
[45] *In.* III.20.21–27.

dishonour Christ and strip him of the title of sole Mediator.[46] Furthermore, veneration of the saints encourages people to call upon them not only as their helpers but also as determiners of their salvation, thereby undermining the very heart of the gospel and engendering superstition in the life of the Church.[47]

The priesthood of Christ and the Eucharist

It is these christological and pneumatological consider-ations which serve to shape Calvin's doctrines of worship and prayer, and it is those same considerations which shape his theology of the Eucharist. We saw in the previous chapter that, as Christ became the object of worship, and liturgical prayers were directed *to* him rather than *through* him and, more particularly, *with* him, so the Eucharist underwent a series of fundamental changes. As the liturgy removed Christ from the midst of the people, so the worshipping faithful were confronted with the inaccessible majesty of the triune God. This not only overwhelmed them – it also generated profound fear, even terror, relieved only by the infusion of grace which was given through the sacrament by a priest who, by virtue of his office, had, to all intents and purposes, become the mediator of salvation. Christ himself was present in the sacrament, of course, but only insofar as he was deemed to become present in the elements of bread and wine through the words of consecration. In keeping with this perception the elevation of the host immediately following the words of consecration became the high point of the liturgy – it became in itself the object of veneration and worship because it was deemed to be the effective cause of the grace it signified.

Calvin's theology of the Eucharist could not have been more different. Near the beginning of his discourse on the Eucharist, immediately following an opening section on

[46] *In.* III.20.21.
[47] *In.* III.20.22.

the signs of bread and wine, he has a section entitled
'Union with Christ as the special fruit of the Lord's
Supper'.[48] Of the importance of this notion of being in
union with Christ to Calvin's doctrine of the Eucharist,
Kilian McDonnell comments:

> Calvin did not consider the sacraments as a necessary
> means of salvation, and though union with Christ was
> not considered as dependent on the sacraments – as is
> also the case in Roman Catholicism – he did consider
> union with Christ as quite unthinkable apart from the
> sacraments. Union with Christ was not considered
> without reference to the Eucharist, or to baptism for
> that matter, just as union with Christ was not
> considered without reference to faith. The Eucharist,
> on the other hand, is possible only in view of a
> preceding and present union with Christ. The grafting
> into Christ, of which Calvin speaks, is at the same time
> a grafting into the body of Christ, a grafting into the
> body of the church.[49]

At the heart of Calvin's section on our union with Christ
stands his key passage on the wondrous exchange (*mirifica
commutatio*), which makes clear that the basis of our union
with Christ in the sacrament is not a miraculous transubstantiation of the elements of bread and wine, brought
about through a prayer of consecration, but rather the active
and living presence in the Spirit of the One who, out of his
measureless benevolence, took upon himself the weight of
our iniquity and clothed us with the righteousness that is
his alone.

What takes place in the Eucharist, therefore, is not the
imparting of grace (understood in terms of a heavenly
substance) but communion with the Mediator.
Accordingly, it is not the consecration of the elements that
gives the Eucharist its efficacy but rather the word

[48] *In.* IV.17.2.
[49] K. McDonnell, *John Calvin, the Church, and the Eucharist* (Princeton:
Princeton University Press, 1967), pp. 184–5.

proclaimed and the activity of the Spirit. Indeed, it is through the preaching of the word that he who *is* the Word, and yet has accommodated himself to the proclaimed word, is sacramentally present in the event of worship. It was for this reason that the sermon was regarded by the Reformers as 'sacramental' of the speech of God, and Reformed churches introduced into their liturgies the 'prayer of illumination' before scripture and sermon, which paralleled the prayer of consecration in the Eucharist, thus providing a proper balance between word and sacrament. It was their conviction that there is no true preaching and no right hearing without *epiclesis*.[50] Interestingly, T. F. Torrance detects in Calvin's writings a conviction that preaching, or teaching the word of God, is an intrinsically *priestly* act. He regarded the sermon, Torrance says, 'not only as a proclamation of the Gospel from the mouth of God but as an offering made to God, assimilated to Christ's one self-offering as the Word become flesh now ascended to the Father'.[51]

That, for Calvin, word and sacrament belong together is evidenced by the fact that he condemned the practice of taking communion only once a year, and advocated weekly communion instead.[52] For him the 'means of grace' were twofold, consisting of both the word and the sacraments. The ministry was a ministry of word and the sacraments, and a minister's task and office was not only to preach and instruct, but also to celebrate the Lord's Supper every week and urge the people to communicate weekly.[53]

On·the controversial matter of the real presence of Christ in the Eucharist, we might sum up Calvin's position by saying that in contrast to the medieval Church's notion of local, spatial presence through the transubstantiation of the

[50] Cf. Wolterstorff, 'Reformed Liturgy', p. 290.
[51] Cf. T. F. Torrance, 'Legal and Evangelical Priests: The Holy Ministry as Reflected in Calvin's Prayers', unpublished notes, p. 12.
[52] *In.* IV.17.46.
[53] Cf. Maxwell, *Outline of Christian Worship*, p. 116. Calvin was never able to implement weekly communion, and it was over this very issue that he was banished from Geneva by the city magistrates in 1538.

elements of bread and wine, Calvin sees the Church being lifted by the Spirit in the act of worship into the presence of God through the High Priest, Jesus Christ. The elements of bread and wine are more than the symbols of this presence – they are also the instruments and organs by which, through the activity of the Spirit, the Lord gives his people his body and his blood so that they might feed on him by faith with thanksgiving.[54] Grace is regarded not as some kind of substance that is caused or imparted to people by the sacrament, but as the personal and gracious presence of God which becomes present through the symbols of bread and wine. It is a relational rather than a physical notion of grace at work here.

Calvin on eucharistic sacrifice

It was the private Mass and the theology of sacrifice which lay at the heart of Martin Luther's invective against the Catholic Church in the sixteenth century. At the same time as he denounced the practice of private Masses he railed against the notions that the Mass is a sacrifice, that it is in any way a meritorious work, and that it might be of advantage to non-communicants, including the dead.

Luther's concerns were Calvin's too. On the subject of sacrifice, he writes:

> ... after Christ's sacrifice was accomplished, the Lord instituted another method for us, that is, to transmit to the believing folk the benefit of the sacrifice offered to himself by his Son. He has therefore given us a Table at which to feast, not an altar upon which to offer a victim; he has not consecrated priests to offer sacrifice, but ministers to distribute the sacred banquet.[55]

As far as Calvin is concerned, the notion of the Mass as a sacrifice of expiation distorts the very nature of the sacrament, and undermines the notion of the sole

---

[54] *In.* IV.17.11.
[55] *In.* IV.18.12.

priesthood of Christ, both in terms of the atoning sacrifice which he offered once and for all at Calvary, and in terms of his ongoing role as High Priest and leader of worship.

This does not mean that there is no sense in which Christians 'offer' and 'sacrifice' to God, but a crucial distinction needs to be drawn between two senses of the term 'sacrifice'. One is the 'sacrifice of propitiation or expiation' for sin, which is Christ's alone. The other is 'a sacrifice of praise and reverence', and 'whatever we do in the worship of God', which believers both owe and render to God, since 'it is given to God only by those who, laden with innumerable benefits from him, pay back to him their whole selves and all their acts'.[56] Calvin is adamant: we must not confuse the two; we must reject both the notion of the 'sacrifice of the Mass' and the conception of the ministry as a 'sacrificing priesthood'.

Calvin's views here bring into sharp focus one of the key differences between medieval and Reformed thought, which Alasdair Heron succinctly articulates in the following way:

> Medieval thought generally tended to operate with a fairly broad conception of 'sacrifice' and 'offering', seeing all kinds of worship, devotion and good works as 'sacrifices' with which God is pleased, and without compromising the supreme and unique sacrifice that was Christ's, the Reformers emphasised the absolute difference in kind and the objective, finished character of the one sacrifice of Golgotha over against any and every other 'sacrifice' that could be brought or offered.[57]

However, at the same time as we note the difference between medieval and Reformed thought, we must also ask whether Calvin's determination to emphasise the disjunction between Christ and us on the issue of sacrifice is itself problematic. This question is posed by Heron, who writes:

---

[56] *In.* IV.18.13 and IV.18.16.
[57] Heron, *Table and Tradition*, p. 168.

> If our sacrifice is only that of sacrifice and praise for
> what Christ has objectively done, that can only mean
> that at the very heart and core of Christian worship,
> *anamnesis* and offering, he stands over against us, apart
> from us, rather than with us.[58]

Moreover, while union with Christ lies at the heart of
Calvin's eucharistic theology

> ... when it comes to the controversial matter of the
> sacrifice of the Mass he is so anxious to avoid any idea
> of repeating or adding to Christ's sacrifice that he also
> seems to rule out our *participation* in his self-offering.
> Our offering becomes simply a response – response to
> him rather than sharing with him in his offering, not
> only of himself for us, but of us with himself.[59]

In making the above comment, Heron puts his finger on
a critical issue, namely, that because of the reaction of
Calvin and his fellow Reformers against the Mass as
sacrifice, they could not develop the idea of the Eucharist
as an offering in a proper way.[60] When Calvin speaks of a
sacrifice of praise he regards it as something the Church
does in the Eucharist, not something Christ does. When he
speaks of thanksgiving he refers to that which the Church
renders for a finished work on the cross, not one which
continues in heaven. The role of Christ in heaven is thus
deemed to be one of intercession rather than offering,
which has the effect of undermining the vicarious
humanity and mediation of Christ in relation to the
Reformed understanding of worship and prayer.

---

[58] Heron, *Table and Tradition*, p. 168.
[59] Heron, *Table and Tradition*, p. 169.
[60] The same point is made by Nugent Hicks, who says that the tendency
to equate sacrifice with the death rather than the life of Christ in medieval
eucharistic thought affected Catholics and Reformers alike, insofar as it
prevented both sides from developing a proper understanding of Christ's
continued offering in heaven – cf. *Fullness of Sacrifice*, pp. 317–19. We shall
return to this issue in Chapter Four, when we consider the influence of
William Milligan on Reformed theology and liturgy in the nineteenth
century.

There is, therefore, an inconsistency in Calvin's eucharistic theology that stems from his strong reaction against the medieval Mass. This inconsistency, however, should not overshadow the fact that, in every other respect, the priesthood of Christ, which stands at the heart of his doctrine of atonement, shapes profoundly his views on prayer, worship and the Eucharist. Perhaps we could leave the matter there were it not for the fact that immediately following his section on prayer in the *Institutio*, he goes on to expound his doctrine of election and predestination. In so doing, he raises further issues concerning the priesthood of Christ that are worthy of our consideration, especially insofar as they reveal another inconsistency in his thinking which was exploited by the federal Calvinists who came after him.

Calvin on election and predestination

The significance of the placement of the doctrine in the *Institutio*

Immediately following his section on prayer Calvin turns his attention to the subject of election. In doing so he picks up a subject on which he had already written at length in his 1552 treatise *Concerning the Eternal Predestination of God*, although at that time he was primarily concerned not with setting forth his own views in a systematic manner but with confronting contrary views. As J. K. S. Reid says of him in that polemical work, 'he does not have before him a clear field through which he may pick his way unimpeded, but a field strewn with obstacles of his opponents' devising'.[61] While the *Institutio*, therefore, does not contain Calvin's first exposition of the doctrine of election, it does contain his most systematic and orderly treatment of the subject.

[61] 'Introduction' to J. Calvin, *Concerning the Eternal Predestination of God*, Geneva, 1552, trans. J. K. S. Reid (London: James Clarke and Co., 1961), p. 10. Cf. David Weir's *The Origins of the Federal Theology in Sixteenth-Century Reformation Thought* (Oxford: Clarendon Press, 1990), pp. 64f., for a very useful account of the polemical background to Calvin's book.

In considering Calvin's section on election in the *Institutio*, the first question that arises is, How are we to interpret its placement within his overall system of thought? This question is pressed upon us by the fact that in earlier editions of the *Institutio* the doctrines of providence and predestination were treated as a single unit and located within the doctrine of God. In the final 1559 edition, however, they have been separated, the doctrine of providence remaining under the doctrine of God, while the doctrine of predestination has been relocated towards the end of the doctrine of salvation, followed only by the chapter on the resurrection of the dead.

The first thing to note is that the relocation of the doctrine is part of Calvin's recasting of his *Institutio* into an entirely new structure and the rearrangement of all his material. This does not in itself mean the doctrine was less important than before.

Karl Barth interprets the relocation as indicative of the fact that for Calvin this doctrine had become the 'consummation' of the doctrine of reconciliation – that is to say, 'the ultimate and decisive word which shed additional light upon all that has gone before.'[62] In accord with this line of thinking, F. Wendel suggests that Calvin deliberately connected his discussion of the doctrine of election with his section on the person and work of Christ rather than his prior section on the doctrine of God in order to show more clearly that it is *in Christ* that election takes place.[63] And of the relationship between the doctrines of providence and predestination in the final edition of the *Institutio*, Wendel comments:

> Just as the doctrine of providence, placed at the conclusion of the doctrine of God, might be said to complete the latter as the keystone finishes an arch, so also does the doctrine of predestination complete and illuminate the whole of the account of the Redemption. The link between predestination and providence

[62] *CD* II/2, p. 85.
[63] *In.* I.15.8.

subsists, then, in the last edition of the *Institutes*, in their two parallel functions.[64]

Clearly, Calvin's relatively late treatment of the doctrine of predestination in the *Institutio* does not diminish its importance for his overall system of thought. But while acknowledging this we must also heed Barth's warning against overestimating its importance. Wendel makes the same point, noting that Calvin developed his doctrine under the sway of 'ecclesiological and pastoral preoccupations rather than in order to make it a main foundation of his theology'.[65]

Accordingly, the doctrine of predestination must not be established as the basic tenet from which all other doctrines of Calvin may be deduced.[66] This is consistent with Calvin's own warning against a certain approach to the issue that seeks to penetrate 'the sacred precincts of divine wisdom'.[67] The proper way to approach the subject of predestination, he says, is not to engage in metaphysical speculation in a futile attempt to satisfy an impious curiosity about the eternal destiny of believers and unbelievers, for that is to search out something that 'the Lord has willed to be hid in himself'.[68] Rather, one must begin with God's revelation through the testimony of scripture.[69]

Scriptural foundations and the priority of grace

Reflecting first of all upon the election of Israel in the Old Testament, Calvin raises two points that become pivotal to his whole doctrine of predestination: first, that by eternal decree one people is peculiarly chosen, while others are rejected; and second, that the basis of this peculiar choice is God's freely given love.[70] Accordingly, God's 'eternal and

[64] F. Wendel, *Calvin: The Origins and Development of his Religious Thought*, trans. P. Mairet (New York: Harper and Row, 1963), p. 268.
[65] Wendel, *Calvin*, p. 264.
[66] *CD* II/2, p. 86.
[67] *In*. III.21.1.
[68] *In*. III.21.1.
[69] *In*. III.21.2.
[70] *In*. III.21.5.

unchangeable plan' in relation to the elect has been founded 'upon his freely given mercy, without regard to human worth'.[71] Conversely, the reprobate are those for whom, by God's 'just and irreprehensible but incomprehensible judgment' 'the door of life' has been barred, and who have been 'given over to damnation'.

For Calvin, the doctrine of election is the ultimate and essential expression of the evangelical doctrine of grace insofar as it asserts that the ground of our salvation lies uniquely and solely in God and nowhere else. He goes to considerable lengths to refute those 'who would bind God's election either to the worthiness of men or to the merit of works'.[72] And to underline the absolutely gratuitous nature of election, he draws a sharp distinction between foreknowledge and predestination.[73] Even though God has foreknowledge of all things, he does not elect people for salvation on the basis of his foreknowledge of their future works and merits. Election, like its counterpart reprobation, is an entirely free act of the divine will by which 'eternal life is foreordained to some, eternal damnation to others'.[74] All people, therefore, are not created in equal condition, but the very inequality of God's grace proves that it is free.[75]

Assurance of salvation

Calvin's strong emphasis here on the gratuitous nature of election implies a point of considerable pastoral significance that he wishes to make, namely, that the elect have a firm assurance of salvation which cannot be undermined or overturned by their failures: 'The elect can sway, fluctuate and even fall, but they will not perish because the Lord will always stretch out his arm to save them.'[76] Besides, their election includes the gift of perseverance, a free gift, independent of their will or their merits, since the

---

[71] *In.* III.21.7.
[72] *In.* III.21.5.
[73] *In.* III.21.5.
[74] *In.* III.21.5.
[75] *In.* III.21.5.
[76] Niesel, *Theology of Calvin*, p. 169.

grace of election is irresistible. The corollary of this is that good works must be viewed not as a *condition* of grace by which one earns God's favour, but rather as a *sign* of one's being in a state of grace.

Calvin's grounding of election in the grace of God means that reprobation, though an essential part of the doctrine, is but its shadow side, the more forbidding aspect to a doctrine derived from God's eternal decree rather than the merits of individual human beings. As Reid points out, 'in general, Calvin, like Augustine before him, is much more disposed to talk about election than about reprobation, and has certainly more to say about it'.[77] The purpose of preaching about reprobation is the banishment of indolence and complacency in believers so that they may be stirred up to depend wholly on God for their security, to enjoy their assurance, and to watch with prayer.[78]

One must ask whether Calvin is right on this score. Does the preaching of reprobation really have the effect of stirring up a proper dependency upon God and a prayerful watchfulness, or does it have the opposite effect of so undermining the believer's assurance of salvation that he or she is driven by anxiety to greater works in the hope of proving that his or her place is truly among the elect? Accordingly, does Calvin's thinking at this point open the door to a contractual or legal moulding of the faith which one detects in the Westminster tradition that followed him? As we shall see, this was the question raised by John McLeod Campbell in his critique of federal Calvinism and the Westminster tradition.

As to the question of justice, Calvin admits that at first glance the mind is disturbed to hear that grace is granted to some and denied to others – the disparity of treatment is indeed offensive to our notions of justice. But then divine justice is not to be measured by human justice. It is not for us, who are all equally condemned, to impose restraints upon God in having mercy on whom he will. Rather, we must marvel at the profundity of the judgements of God,

---

[77] Calvin, *Eternal Predestination*, p. 17.
[78] Calvin, *Eternal Predestination*, VIII.8, pp. 132–3.

including all disputations, and exclaim with Paul, 'O man, who art thou that contendest against God?'[79]

Christological considerations

What is the relationship between Christ and the eternal decree in Calvin's thought? As High Priest Christ is the *mediator* of God's elective decree, and as the eternal Son of God he is, together with the Father, also the *author* of election.[80] He is the One in whom the promises of salvation find their guarantee, and he is the One in whom the elect find full assurance of their salvation. As far as Calvin is concerned, there is an inextricable link between predestination and Christology. Insofar as this link is maintained he refuses to examine the predestination of an abstract humanity which does not exist apart from the person of Christ. 'It is in the fact that election is founded upon Jesus Christ', Wendel comments, that Calvin 'finds assurance of the certitude of salvation. Communion with Christ ought to relieve us of all doubt on this point: it is the proof of our election.'[81]

Despite Calvin's determination to maintain a strong link between election and Christology we are obliged to ask whether the link is forged in such a way that Christology plays only a subordinate role to a doctrine that at its deepest level is controlled by presuppositions which bypass the person and work of Christ. This is a criticism voiced by Reid, who notes that Calvin's reference to Christ as the *author* of election 'only appears once in the *Institutio*, the flicker of a flame which promises more light, but whose promise is never fulfilled'.[82] With one brief exception, when referring to the grounds of predestination, Calvin directs one's attention overwhelmingly to God in general rather than to Christ in particular. As Reid points out:

[79] Calvin, *Eternal Predestination*, VIII.5, p. 126.
[80] *In.* III.22.7.
[81] Wendel, *Calvin*, p. 274.
[82] J. K. S. Reid, 'The Office of Christ in Predestination', *Scottish Journal of Theology* 1 (1948), p. 9.

Despite all that is said concerning the place of Christ in election, the *Leitmotiv* of Calvin's presentation of the doctrine is that Predestination belongs to God. Predestination is certainly in Christ, and even *per Christum*, and in a sense *propter Christum*; but for its primary grounds we have to penetrate, warily it is true, into the *divinae sapientiae adyta* (inmost recesses), and there we find it lodged in an *arcanum consilium*.[83]

In the last resort, Reid continues, this *arcanum consilium* is that of a God into whose counsels Christ has not been admitted, and the inmost recesses of whose wisdom Christ has not illuminated. This is evident in a chance phrase which Calvin uses at least once, *'gratium istam Dei praecedit electio'*,[84] thus making election prior to grace. 'Who, then,' asks Reid, 'is this God who determines men's election before grace becomes operative?'[85]

Taking the same line of argument a little further, Karl Barth writes:

> The electing God of Calvin is a *Deus nudus absconditus*. It is not the *Deus revelatus* who is as such the *Deus absconditus*, the eternal God. All the dubious features of Calvin's doctrine result from the basic failing that in the last analysis he separates God and Jesus Christ, thinking that what was in the beginning with God must be sought elsewhere than in Jesus Christ. Thus with all his forceful and impressive acknowledgment of the divine election of grace, ultimately he still passes by the grace of God as it has appeared in Jesus Christ.[86]

For Barth, as for Reid, the decisive weakness of Calvin's doctrine of election is that it is ultimately grounded in a hidden divine decree that exists apart from God's self-disclosure in Jesus Christ. While this might appear to

---

[83] Reid, 'Office of Christ', p. 12; cf. also, Calvin, *Eternal Predestination*, p. 40.
[84] *In.* III.22.1.
[85] Reid, 'Office of Christ', p. 12.
[86] *CD* II/2, p. 111.

preserve doctrinally the freedom and sovereignty of God, it does so only at the expense of the grace by which all of creation has been reconciled to God in Christ, and after introducing a dichotomy into the Godhead – Is Christ *fully* God or not? – the eventual result being that God's Yes to humankind in election is overwhelmed by his No in reprobation.[87]

Universal or limited atonement?

Inconsistencies in Calvin

The consequence of this tendency to ground election in a hidden divine decree rather than the person and work of Christ is a doctrine of atonement characterised by a diminished appreciation of both the vicarious humanity of Christ and the nature of his priesthood. This in turn raises the question of whether Calvin is a proponent of limited atonement. That is to say, no matter how much Calvin might stress elsewhere in his *Institutio* the once and *for all* nature of Christ's priesthood and reconciling exchange, as soon as he expounds a doctrine of election that assumes a hidden divine decree which is prior to grace and which divides the elect from the reprobate, then we are bound to ask whether the result can be anything other than a reconciling exchange which to all intents and purposes is null and void for all but the elect and a priesthood which fails to represent and offer hope to the reprobate.

Universal atonement, but restriction of faith to the elect

For many years it was widely and rather uncritically assumed in Calvinist circles that Calvin advocated a position of limited atonement. A resurgence of interest in the issue has emerged in recent decades, however, due in large part to the publication in 1979 of R. T. Kendall's book *Calvin and English Calvinism to 1649*, which opens with the

---

[87] *CD* II/2. Cited by C. Gunton, in 'Karl Barth's Doctrine of Election as Part of his Doctrine of God', *Journal of Theological Studies* 25 (1974), p. 382.

emphatic claim that *universal* atonement is fundamental to Calvin's doctrine of faith and assurance, and goes on to posit that, as far as Calvin is concerned, if Christ did not die for the sins of *all* humankind, then one cannot be certain that one's sins are forgiven.[88]

If this is so, how are we to regard those passages of Calvin's, including those on predestination, which suggest something far less universal in scope? Kendall addresses this question by noting a distinction in Calvin's thinking between *universal atonement*, the basis of which is the *salvific* work of the *crucified* Christ in his death on the cross, and the *faith of the elect*, the basis of which is the *intercessory* work of the *ascended* Christ at the Father's right hand. It is Calvin's view, says Kendall, that while Christ died for all, 'he himself declares that he does not *pray* for all the world'; such intercession is for the elect only.[89] While Christ's priesthood on the cross at Calvary is for all humankind – he truly dies for the sins of the world – his ongoing priesthood is for the elect only. The decree of election in Calvin's thought is not rendered effective in Christ's *death* but in his *ascension and intercession* at the Father's right hand.[90] It is the ascension and not the death of Christ which 'opened the way into the Heavenly Kingdom, which had been closed through Adam'.[91] Calvin's position, then, despite his saying that Christ died for all, still requires that one be among the number of the elect to be saved, for saving faith is limited to the elect.[92]

Kendall's interpretation of Calvin on this point is consistent with what Calvin himself teaches on the tension between the universal promises of salvation and the reality of saving faith for the elect. 'When we receive the promises in faith,' he writes, 'we know that then and only then do

---

[88] R. T. Kendall, *Calvin and English Calvinism to 1649* (Oxford: Oxford University Press, 1979), pp. 13–14. He cites Calvin's commentary on John 3:16 and 15:9.

[89] *Sermons on Isaiah's Prophecy*, 145, cited by Kendall, *Calvin and English Calvinism*, p. 17.

[90] Kendall, *Calvin and English Calvinism*, p. 16.

[91] *In.* II.16.16.

[92] Kendall, *Calvin and English Calvinism*, p. 17.

they become effective in us. On the contrary, when faith is snuffed out, the promise is abolished at the same time.' Only those whom God has illumined may seek after the promises of salvation, and God illumines only those who are predestined to salvation.[93]

Recognising the ambiguity which surrounds faith, Calvin draws a distinction between the *regenerating* faith of the elect and the *temporary* faith of the reprobate. There are some among the reprobate, he says, who respond positively to the word and in so doing produce evidence of a kind of faith. When this happens, there are many similarities between the elect and the reprobate – even to the point that the reprobate may share 'almost the same feeling as the elect'.[94] However, in contrast to the true believer, the faith of the reprobate is temporary. Eventually it fails and falls away, while the faith of the true believer, though imperfect and subject to anxiety and fear, ultimately triumphs.[95] The temporary faith of the reprobate is further characterised by a false confidence in their eternal destiny and a dangerous self-reliance insofar as their trust is in their own faith. Therefore Calvin prompts Christians to self-examination, not in relation to their holiness or their works, but in relation to their belief in Christ, in whom they experience divine mercy and find the proper assurance of their election. 'We shall not find assurance of election in ourselves', he says, for Christ is 'the mirror wherein we must, and without self-deception may, contemplate our election'.[96] It is important to note that self-examination is understood by Calvin in terms of directing one's gaze not towards oneself and one's faith but to Christ, who is the object of one's faith. As A. N. S. Lane points out, proper self-examination asks not 'am I *trusting* in Christ? but am I trusting *in Christ*?'[97]

---

[93] *In.* III.24.17.
[94] *In.* III.2.11.
[95] *In.* III.2.17–18.
[96] *In.* III.24.5.
[97] A. N. S. Lane, 'Calvin's Doctrine of Assurance', *Vox Evangelica* 11, 1979, p. 46, cited by M. C. Bell, *Calvin and Scottish Theology: The Doctrine of Assurance* (Edinburgh: Handsel Press, 1985), p. 39.

In sum, there seems to be solid support for Kendall's assertion that while Calvin taught a doctrine of universal atonement, he also taught a doctrine of predestination in which faith is limited to the elect. As Charles Bell comments, he could do this because, unlike the federal Calvinists who followed him, he did not link the doctrine of election and atonement in a logical order of cause and effect.[98]

Theory of universal atonement in question

Not all scholars, though, have been convinced by Kendall's thesis concerning the doctrine of universal atonement in Calvin's writings. In 1981 Paul Helm published an article, 'Calvin, Calvinism and the Logic of Doctrinal Development',[99] which he expanded into a book the following year, *Calvin and the Calvinists*.[100] In the first chapter of that book he states categorically 'that Calvin taught that Christ's death procured actual remission of sins for the elect, and that in dying Christ died specifically for the elect'.[101] The rest of the book is devoted to substantiating that claim and at the same time refuting Kendall's thesis.

Helm's counter-thesis rests upon his ability to prove that for Calvin salvation is for the elect alone. In this regard, he cites three passages from the *Institutio* – III.21.7, III.22.7 and III.22.10 – all of which are taken from Calvin's teaching on election, and all of which clearly state in their own way that while the world in general has been left to its own destruction, to which it has been destined, God has graciously elected some to salvation. This leads Helm to conclude that while Calvin never committed himself 'in express terms' to a doctrine of limited atonement, that he was committed to it in practice is abundantly clear from his

---

[98] Bell, *Calvin and Scottish Theology*, p. 17.
[99] P. Helm, 'Calvin, English Calvinism and the Logic of Doctrinal Development', *Scottish Journal of Theology* 34 (1981), pp. 179–85.
[100] P. Helm, *Calvin and the Calvinists* (Edinburgh: Banner of Truth Trust, 1982).
[101] Helm, *Calvin and the Calvinists*, p. 11.

teaching on election. 'For it might be said', he writes, 'that since, for Calvin, all for whom Christ died are saved, and not all men are saved, it follows that Christ did not die for all men.'[102] Taking this line of thinking still further, he refers to Calvin's 'striking' reference to Christ as the 'author of election', and asks, 'If Christ is the author of election and the elect are a definite number, how can it be that Christ would die for some whom he had not elected?'[103]

In assessing the merits of Helm's argument it should be noted that the only three passages of Calvin's works to which he refers are all taken from his teaching in Book III on predestination, while other sections of his works are not brought into consideration. As Charles Bell rightly points out, these three passages say nothing about the extent of the atonement per se; rather, they merely affirm that the elect shall be saved and kept by Christ their Head.[104] The fact that Helm confines himself to references taken from Calvin's teaching on predestination seems to justify Bell's accusation that he does what Calvin himself refused to do, namely, begin with a doctrine of election and from it logically deduce a doctrine of limited atonement:

> At no point does Calvin link the doctrines of election and atonement in a pattern of logical dependence or cause and effect. For this reason, he is able to teach a doctrine of predestination in which faith is limited to the elect, and, at the same time, to give proper consideration to Scripture passages which clearly teach universal atonement.[105]

'What Calvin does teach', Bell continues, 'is that there is no salvation, no participation in the benefits of Christ's work apart from union with Christ.'[106] As Calvin himself puts it,

---

[102] Helm, *Calvin and the Calvinists*, p. 17.
[103] Helm, *Calvin and the Calvinists*, p. 20.
[104] C. Bell, 'Was Calvin a Calvinist?', *Scottish Journal of Theology* 36 (1983), p. 536.
[105] Bell, 'Was Calvin a Calvinist?', p. 536; cf. also, Bell, *Calvin and Scottish Theology*, p. 17.
[106] Bell, *Calvin and Scottish Theology*, p. 17.

'as long as Christ remains outside of us, and we are separated from him, all that he has suffered and done *for the salvation of the human race* remains useless and of no value for us'.[107]

Alongside this key reference to the scope of salvation, Bell cites in a footnote several other passages which support his general contention that 'Christ's death, according to Calvin, was an expiation for the sins of the entire world, but the benefit of the atonement requires application and this comes about through the work of the Holy Spirit, whose gifts to us are saving faith and participation in the work of Christ.'[108]

At the same time as Helm's interpretation of Calvin is vulnerable to criticism on the grounds of the causal link that is made between predestination and atonement, it is also vulnerable to criticism on the grounds of a lack of connection between the atonement and the incarnation. Helm interprets the atonement through the event of the cross alone, thus rendering the incarnation a mere prelude to the atonement rather than something that has atoning significance in itself. As we have already mentioned, however, this line of thinking would have been foreign to Calvin, who described the priesthood of Christ both in terms of what transpired on the cross, and in terms of (1) the assumption of our humanity in the incarnation; and (2) the ongoing representation of our humanity before the Father in the ascension. Trevor Hart sums up this dynamic when he says that for Calvin 'the incarnation is no temporary episode in the life of God, but rather a permanent involvement in the human situation'.[109]

In summary it would seem, on the basis of both individual passages and the larger doctrinal picture in Calvin's works, that Helm's interpretation of his thinking cannot be sustained. The evidence supports Kendall's assertion that Calvin taught universal atonement.

---

[107] *In*. III.1.1 (italics mine), cited in Bell, *Calvin and Scottish Theology*, p. 17.
[108] Bell, *Calvin and Scottish Theology*, p. 17.
[109] T. Hart, 'Humankind in Christ and Christ in Humankind: Salvation as Participation in our Substitute in the Theology of John Calvin', *Scottish Journal of Theology* 42 (1989), p. 72.

Does Christ pray for all, or only for the elect?

The question of limited atonement aside, of more urgent concern for us in this book is Kendall's other assertion that Calvin taught that while Christ died for all, *he does not pray for all*, that his prayers are limited to the elect only. The reason for our concern here is that if Kendall is correct, then Calvin is guilty not only of shifting the problem of assurance from the area of Christ's atonement to that of his intercession,[110] but also of breaking up the unity between Christ's priestly atonement (effective for all) and his priestly intercession (effective only for some). This is where Bell is critical of Kendall. He says it is only when Calvin is commenting on Christ's prayer in John 17:9 that Christ's intercession is said to be limited to the elect. Apart from that occasion, Calvin never develops his teaching on the subject. In fact, argues Bell, the emphasis in his teaching overall is on the unity of the death and intercession of Christ, and upon the idea that Christ's intercession flows from his sacrificial death, which was made on behalf of all.[111]

While Bell's final statement is convincing concerning the unity of Christ's death and intercession, less convincing is his assertion that Calvin never developed his teaching on the scope of Christ's intercessions. In his section on prayer in the *Institutio*, Calvin tackles the Sophists, who were claiming that while Christ is the mediator of redemption, believers are mediators of intercession. By way of reply, Calvin refers to scripture, asking:

> For when John says, 'If anyone sins, we have an advocate with the Father, Christ Jesus' (1 John 2:1), does he mean that Christ was an advocate for us once for all, or does he not rather ascribe to him a constant intercession?[112]

While Calvin's main purpose in quoting this Johannine text is to argue that Christ's mediatorial role is indeed ongoing

---

[110] The problem has already been shifted one step by Calvin's limitation of faith to the elect. Cf. Bell, *Calvin and Scottish Theology*, pp. 18, 22–24.
[111] Bell, *Calvin and Scottish Theology*, p. 19.
[112] *In.* III.20.20.

and did not end with what he accomplished on the cross (thus confirming Bell's argument concerning the unity of the death and intercession of Christ) he is also hinting at the *scope* of Christ's intercessions, a scope that is all-inclusive: 'If *anyone* sins, we have an advocate.' From this it can be inferred that Christ the Mediator intercedes for all people, for *all have sinned* and fallen short of the glory of God, and all are therefore in need of an advocate with the Father. As Trevor Hart notes, 'far from the doctrine of total depravity in Calvin being an accurate measure of his opinion of humanity, it would be better regarded as a reflection of the breadth and richness which he perceives in the salvation wrought in Christ, the refashioning of fallen humanity and its exaltation at the right hand of the Father'.[113]

What Calvin at this point only infers is immediately made explicit in what follows. Commenting on 1 Timothy 2, he writes:

> For, after previously saying that intercession is to be made for *all* men, Paul, to prove this statement, soon adds that 'there is one God, and ... one mediator' (1 Tim. 2:5). Augustine similarly explains it when he says: 'Christian men mutually commend one another by their prayers. However, *it is he for whom no one intercedes, while he intercedes for all, who is the true mediator.*'[114]

That Calvin believes that Christ prays for all those for whom no one else intercedes – elect and reprobate together – is a point of considerable significance. As Trevor Hart observes, 'not only does Calvin insist upon the integrity of the humanity of Christ in his life and death, he will accept no lessening of its integrity even after the ascension'.[115] The One, in whom all humanity is represented in his incarnation, death and resurrection, continues to represent all humanity in his ascension. And Hart further comments:

[113] Hart, 'Humankind in Christ', p. 73.
[114] *In.* III.20.20 (italics mine).
[115] Hart, 'Humankind in Christ', p. 72.

> Calvin discerns a salvific significance in the humanity
> of the Saviour which makes a nonsense of any attempt
> to interpret salvation in wholly extrinsic terms. ...
> Atonement does not consist simply in a debt being
> paid, or in the non-reckoning of sin and guilt alone.
> The wider context is ... the establishing a new
> humanity in a new relationship with God, the
> exaltation of humanity to a previously unknown
> glory.[116]

Calvin places himself firmly within the tradition of
Chalcedonian orthodoxy in this regard. The hypostatic
union between the Father and the Son is an atoning union,
wherein God takes our 'polluted flesh' into the very life of
the Godhead, and, purging it of all that separates it from
him, establishes it in the filial relationship of the Son to the
Father in the Spirit, thus making it his humanity. Insofar as
this happens we are established and vindicated as truly
human, sharing in the new humanity of God himself. This
is the essential meaning of the wondrous exchange established
through the priesthood of Christ.

Not everyone is *in Christ*

Having said all that, as we have already noted, Calvin is
equally clear that not everyone is *in Christ* simply by virtue
of what he in his priestly mediation has done and
continues to do on their behalf. It is the Holy Spirit who
establishes union and communion with Christ, bestowing
upon those whom God has called the benefits of Christ,
awakening and sustaining faith, enabling them to lay hold
of the gift of forgiveness and to truly repent, and
conveying to them the very life of Christ. Accordingly,
faith is nothing less than 'a firm and certain knowledge of
God's benevolence towards us'.[117]
    In this context, Calvin's doctrine of election must be seen
as an attempt to provide pastoral assurance to those who

---

[116] Hart, 'Humankind in Christ', pp. 73–4.
[117] *In.* III.2.7.

are in Christ but who perhaps are plagued by doubts concerning their salvation. The elect need not be anxious. They have certain knowledge of their salvation. Why? Because of God's eternal decree in their favour. This decree is grounded in the merciful but hidden will of God rather than the merits of human beings. It is revealed in the person and work of Christ the High Priest and sealed through the activity of the Holy Spirit, who brings forth the faith by which the elect are united with their Saviour.

Unfortunately, as we have also seen, Calvin's doctrine of election has a number of inconsistencies. No matter how christological it appears to be, at its deepest level it is grounded in a divine decree that has been made apart from Christ and prior to grace. As J. K. S. Reid says, 'Predestination *sola gratia*, which is the true defence for which Calvin seeks, is allowed to relapse and degenerate into the Predestination *sine gratia* or at least *ante gratiam*.'[118] This has two consequences. The first is identified by Charles Bell, who points out that Calvin's emphasis on saving faith (rather than the vicarious faithfulness of Christ) undermines the very assurance which he seeks to give the elect.[119]

The second consequence is that the contradiction between the unbiblical notion of a hidden will of God and the biblical notion of God fully revealing his will for humanity in Jesus Christ tends to result in the former gaining ascendancy and eventually becoming the doctrine under which all other Christian doctrines, and most notably that of soteriology, are subordinated. The keystone to Christian doctrine so easily becomes the foundation stone. As we shall see in the next chapter, this is precisely what happened under the Westminster tradition.

Concluding comments

The inconsistencies demonstrated by Calvin with regard to his doctrine of predestination should not be allowed to overshadow the extent to which he developed the

---

[118] Reid, 'Office of Christ', p. 174.
[119] Bell, *Calvin and Scottish Theology*, p. 32.

implications of the human obedience of Christ in a doctrine of atonement. T. F. Torrance goes so far as to say that Calvin was, in fact, 'the first great theologian since the Early Church to give a full and satisfactory account of the saving significance of the humanity of Jesus, and of the life of the Church as union with Christ through the power of the Spirit sharing in his New Humanity'.[120] Calvin's doctrine of the priesthood of Christ enabled him to give proper place to the mediatorship of Christ and to refute alternative notions of human mediation and priesthood so that the saving, vicarious humanity of Christ was the crucial factor in defining the nature of the Church's life of prayer and worship.

The Early Scottish Reformed Tradition: John Knox and John Craig

John Knox and the *Scots Confession*, 1560

Calvin, Knox and the reformation of worship and theology in Scotland

The theology of Calvin had a significant influence on Reformed theology in Scotland, where John Knox was a pivotal figure in the Scottish Reformation. Unlike Calvin, he produced no systematic treatment of his theology, but rather made his mark as a preacher and defender of the Protestant faith. The influence of Calvin is most visibly discernible in the introduction of his service book to Scotland and in the drafting of the *Scots Confession* of 1560. Knox was a key personality in both these events.

Knox, who had been in exile from England under the reign of Mary, was not the first to introduce Reformed theology to Scotland, but he was the one who brought Calvin's service book to Scotland, where it became the basis

---

[120] Torrance, 'The Place of the Humanity of Christ in the Sacramental Life of the Church', p. 4.

for Knox's own service book, which passed through about seventy editions, and was commonly known as the *Psalm-Book* or *Book of Common Order*. It was adopted by the General Assembly in 1562, and continued in use in Scotland until the Westminster Directory supplanted it in 1645. William Maxwell notes a number of features in Calvin's service book that distinguished it from the Roman liturgy:[121] It was in the vernacular rather than in Latin; people were encouraged to share in the service as participants – they were no longer passive observers; psalms were cast in metrical forms which were easily learned and encouraged congregational participation; the scriptures were translated, and preaching was restored to prominence; weekly communion was advocated; and the number of sacraments was reduced to two – baptism and communion. These distinguishing features were all grounded in Calvin's understanding of worship as an event in which the whole people of God are brought by the activity of the Holy Spirit to share and participate regularly in the Son's worship of the Father. Calvin's doctrine of the sole priesthood of Christ and the derivative priesthood of all believers is clearly present throughout.

If Calvin's influence in Scotland was felt through the introduction of his service book by Knox, it was felt just as much through the *Scots Confession* of 1560, the drafting of which was attributable to Knox and his friends, who had been asked by Parliament to provide a statement of the Reformed faith which could be established in Scotland. Whereas other Reformation confessions, such as the *Heidelberg Catechism*, tended to have an anthropocentric starting point, the *Scots Confession* was strongly theocentric and trinitarian. It began not by describing the human condition but by confessing and acknowledging one God, Father, Son and Holy Ghost, 'to whom only we must cleave, whom onelie we must serve, whom onelie we must worship, and in whom onelie we must put our trust'. As T. F. Torrance puts it:

---

[121] W. D. Maxwell, *A History of Worship in the Church of Scotland* (London: Oxford University Press, 1955), pp. 50–1.

It is clear in the *Scots Confession*, as in Knox's *Genevan Liturgy*, that the doctrine of the Trinity is not added on to a prior conception of doctrine of God, but belongs to the basic and essential content of the doctrine of God – there is no other content but Father, Son and Holy Spirit. This clearly reflects the approach of John Calvin in chapter 13 of the first book of his *Institutes of the Christian Religion*.[122]

Justification by faith

To appreciate the decisive contribution of John Knox to Reformed worship and theology we have to understand not only the continuity of his thinking with that of Calvin, but also his distinctive way of dealing with the doctrine of justification. While the doctrine of justification was central to the Reformation, T. F. Torrance has noticed that the expression 'justification by faith' is hardly ever found in Knox's works – 'For when he did speak of justification,' he says, 'he preferred to be more concrete and to use an expression like "justification through the blood of Christ".'[123] That is to say, he directs our attention immediately to Christ and his salvific acts. Evidence of this is to be found in the *Scots Confession*, in relation to which Torrance highlights three distinguishing features. First, he says, 'there is no separate article on justification. It has no place of its own; rather does justification belong to the inner texture of the Gospel and becomes evident as its cutting edge.'[124]

Second, what is absolutely central to the *Confession*, observes Torrance, is Jesus Christ, and the union of God and humankind in him. Justification stems from this hypostatic union, 'the wondrous conjunction betwixt Godhead and Manhood',[125] and is grounded in the saving

---

[122] T. F. Torrance, *Scottish Theology: From John Knox to John McLeod Campbell* (Edinburgh: T&T Clark, 1996), pp. 6–7.
[123] Torrance, *Theology in Reconstruction*, p. 151.
[124] Torrance, *Theology in Reconstruction*, p. 151.
[125] *Scots Confession*, Articles 7 and 8.

Humanity of the One who is both fully God and fully human – that is to say, in his atoning obedience and oblation to God, through which our humanity has been clothed with his holy life.[126] In other words, justification should not be reduced to the forensic non-imputation of sin, for, as Torrance puts it, it is also a sharing in 'the positive righteousness of his obedient and loving life lived in perfect filial relation to the Father from the cradle to the grave'. [127]

By grounding justification in the hypostatic union, Knox is pointing to something that cannot be undone or defiled. This is evident in his teaching on baptism. In his 1556 essay, 'Ansueris to sum Questionis concerning Baptisme, Etc.', he says that in baptism we are received in league with God our Father and clothed with Christ's justice, which is permanent and cannot be defiled.[128]

The same sense of being clothed with Christ's justice or righteousness is evident in Knox's baptism liturgy, wherein the presiding minister declares that 'the justice of Jesus Christ is made ours by baptism' and we experience 'Regeneration, which standeth chiefly on these two points – in mortification, that is to say, a resisting of the rebellious lusts of the flesh, and in newness of life, whereby we continually strive to walk in that pureness and perfection, *wherewith we are clad in Baptism.*'[129] Interestingly, in the baptism liturgy no vows are asked of the parents

---

[126] Torrance, *Theology in Reconstruction*, p. 151. Torrance draws attention to 'a sentence that comes from the *Form of Confession* in the *Book of Common Order*: "We must always have our refuge to the free justice which proceedeth of the obedience which Jesus Christ hath prayed for us" ', of which he says that 'what Knox refers to there is the fact that the prayer of Jesus was part of his atoning obedience and oblation to God – it was the worship of God the Father with his Life'.
[127] Torrance, *Theology in Reconstruction*, p. 156.
[128] *The Works of John Knox*, Vol. 4, collected and ed. by D. Laing (Edinburgh: Woodrow Society, 1855), p. 123. Commenting on this decisive passage, Iain Torrance says that 'Knox is pitting himself against, and distinguishing his thought from, the alternative account which turns the doctrine of justification into one of infused righteousness' (I. Torrance, 'Patrick Hamilton and John Knox: A Study in the Doctrine of Justification by Grace', *Archiv für Reformationsgeschichte* 65 (1974), p. 182).
[129] *Knox's Liturgy*, 1868, p. 136 (italics mine).

presenting their child for baptism. Rather, the father is asked to recite the Apostles' Creed. This act serves to highlight the fact that justification is grounded not in whatever saving faith one might think one has (for oneself and one's children), but in what God has accomplished in Christ and clothed one with by his Spirit.

Following on from this grounding of justification in the hypostatic union, the third feature to which T. F. Torrance draws our attention is the link in the *Scots Confession* between justification and the resurrection and ascension of Christ. The link is of crucial importance insofar as it serves to define justification not merely in terms of the forgiveness of sins, but in terms of being 'lifted up above and beyond ourselves to live out of the risen and ascended Christ, and not out of ourselves'.[130]

Justification here is defined both christologically and eschatologically, about which Torrance comments:

> In none of the Reformers was the stress upon incarnational union so strong as in Knox; and in none of them was the place given to the *parousia* so powerful; while it is Knox's highly distinctive doctrine of the ascension that links those two together, or rather reveals the relation of the incarnation to the *parousia*. It is in the ascension that we have *the fruit* of the incarnation (including the death and resurrection) of Christ, and it is in the parousia that we have the full *fruit* of the ascension.[131]

For Knox and the *Scots Confession* the ascension is not an addendum to the story of salvation. It is one of the great salvation events along with the death and resurrection of Christ.[132] As Torrance notes, it constitutes the inauguration of the kingdom of God over the whole creation,[133] which,

---

[130] Torrance, *Theology in Reconstruction*, pp. 151–2.
[131] Torrance, *Theology in Reconstruction*, p. 152.
[132] In the *Scots Confession*, Article 11 (on the ascension) is as long as Articles 10 and 11 (on the death and resurrection of Christ) combined. In Knox's theology the doctrine certainly was not a mere footnote to the faith as, sadly, it largely is today.
[133] Torrance, *Scottish Theology*, p. 21.

for Knox, had intensely practical implications. From his heavenly throne the merciful Saviour, by whom God will judge the world, rules the world even now. Thus, Torrance observes,

> ... when Knox thinks of Scotland, he sees the whole of its history under the hand and personal direction of God through his 'gentle chastening' – which is gentle even in the midst of dire calamities because in them God is working out his purpose of redemption.[134]

Furthermore, the ascension completes the incarnation event, drawing the saving work of Christ up into eternity, into the ultimate mystery of God. Through it, the union of God and humanity that took place in the person of Christ has been brought into the immediate presence of the Father, where Christ wears our human life, standing in for us, interceding for us as our Advocate, High Priest and only Mediator. In it, Christ has opened the heavens into which people may appear before the throne of the Father's mercy. Christ's ascension, therefore, constitutes the ground of Christian comfort and assurance, for it is the ascended Christ who sends us his Spirit, the Comforter. Consequently, as Torrance astutely observes, 'the full meaning of the ascension is to be discerned in relation to the outpouring of the Holy Spirit upon the Church'.[135]

The doctrine of election

Knox's grounding of justification in the hypostatic union of God and humankind in Christ has further implications. Nowhere in the *Scots Confession* is this clearer than in Articles 6, 7 and 8, which focus on the incarnation of Christ Jesus, the mediatorial union of God and humanity in Christ, and the doctrine of election. As both Barth and T. F. Torrance observe, it is particularly noteworthy that

---

[134] Torrance, *Scottish Theology*, p. 9.
[135] Torrance, *Scottish Theology*, p. 22.

election is expounded in terms of Christology, for it is thus understood as the activity of God *in Christ*.[136] God's eternal purposes are not worked out apart from Christ or behind his back, for he is himself eternally very God of very God.

As with Calvin, then, the *Confession* stresses that election has to be understood strictly in *Christ alone*, and that in the last resort faith must rest in the eternal, incomprehensible and immutable counsel of God. That this points not to a darkness in God but rather to a degree of impropriety in all our statements about him is evident in the conspicuous absence from the *Confession*'s Article on Election of any explicit reference to a double decree. While there is indeed a reference to 'the reprobate' the *Confession* stops short of tracing the fact of damnation back to the eternal will of God.

This reflects the influence of Knox, who, while acknowledging in his treatise on predestination[137] the fact that some people are saved and some are damned, which might appear to indicate that there are two wills in God, also implies very strongly that there is only *one* will which is 'secrete and hid from us, reserved in his eternall wisdome, to be revealed at the glorious coming of the Lord Jesus'.[138] Therefore, 'neither yet do we understand nor affirme, that God's absolute ordinance is the principall cause of reprobation, of sinne, and damnation'.[139]

If we want to understand the proper basis of reprobation we are better to focus our attention, not on the eternal will of God, but on the reality of sin, the root cause of which, argues Knox, is to be found in 'the malice of the Devill, and that free consent of man to rebellion, whose will was

---

[136] K. Barth, *The Knowledge of God and the Service of God According to the Teaching of the Reformation: Recalling the Scottish Confession of 1560*, trans. J. L. M. Haire and I. Henderson (London: Hodder and Stoughton, 1938), p. 69; and, Torrance, *Scottish Theology*, p. 14.
[137] Knox's treatise on predestination, entitled 'An Answer to the Cavillations of an Adversary Respecting the Doctrine of Predestination', was published in 1560. At over 400 pages it constitutes Knox's most elaborate production and is itself a foretaste of the dominance that the doctrine was to have in later Calvinism. Knox's treatise is included in *The Works of John Knox*, ed. D. Laing, Vol. 5 (Edinburgh, 1858).
[138] *Works*, Vol. 5, p. 113.
[139] *Works*, Vol. 5, p. 112.

neither inforced, neither yet by violence of God's purpose compelled to consent, but he, of free will and readie mynd, left God and joyned with the Devill'.[140] Out of the one corrupt mass of humanity, God has called forth his elect while all others are simply left to languish in their corruption.[141] For the elect there is unmerited mercy, for the reprobate there is simply the outworking of natural justice.

Insofar as Knox refuses to trace the fate of the reprobate back to an inscrutable divine decree, he differs from Calvin. But in other respects he and Calvin are of one mind. Regarding the person of Christ, Knox follows Calvin in viewing him not only as the One in whom the elect receive life but as the One who 'in respect of his humanity' is also rightfully 'called the Elect'.[142] He is the Elect One – in him election becomes and operates as mediation.

Interestingly, in the *Scots Confession*, which was drafted after the treatise on predestination, Knox's restriction of the election of Christ to his human nature is absent, reflecting either a different line being taken by Knox or the fruits of collaboration with his co-authors. As Barth notes approvingly, under the section on election in the *Confession*, there is 'simply presented the doctrine of the true Godhead and the true manhood of Jesus Christ, and the necessity and reality of both in the unity of the person of the Mediator'.[143]

Unfortunately, as Barth also points out, Knox and his fellow-workers fail to develop more fully the implications of this hypostatic union for the doctrine of election.[144] The one element not clearly present in either the *Confession* or Knox's treatise on predestination, is that of Christ as *Electing God*. It is one thing, acknowledging the humanity of Christ, to see him as the Elect One. It is quite another thing, acknowledging his divine nature as well, to see him as the Electing God. Indeed, when Christ is seen as the Electing God there can be no division any more between God's mercy and his justice. Nor can there be any possibility of either an eternal

[140] *Works*, Vol. 5, p. 113.
[141] *Works*, Vol. 5, pp. 125–6.
[142] *Works*, Vol. 5, p. 131.
[143] *CD* II/2, p. 62.
[144] *CD* II/2, p. 154.

decree that is made apart from Christ (Calvin), or a divine decision that leaves a significant proportion of the mass of humanity to languish in its own corruption and iniquity (Knox). There is just one decree, one covenant, all of grace, of which Christ is both Mediator and Author.

One of the effects of this failure is to be seen in Knox's teaching on the relationship between election and the assurance of salvation. On the one hand, he is emphatic in saying we need not fear on account of our weaknesses and imperfections because 'as they did not stoppe his mercie to elect us in Christ Jesus, so can they not compel him now to refuse us'.[145] That is to say, the doctrine of election is the basis of the Christian proclamation of assurance.

However, by grounding this assurance in the election of God, the question is begged: How does one know one is included among the elect? From Knox's correspondence it appears that he was seriously confronted with this problem in the person of his mother-in-law Mrs Bowes, with whom he corresponded at great length on the issue. James McEwen notes that in response to her persistent self-doubt Knox, driven more by pastoral than by theological concerns, eventually advocates the 'perilous method of self-inspection':

> Election should produce certain fruits, and if the fruits are there, we can be reasonably certain of our election. Mrs Bowes is not, therefore, to despair of her election because of isolated lapses into sin. But if we find in ourselves a steady delight in some evil course, persistent wrong-doing, an ingrained aversion to godliness, then we do well to doubt our election and to be seriously alarmed.[146]

---

[145] *Works*, Vol. 5, p. 27.
[146] J. S. McEwen, *The Faith of John Knox* (London: Lutterworth Press, 1961), p. 73. On this same matter, Charles Bell writes: 'In fairness to Knox, it must be pointed out that Mrs Bowes appears to have been almost neurotic in her doubts concerning her salvation. Knox often directed her to Christ crucified and the promises of the Gospel for assurance, but nothing would satisfy her. The frustration that this brought to Knox is apparent at times in their correspondence. Because of his love for her, however, he sought again and again to assuage her fears. And whereas he so often directs us away from ourselves, here was a case in which he surely felt he must try all possible arguments' (*Calvin and Scottish Theology*, p. 64).

As much as one might sympathise with Knox's pastoral concerns, his grounding of Christian assurance in something which is discernible within oneself rather than in Christ (the Electing God), actually has the opposite effect to that intended. McEwen writes:

> It is an extraordinary thing that Knox did not clearly realise – none of the Reformers apparently realised – that by grounding assurance on election, rather than on merit, they were only pushing the problem of assurance back one stage, and pushing it into what appeared to be an even more terrifying form. For if salvation depends on merit, and I doubt of my salvation, I can at least do something about it: I can try harder to be good. But if salvation depends on God's election, and I doubt my election, I land in complete and hopeless paralysis. There is nothing I can do about that. If God has not elected me, what hope or help have I? Apparently none.[147]

While Knox fails to recognise Christ as the Electing God his thinking overall is nevertheless controlled by his understanding of the reconciliation wrought by God through the hypostatic union and vicarious humanity of Christ. Article 9 of the *Scots Confession* is dominated by the language of sacrifice, and while traditional forensic language is used, as T. F. Torrance correctly notes, 'the atoning sacrifice is not to be understood as fulfilled by Christ merely as man (which would imply a Nestorian Christology), but of Christ as the one Mediator between God and man who is himself God and man in one Person'.[148] Consequently, the atonement effected in and through the death of Christ should not be seen as the act of the man Jesus placating God the Father, but as a propitiatory sacrifice in which God himself draws near to humankind and draws humankind near to himself. As Calvin pointed out in his *Institutio*, God does not love us because of what Christ has done, but it is because he

---

[147] McEwen, *Faith of John Knox*, p. 72.
[148] Torrance, *Scottish Theology*, p. 18.

first loved us that he came in Christ to exercise his mercy and reconcile us to himself.[149]

Thus understood, there is no suggestion in either the *Scots Confession* or any of Knox's writings that Christ's atoning sacrifice was offered only for some people and not for all. Christ was not merely the instrument in the hands of the Father for the salvation of a chosen few. This is confirmed in Article 11 of the *Confession*, which speaks of the ascension of Christ, his ongoing role as Priest, Advocate and Mediator, and his eventual return as Judge. At the same time as the Article vividly declares that 'the stubburne, inobedient, cruell oppressours, filthie personis, idolaters, and all such sortes of unfaithfull, sall be cast in the dungeoun of utter darknesse, where their worme sall not die, nether zit their fyre sall be extinguished', it neither draws a contrast between these people and those others who might be described as good, righteous and pious,[150] nor directs one's attention, as one might expect, to what one must do to avoid this terrible judgement. Instead, attention is drawn solely to the being and work of Christ, the High Priest, Advocate and Mediator. The final advent of Christ will be a day, not of terror, but of 'refreshing and restitution' of all things, in which those who from the beginning have suffered violence, injury and wrong, for righteousness' sake, through the mediation of Christ shall inherit that blessed immortality promised from the beginning. It will be the day when all secrets will be revealed, God's great work will be unveiled, and a separation will take place, not between the righteous and the unrighteous, but between believers and unbelievers.

Commenting on this emphasis, Barth writes:

> What we have here is not just the usual view which people hold about the Last Judgement. In the

---

[149] *In.* II.16.4.

[150] The Article describes those who are accepted by Christ and partake of eternal life not as the good and the righteous, etc., but simply as those 'that have suffered violence, injurie and wrang'. In other words, there is no division here between the eternally elect and the eternally reprobate, nor between the righteous and sinners defined in moral terms. It thus avoids any sense of works-righteousness or self-justification.

judgement of Jesus Christ which we must all go to meet, it is not a question of establishing that some are righteous and the others sinners. In God's decision and man's election and in the death and resurrection of Jesus Christ it has already been decided that in ourselves and by ourselves we are *all* sinners, but that being saved through the complete incarnation of the Son of God we are *all* righteous ... In face of this judgement there can be only one question, namely Do I really look *for Him*? Do I *believe* that He is my only and my complete salvation? That and that alone is what will be decided at the Judgement.[151]

John Knox on the Eucharist

In 1550, while serving as preacher at Berwick in England, Knox was summoned before the Council of the North for Public Affairs, where he delivered 'A Vindication of the Doctrine that the Sacrifice of the Mass is Idolatry',[152] in which he contrasts the Lord's Supper and the Mass:

In the Supper of the Lord, confes we our selves redeamit from sin by the death and blud of Jesus Chryst inlie. In the Masse, crave we remissioun of sinnes, yea, and what so ever thing we list, by working of that same work, whilk we presentlie do our self.

Knox thus rejects the Roman notion that the priest performing Mass is attempting to procure remission of sins for those who are participating. We already have remission of sins: Christ has died for us. As Iain Torrance comments, we 'approach the Lord's Table for our reassurance that, our sins notwithstanding, we have a Mediator, clad with whose righteousness we stand before God'.[153]

In tune with Calvin, Knox's attack upon the Mass and his reformation of it, is characterised by a renewed

---

[151] Barth, *Knowledge of God*, pp. 98–9.
[152] Cf. *Works*, Vol. 3.
[153] Torrance, 'Patrick Hamilton and John Knox', p. 183.

emphasis upon the sole mediatorship of Jesus Christ, and his once-for-all atoning sacrifice on the cross, which brought with it a fresh emphasis upon the vicarious humanity of Christ in atonement and worship as the sole Mediator and High Priest before God. Evidence of this is to be found in the *Scots Confession*, where, under Article 21 on the sacraments, it is declared that

> ... the unioun and conjunction, quhilk we have with the body and blude of Christ Jesus ... wrocht be operatioun of the haly Ghaist, who by trew faith carryis us above al things that are visible, carnal, and earthly, and makes us to feede upon the body and blude of Christ Jesus, *quhilk was anes broken and shed for us, quhilk now is in heaven, and appearis in the presence of the Father for us.*[154]

The important thing to note here is that the risen and ascended Christ, who now is in heaven and who appears in the presence of the Father for sinners, is none other than the crucified Christ, whose body was broken and blood shed for sinners on the cross. The sacrificial and intercessory aspects of Christ's mediatorial role are part of the *one* priesthood exercised by the same divine–human person. Accordingly, the humanity of Jesus the High Priest is just as important to his intercessory role (in heaven) as it was to his sacrificial role (on the cross). Just as all were vicariously represented in the humanity of the crucified Christ at Calvary, so all are vicariously represented in the humanity of the ascended Christ in the presence of the Father.

Torrance notes how very important the humanity of Christ was to Knox, especially as he hammered out his theology of the Eucharist:

> The important point here can be put like this: if what Christ did was an act only as God for us, then that demands an answer from man corresponding to

it: hence the notion of a human priesthood to convey to man what God has done. But if Christ acted, not only as God, but as man, and has once for all offered man's sacrifice, man's response to God, then our sacrifice is already made, and our response to God is already offered. This does not mean that we do not have to worship God in sacrifice and oblation, but it does mean a) that our sacrifice is mainly one of thanksgiving and praise (the meaning of 'Eucharist') for what has been offered on our behalf, and b) that whatever we offer, even by way of thanksgiving, praise, and prayer, ourselves in living sacrifice, etc., we offer only by 'the hand of Christ'. 'Christ is our right hand by whom we offer anything unto the Father' – cited by Knox from Ambrose.[155]

In conjunction with this strong emphasis on the priesthood of Christ, both at Calvary and at the right hand of the Father, Knox views the Eucharist not merely as the event through which one receives Christ and his gifts (won for all sinners at Calvary), but also as the event at which, in union with him who continues to intercede for sinners, one engages in prayer. It is in prayer and intercession, observes Torrance, 'that Knox discerns the true "priestly character" of the holy ministry, involving not only the prayer of thanksgiving but also of inter-cession in Christ'.[156] Accordingly, there is a very real sense in which, for Knox, the Eucharist is not only 'that most blessed conjunction, union and societie quhilk the elect have with their head Christ Jesus';[157] it is also the means of one's participation in the new humanity of Christ. The Eucharist is not only a meal of thanksgiving; through the act of intercession it becomes a means of sharing in the saving ministry of Christ in the world. Perhaps this is why Knox viewed prayer as part of the

---

[155] Torrance, *Scottish Theology*, p. 42.
[156] Torrance, *Scottish Theology*, p. 44.
[157] *Scots Confession*, Article 21.

'eucharistic sacrifice' and gave such attention to prayers for the poor.[158]

John Knox on prayer

In 1554 Knox published a treatise on prayer[159] in which, as with his doctrine of the Eucharist, the human priesthood of Christ is of central importance. One discerns within the treatise both advice on a number of pragmatic issues to do with prayer – what prayer is; what is to be observed in it; why it should be engaged in; why God defers in granting prayers; what the link is between prayer and fasting; the readiness of God to hear prayers; and so on – and also an articulation of those theological presuppositions upon which a proper doctrine of prayer is based, all of which are anchored in the person and work of Christ the Mediator: the basis for one's hope in prayer; the necessity of a Mediator; by whom it is that Christians pray; erroneous belief in the intercessions of the saints; erroneous thinking of angels as mediators; Jesus Christ the only Mediator; and so on.

Interestingly, the theological presuppositions are brought to bear constantly on the pragmatic issues, as in the case of the definition of prayer that constitutes the opening section of the treatise. There prayer is defined as 'ane earnest and familiar talking with God, to whom we

---

[158] In his debate with the Abbot of Crossraguel Knox included prayer and 'liberalitie toward the poor' in his list of 'sacrifices called Eucharistic', together with 'thanksgiving, the mortification of our bodies, and the obedience that we give to God'. Of course, this is not to be confused with the 'one Sacrifice which is the greatest, and most of all called *Propitiatorium*, which is that sacrifice whereby satisfaction is made to the justice of God' (*Works*, Vol. 6, p. 198). Rather, as we have already seen, it is the Church's response to what has already been offered once and for all in Christ. It is sacrifice in a derivative or secondary sense. Cf. Torrance, *Scottish Theology*, pp. 42–3.

[159] 'A Declaration of the True Nature and Object of Prayer', *Works*, Vol. 3, pp. 89–105. T. F. Torrance describes this treatise as 'one of the most important documents for the understanding of the theology of the Scottish Reformation' (*Scottish Theology*, p. 42). On Knox's understanding of prayer, cf. also his 'Exposition of the Sixth Psalm of David', 1554, pp. 119–56.

declair oure misereis, whois support and help we implore
and desyre in our adversiteis, and whom we laude and
prais for oure benefittis receaved'.[160] Taken on its own this
working definition suggests that prayer is very much a
human activity by which one is able to establish a line of
communication with God. But just a few words later,
under a brief section called, 'How the Spirit maketh inter-
cessioun for us', it becomes very clear that prayer is not
something that belongs in the realm of human initiative
and activity at all. Rather, as Knox puts it, it is the *'Halie
Gaist'* that 'steireth up our myndis, giving unto us a desyre
or boldnes for to pray, and causeth us to murne when we
ar extractit or pullit thairfra'.[161] By the end of the treatise
one is made strongly conscious not just of the activity of
the Spirit in stirring up our minds to pray, but of the fact
'that without our Mediatour, Foirspeaker, and Peace-
maker, we enter not into prayer'.[162] In other words, there is
such an interweaving of pneumatology and Christology in
this treatise that by its end the reader is left with the
indelible impression of prayer as a trinitarian event
involving the Spirit and the Son. One is reminded at this
point of the early Church which for the first three centuries,
as we noted in Chapter One, addressed its liturgical
prayers in a very trinitarian way *to the Father, through the
Son, in the Spirit.* The parallel is striking, constituting a
good example not only of the resonance between Reformed
and patristic theology on the subject of prayer, but also of
the way in which Knox's treatise needs to be read – not in
a piecemeal manner but as a whole, so that practical
instruction is theologically informed.

    As far as the priesthood of Christ is concerned in this
treatise, only a 'perfyte Mediatour' who stands on both
sides of the God–human divide and has the 'trust and
favour of both parteis' is able to bring about true
and complete reconciliation.[163] Jesus Christ is that person,

---

[160] *Works*, Vol. 3, p. 83.
[161] *Works*, Vol. 3, p. 85.
[162] *Works*, Vol. 3, p. 94.
[163] *Works*, Vol. 3, p. 95.

both on the cross at Calvary and in his continual intercessions before the Father. As for the spurious notion that he
fulfilled his mediatorial role on the cross but assigned the
subsequent task of intercession to his 'Sanctis and Holie
Men', Knox writes scornfully, 'as thocht that Jesus Chryst
had bene but one hour our Mediatour, and efter had
resignit the office unto his servandis!'[164] The way in which
he seems to labour the point suggests this was a major
issue in the Church that needed addressing. 'Sum say,' he
writes, 'we will use but one Mediatour, Jesus Chryst, to
God the Father; but we must haif Sanctis, and chieflie the
Virgin Mary, the mother of Jesus Chryst, to pray for us
unto him.'[165] Knox is strongly opposed to this view. For
him, as for Calvin, the Roman tendency to set up others
alongside Christ as mediators of prayers detracts from the
honour that is due to him alone. It also constitutes a failure
to perceive God's 'infinit kyndnes, gentilnes, and love
toward mankynd'[166] which is mediated to the world in and
through Christ.

John Knox on discipline

One issue, which emerges from a review of Knox's
writings, is the nature of the relationship that obtains
between justification and ecclesiastical discipline. Not only
does he regard discipline as one of the marks of the true
Church, but in his liturgy there is a separate Order of
Ecclesiastical Discipline, and in the Order for the
Administration of the Lord's Supper there is a lengthy
Exhortation to self-examination. A question arises: Does
this strong emphasis on ecclesiastical discipline and self-
examination in Knox's writings introduce a kind of
legalism that undermines his otherwise uncompromising
emphasis on the unconditional grace of God?

In the Order of Ecclesiastical Discipline, the nature and
purpose of discipline is likened to the

---

164 *Works*, Vol. 3, p. 96.
165 *Works*, Vol. 3, p. 98.
166 *Works*, Vol. 3, pp. 96 and 98.

... sinews in the body, which knit and join the members together with decent order and comeliness. It is a bridle to stay the wicked from their mischiefs. It is a spur to prick forward such as be slow and negligent, yea, and for all men it is the Father's rod, ever in readiness to chastise gently the faults committed, and to cause them afterward to live in more godly fear and reverence. Finally, it is an order left by God unto His Church, whereby men learn to frame their wills and doings according to the law of God, by instructing and admonishing one another, yea, and by correcting and punishing all obstinate rebels and contemners of the same.[167]

Thus described, discipline is regarded as a divinely ordained means of encouraging the people of God to 'learn to frame their wills and doings according to the law of God'. Expounding the logic of this sentiment, and noting the close link between the Lord's Supper and discipline in Knox's liturgy, James McEwen argues that the discipline which the Reformed Church insisted upon exercising was an expression of neither legalism nor over-scrupulous moralism. Rather, he says, its basis was the 'sense of the "numinous", or the "altogether holy", in the Lord's Supper – and the deep conviction that this holiness must not be profaned by allowing the careless or the deliberately wicked to approach the Holy Table, at the sacred moment when the Lord and the participants were (as Knox put it) "knitted together" '.[168] McEwen continues:

Such scandalous persons must be exhorted to repent, and remedial discipline must be applied in the hope that they might be led to a better frame of mind. If this failed, they must be debarred, until they repented, from presenting themselves at the Lord's Table. This exclusion from the Sacrament – remedial, and it was to

---

[167] *Book of Common Order*, 1868 (1901 reprint), otherwise known as *Knox's Liturgy*, pp. 31–2.
[168] McEwen, *Faith of John Knox*, p. 60.

be hoped temporary – was what Knox understood by 'excommunication'. Knox's excommunication had nothing to do with consigning a soul to eternal damnation: it, and the whole discipline of the Kirk, were directed to one end – the protection of this central element of the Church's life from profanation.[169]

The view that the aim of Knox's *Exhortation* is to prevent profanation of the sacrament rather than exclude sinners from the Table is supported by the following declarations, which follow his pronouncement of excommunication:

> This I pronounce *not, to seclude any penitent person*, how grievous soever his sins before have been, so that he feel in his heart unfeigned repentance for the same; but only such as continue in sin without repentance ... For the end of our coming thither is *not to make protestation that we are upright or just in our lives*; but contrawise, *we come to seek our life and perfection in Jesus Chris* ... Let us consider, then, that *this Sacrament is a singular medicine for all poor sick creatures, a comfortable help to weak souls, and that our Lord requireth no other worthiness on our part, but that we acknowledge our naughtiness and imperfection.*[170]

Despite these assurances, however, by elevating discipline to the level of a mark of the true Church, and relating it in this way to the word and sacraments, Knox plants a seed of confusion in relation to the nature of grace. This is a point made by Charles Bell, who argues that 'the subse-

---

[169] McEwen, *Faith of John Knox*, p. 60. In the Exhortation, the presiding minister declares: 'In the name and authority of the eternal God, and of His Son, Jesus Christ, I *excommunicate from this Table* all blasphemers of God, all idolaters, all murderers, all adulterers, all that be in malice or envy; all disobedient persons to father or mother, Princes or Magistrates, Pastors or Preachers; all thieves and deceivers of their neighbours; and finally, all such as live a life directly fighting against the will of God: charging them, as they will answer in the presence of Him who is the righteous judge, that they presume not to *profane this most holy Table*' (Cf. *Knox's Liturgy*, pp. 122–3 (italics mine)).
[170] *Knox's Liturgy*, pp. 122–3 (italics mine).

quent emphasis placed on self-examination, and examination by the clergy and elders, can lead to that "legal strain" in Scottish theology of which the Marrow men later complained, which led in practice to what they called, following Calvin, "legal repentance"; that is, the idea that repentance precedes grace in God's order of salvation'.[171] Knox's 'dominating concern for godly discipline, a godly church, and godly Table fellowship at the Lord's Supper', Bell goes on to suggest, 'is moving in the direction of self-examination. For the tendency is to take our eyes off what we are *in Christ*, who is our sanctification, and to dwell instead on what *we must do* to keep covenant with God, and to be worthy to partake of the sacrament.'[172]

Perhaps the danger referred to by Bell might have been avoided if Knox's teaching on discipline had been accompanied by a stronger pneumatology. When discipline is not grounded in a proper doctrine of the Holy Spirit it tends to become a predominantly institutional process. It is also, more often than not, dominated by a moralistic agenda as those charged with leadership responsibilities seek to preserve the purity and holiness of the Church they serve, and control and manage admission to the Lord's Table. But when discipline is understood pneumatologically, then it is understood within the context of being part of that *koinonia* which shares in the life of him who was judged in the place of the ungodly and in whom they have been justified. As T. F. Torrance agues, 'this does not mean that the Church is prohibited from "fencing the Table", by excluding from participation in the Eucharist the lapsed who have denied their Baptism or the impenitent and insincere, but it does mean that the Church must exercise its discipline *with the authority of the Son of Man*, and not with the authority of Priests and Scribes and Pharisees'.[173]

By what means does the Son of Man exercise his authority? It is by the word, says Torrance, and it is by the

---

[171] Bell, *Calvin and Scottish Theology*, p. 48.
[172] Bell, *Calvin and Scottish Theology*, p. 48.
[173] T. F. Torrance, 'Eschatology and the Eucharist', in *Intercommunion*, eds D. Baillie and J. Marsh (London: SCM Press, 1952), p. 341.

word that he judges and divides between people.
Therefore, 'it is when the Son of Man, Christ crucified and
Christ to come, is proclaimed with power in all His saving
grace and judgment, that the Table is kept holy and
undefiled; and it is then when His Word and authority are
glorified that it is indeed the Lord's Table and the Lord's
Supper, and not a private supper owned and administered
on exclusive principles by the Church'.[174] Thus understood, discipline is a function of the word proclaimed
rather than a mark of the true Church in its own right.

John Craig's *Catechism*, and the *Negative Confession*, 1581

In continuity with the *Scots Confession*

Following its production in 1560 and ratification in 1567 by
the first Parliament of the infant King James VI, the *Scots
Confession* was used by the Church of Scotland as a
yardstick of Reformation orthodoxy in a context of
Protestant–Catholic polarisation and conflict. Suspected
Romanists were invited to subscribe to it and, following a
Privy Council decree in 1578, refusal to do so was
a punishable offence. It remained the official doctrinal
statement of the Church of Scotland until superseded by the
adoption of the *Westminster Confession* in 1647, although it
did experience some revival in status when the *Westminster
Confession* was for a while stripped of its legal standing.

Around 1580, as the effects of the Counter-Reformation
began to be felt, the Protestant–Catholic tension was
increasing. In the face of this tension, and to allay some
suspicion that he was wavering, King James deemed it
necessary to make a strong declaration of his allegiance to
the Protestant faith. Because it was commonly believed
that many papists subscribed to the *Scots Confession* deceit-
fully, mere endorsement of it was not enough. The King
therefore commissioned John Craig, one of his chaplains

---

[174] Torrance, 'Eschatology and the Eucharist', p. 341.

and a preacher of some repute, to draft a short confession that no papist could possibly sign. The result was the *Negative Confession*, sometimes called the *King's Confession*, produced in 1581, the same year that Craig produced a *Catechism* for instructing children in the Faith. Craig had been a Dominican monk before his conversion to the Reformed faith in 1536, the catalyst for his conversion being his discovery of Calvin's *Institutio* while in Italy. Upon his return to Scotland he became a close colleague of John Knox's, serving with him for a while at St Andrew's.

Given Craig's background, it is not surprising that there is a strong sense of continuity theologically between his *Catechism* and both the *Scots Confession* and Calvin's *Institutio*. In the opening preface of his *Catechism* he refers the reader to the *Institutio* for 'further confirmation of the Biblical nature of this doctrine', and included within the opening statement of the *Negative Confession* is an explicit endorsement of the *Scots Confession*. Referrals and endorsements aside, the theological continuity is most evident in the central place given in the *Catechism* to the mediatorial role and redemptive work of Christ, of people's union and communion with him through the Holy Spirit, and of their participation in his saving and sanctifying humanity. And that which is explicitly stated in the *Catechism* is presupposed in the *Negative Confession*, wherein Craig denounces one papist practice after another, thereby distinguishing Reformation theology sharply from that of the Roman Church (which, it should be remembered, he had earlier served while a member of the Dominican Order, so he was no stranger to Roman practices and ways of thinking).[175]

Interrelation between union with Christ, justification and faith

The first fruit of faith, according to Craig's *Catechism*, is union with Christ. There are two aspects to this union. In

---

[175] While the *Negative Confession's* anti-papist rhetoric is offensive to the modern ear, cognisance should be taken of both the context in which it was written and the underlying theological issues, which have ongoing relevance.

the incarnation there was a *carnal* union, in and through which divine 'life and righteousness' was 'placed in our flesh' and our flesh was 'joined personally with the Fountain of life'.[176] In other words, there was a sanctification of sinful human flesh in the holy flesh of the Saviour.[177] But all of this is of no avail to people without their *spiritual* union with Christ, by which and through which they participate in all his graces and merits, namely, 'justification and peace of conscience'.[178]

If the first fruit of faith is union with Christ, the second fruit of faith, according to the *Catechism*, is justification, defined in terms of the 'remission of sins' and 'imputation of (God's) justice'.[179] God's justice is able to forgive sin, the *Catechism* teaches, because 'Christ satisfied abundantly the justice of God for us'. His justice, defined in terms of his 'perfect obedience', has been imputed to sinners by virtue of their union with him. It is Christ who justifies – faith is but the 'instrument of our justification', the means by which sinners receive that which is offered to them in the preaching of the gospel.

The third fruit of faith, according to the *Catechism*, is good works, borne of 'continual faith and repentance'.[180] Repentance here is defined as 'the hatred of sin and the love of justice', is deemed to come from 'the fear of God' (generated by 'the preaching of the Law') and 'the hope of mercy' (generated by 'the preaching of the Gospel') and by the Spirit, who regenerates us 'through the death and resur-

---

[176] 'Craig's *Catechism*, 1581', which is published in T. F. Torrance's *The School of Faith: The Catechisms of the Reformed Church* (London: James Clarke and Co., 1959), p. 113.

[177] It is worth nothing that the *Catechism* views sanctification as something which began in the incarnation rather than something that only happens in us subsequent to our being justified. Cf. Craig's *Catechism, School of Faith*, p. 112, where, in response to the question, 'Why was He (Christ) conceived by the Holy Spirit?' the answer is given, 'That He might be without sin, *and so sanctify us*' (italics mine).

[178] Craig's *Catechism, School of Faith*, p. 124. This does not mean that there are two different unions, as though one's salvation is incomplete without both of them in place. Rather, it means that there is one union with Christ, which he has established through his life, death and resurrection and in which he gives those whom he calls to share through the gift of his Spirit.

[179] Craig's *Catechism, School of Faith*, p. 125.

[180] Craig's *Catechism, School of Faith*, pp. 125–6.

rection of Christ', and works in us 'continual mortification of our lusts and newness of life'.[181]

Two important points worth noting here are the interrelation between union with Christ, justification and faith, and the fact that justification, repentance and good works stem from one's union with Christ rather than the other way round. In other words, union with Christ is not something with which one is rewarded *after* one has repented, demonstrated good works and been justified. It is the *first*, not the last, fruit of faith.

Salvation, election and assurance

The strong Christology implicit in the *Confession*'s teaching on our union with Christ is reinforced in its teaching on his redemptive work, where special attention is given to his priestly office, and in particular to his obedience and prayer as part of the atoning passion offered in satisfaction of God's wrath.[182] Christ died for all sinners, the *Catechism* teaches, suffering for them all in 'both body and soul', sustaining 'the person of guilty men', taking upon himself their curse and punishment, thereby giving them God's blessing. He suffered the 'anguish of death and pain of hell', sustained by 'faith, patience and prayer to His Father'.

Especially noteworthy is the question in the *Catechism*, 'What comfort do we have in the person of the Judge?' to which the reply is given, 'Our Saviour, Advocate and Mediator only shall be our Judge.'[183] According to this teaching, people shall be judged by none other than the One who was judged in their place, who through his suffering removed their curse and gave to them his blessing. As Torrance astutely comments, 'with John Craig there was no concept of God as Judge behind the back of Christ'.[184] This is reinforced by his teaching on election,

[181] Craig's *Catechism*, *School of Faith*, p. 126.
[182] Craig's *Catechism*, *School of Faith*, pp. 110f.
[183] Craig's *Catechism*, *School of Faith*, p. 117.
[184] Torrance, *Scottish Theology*, p. 51.

which, in its emphasis not on an eternal, immutable divine decree but on people's adoption with Christ and their union and communion with him through the Spirit, is equally christocentric: 'From what source does our stability derive?' asks Craig in his section on the cause and progress of salvation. 'From God's eternal and constant election *in Christ*.'[185]

However, as with Knox, Craig's christocentric approach to the subject of election falls short of affirming Christ as the *Electing God*. This delivers the same result, namely, a disjunction between divine mercy (for the elect) and divine justice (for the reprobate), and ultimately, a lack of assurance of salvation – despite deeming assurance to be of the essence of faith. While God's election 'is clear and certain in itself', teaches the *Catechism*, 'it is not always certain to us in particular'. Therefore, in seeking certainty of salvation Christians are advised not to begin with God's eternal decision, whatever that might be in relation to particular individuals, for if that is their starting point then they 'shall wander in darkness'. Rather, they must look to God's election as 'it may be felt and known by its fruits'. While this might be troublesome to them in the short term, and even bring 'some to desperation', 'at length it brings great peace of conscience'.[186]

Ecclesiastical discipline

While Craig emphasises the work of the Spirit in effecting union and communion with Christ, he also says that God uses three main instruments to bring people into union and to maintain them in it: 'the Word, the Sacraments, and the Ministry of men'.[187]

Of the third instrument, the 'Ministry of men', Craig speaks of the 'discipline' by which, at the judgement of the elders, the likes of 'infidels and public slanderers of the Church' will be excluded from the sacrament 'lest they

---

[185] Craig's *Catechism, School of Faith*, p. 161.
[186] Craig's *Catechism, School of Faith*, p. 163.
[187] Craig's *Catechism, School of Faith*, p. 146.

should hurt themselves, slander the Church, and dishonour God'. Such is the importance of discipline in the life of the Church that Craig follows John Knox in elevating it to be a mark of the Church, along with the word and the sacraments.[188] Comments made in relation to Knox's view of ecclesiastical discipline also apply here.

While a 'legal' understanding of repentance is always a potential consequence of discipline being elevated to a mark of the true Church, it is partially counter-balanced in the *Catechism* by the portrayal of self-examination in non-legalistic and non-moralistic categories. Craig suggests that the purpose of self-examination according to 1 Corinthians 11:28 is to determine whether or not one is a 'lively' member of Christ, and this is achieved through discernment of the fruits of 'knowledge, faith and repentance' in one's life.[189] Of course people will always discern that their faith is imperfect and that they are unworthy and sinful creatures, but this should not keep them away from the Lord's Table, says Craig, provided only that there is no hypocrisy in them.[190]

Prayer

The *Catechism*'s main section on prayer follows the ordering of petitions contained in the Lord's Prayer. It is preceded by a general discourse on the subject of prayer in which prayer is defined as 'a humble lifting up of our minds and hearts to God'.[191] This entails being moved by the Holy Spirit to pray fervently in the name of Christ – for he is the Mediator of prayer[192] – for those 'things promised or commanded in the Word'. It is not a matter of following 'our own imagination', for then 'our prayer would be but

---

[188] Craig's *Catechism, School of Faith*, p. 160.
[189] Craig's *Catechism, School of Faith*, pp. 151, 158.
[190] Craig's *Catechism, School of Faith*, pp. 151, 158.
[191] Craig's *Catechism, School of Faith*, p. 136.
[192] Craig's *Catechism, School of Faith*, p. 137. While the *Catechism* does not say explicitly that Christ is the Mediator of prayer, it is implied in the statement that we should pray in the name of Christ because of 'God's commandment and promise to hear us in so doing (John 16:23)'.

vanity'.[193] In other words, prayer is not mere self-expression. Nor is it something that Christians do out of their own strength and resources. Rather, it is something they do through Christ and in the Spirit as they earnestly seek the mind of Christ.

The *Catechism* further distinguishes between prayer and thanksgiving. Whereas prayer is petitionary in nature, devoted to seeking the mind and will of Christ, thanksgiving is a simple acknowledgement of Christ 'as the Author and Fountain of all good things'.[194] All prayer should be bracketed by thanksgiving,[195] and while prayer may cease for a time thanksgiving never ceases 'because we always have benefits from God'.[196] The only sacrifice that Christians make to God is this: a sacrifice of praise or thanksgiving.[197]

Conclusion

In the above consideration of Calvin, Knox and Craig we have identified a strong resonance of thought which not only unites them with one another but which also places them firmly in theological continuity with Athanasius and Nicene orthodoxy. We have paid particular attention to the importance which all of them attached to the notion of being in union with Christ – 'carnally' (to use the language of John Craig) through the hypostatic union of God and all humankind in the person of Christ, and 'spiritually' through the activity of the Holy Spirit who brings individual persons to participate in the life of Christ and his benefits.

In keeping with this emphasis, Calvin, Knox and Craig articulated their theology of worship in a thoroughly

---

[193] Craig's *Catechism, School of Faith*, p. 138.
[194] Craig's *Catechism, School of Faith*, p. 144.
[195] Craig's *Catechism, School of Faith*, p. 145: In response to the question, 'How should we begin and end our prayer?', the *Catechism* responds, 'Evermore with thanksgiving to God'.
[196] Craig's *Catechism, School of Faith*, p. 145.
[197] Craig's *Catechism, School of Faith*, p. 145.

trinitarian way, understanding it as an activity which stems from being in union with Christ through the Spirit, and which constitutes an act of participation in the worship that Christ offers eternally to the Father in our name and on our behalf. In the same way, prayer is portrayed in terms of one's being united through the activity of the Spirit with the prayer of Christ, whose prayer precedes one's own and who continually intercedes for sinners.

At the heart of this trinitarian view of worship and prayer lies the mediatorial role of Christ, understood not only in terms of his death on the cross, but also in terms of his saving life and obedience on humanity's behalf, thereby giving equal emphasis to the 'active' obedience of Christ (in his life) and his 'passive' obedience (on the cross). The atonement here is regarded not as an act of God done *ab extra* upon humankind, but as an act of God done *ab intra*, from within the depths, and indeed limitations, of the human condition. The Son's incarnational assumption of the human condition was therefore nothing less than a reconciling, healing, sanctifying and recreating activity in which, by making himself one with all people, he both took what was theirs and imparted to them what is his. This is the 'wondrous exchange' which lies at the heart of Calvin's soteriology, and which is taken up by Knox and Craig.

This means that for these early Scottish Reformers, to be united with Christ is not merely a matter of benefiting from the non-imputation of sin through his death; rather, it is to be actively joined to him by the Spirit in his life of faith, obedience, prayer and worship. Believers are therefore exhorted to look away from *their* own faith, obedience, prayer and worship to what *Christ* does for them in their place and on their behalf. Their union with Christ is not something that occurs as a result of their being justified by an act of their faith as such. Rather, their union with Christ and the sanctification of their humanity through the incarnation is the basis for their justification.

Union with Christ is the basis for everything that follows in the Christian life, the most visible expression of which is the Eucharist, conceived as that act, instituted by Christ himself, through which Christ gives himself to his people in such a way (through the 'wondrous exchange') that his life becomes theirs and their lives, sanctified by the Spirit, ascend in him, through him and with him to the Father. In this regard, Calvin and the early Scottish Reformers considered union with Christ quite unthinkable apart from the Eucharist – not that union with Christ was considered dependent upon it, rather it was regarded as an indispensable pledge, witness and strengthening of the union Christians have with Christ through faith. Accordingly, their theology may be described properly as eucharistic.

We also argued in this chapter that despite their very strong appreciation of the vicarious humanity and priesthood of Christ in relation to both atonement and worship, Calvin, Knox and Craig shared two weaknesses. First, Calvin's reaction against the medieval notion of sacrifice meant that he, and those who transplanted his theology on to Scottish soil, never developed the idea of Eucharist as an offering in a proper way. Second, their failure to allow their Christology to shape their doctrine of election and predestination as thoroughly as other doctrines left their soteriology and understanding of the Christian life vulnerable to the possibility of being recast in a more legalistic, contractual and introspective mould as the doctrine of predestination gained greater prominence and people, uncertain of their own election, sought assurance not in Christ but in their own faith and works. In the next chapter we will assess the extent to which this scenario became a reality in the Westminster tradition.

3

Federal Calvinism and the Westminster Tradition, and their Legacy in Reformed Liturgical Developments

Key Questions

If the doctrine of predestination expounded by Calvin and the early Scottish Reformers of the sixteenth century left their soteriology and understanding of the Christian life vulnerable to the possibility of being recast in a more legalistic, contractual and introspective mould, the question which must be asked is, To what extent did this actually happen as Calvinism became a real force on the Reformed ecclesiastical landscape in seventeenth-century Britain? T. F. and J. B. Torrance stand within a school of thought which claims there are significant and irreconcilable differences between the Calvinistic doctrines of the seventeenth-century Westminster documents and those doctrines expounded by Calvin himself in the sixteenth century and built upon by the 'older Scottish tradition', of which John Knox and John Craig were leading figures. In recent years this claim has been challenged, most notably by Paul Helm, Robert Letham and Richard Muller, who claim continuity rather than discontinuity, and faithfulness rather than distortion in relation to Calvinism's development of Calvin's doctrinal system.

The debate tends to concentrate on three interrelated issues: (a) The extent to which Calvin's Genevan successor, Theodore Beza, rather than Calvin himself, determined the direction of Reformed theology, especially in Great Britain; (b) The influence of federal theology on the Westminster tradition; and (c) The influence of Puritanism, and in particular William Perkins, on Reformed doctrine and worship. It is to these issues that we will now turn before we conclude the chapter with a brief survey of the key doctrinal features of the Westminster documents, especially as they pertain to the priesthood of Christ.

Theodore Beza and John Calvin: Continuity or Discontinuity?

The effects of a greater stress on the doctrine of predestination

Michael Jinkins describes Theodore Beza as 'the chosen successor to Calvin's place of leadership, the man groomed as guardian of the Genevan Reformation'.[1] Clearly, there was a close affinity between Calvin and his successor – at least on a personal level. However, it is not quite so clear that the same affinity can be assumed on a theological level. In recent years a range of scholars, including Ernst Bizer, Walter Kickel, Brian Armstrong, Robert Kendall, J. B. and T. F. Torrance and Basil Hall have drawn attention to significant differences between the theological systems of the two men.[2] T. F. Torrance, for example, attributes to Beza the development of a 'rationalistic supralapsarian form of Calvinism ... which was to leave its mark on Scottish Theology'.[3]

Kendall shares this opinion of Beza and, in chapter 2 of his book, *Calvin and English Calvinism to 1649*, provides a useful summary of Beza's theological system. He notes the dominating influence of the doctrine of predestination, which has several effects. To begin with, it carries with it a doctrine of limited atonement – Christ is regarded as the Redeemer of the elect only. Accordingly, says Kendall of Beza, the ground of assurance of salvation must be sought

---

[1] M. Jinkins, 'Theodore Beza: Continuity and Regression in the Reformed Tradition', *Evangelical Quarterly* 64 (1992), p. 132.

[2] As Richard Muller notes, for most of this century, scholarship was generally content to accept the generalisations and arguments of nineteenth- and early twentieth-century German historians who under-stood Calvin as standing in continuity with later Reformed theology. In particular, it was held that predestination was the fundamental principle of Reformed theology. Cf. R. Muller, 'Calvin and the "Calvinists": Assessing Continuities and Discontinuities Between the Reformation and Orthodoxy' (Part 1), *Calvin Theological Journal* 30 (1995), pp. 345–8.

[3] Torrance, *Scottish Theology*, p. 60. Not only on Scottish theology but on English theology too. Jinkins notes the influence of Beza on Thomas Cartwright, together with a number of other English Reformed scholars who were on the continent during the last part of the sixteenth century. Cf. 'Beza: Continuity and Regression', pp. 138–9.

elsewhere than in Christ, for Christians cannot be certain that they are among the elect for whom Christ died: 'While Calvin thinks looking to ourselves leads to anxiety, or sure damnation, Beza thinks otherwise. Sanctification, or good works, is the infallible proof of saving faith.'[4] Kendall identifies in Beza's theological system an implicit distinction between faith and assurance, accentuated by his insistence that believers must 'apply' Christ to themselves: 'Consistent with his doctrine of limited atonement, Beza states that it is hardly enough to believe that "Jesus Christ came to save sinners"; rather one must "particularlye applye" Christ "to himself", the promise of his salvation.'[5] We have in this understanding of faith, says Kendall, the seed of voluntarism – that is, the view that faith is an act of the will that is rewarded. 'To Calvin', writes Kendall, 'looking to Christ *is* faith; Calvin could point men directly to Christ since Christ died for all. Beza begins not with Christ but with faith; faith, if found, is rewarded with salvation in Christ'.[6]

Kendall goes on to note that this *ordo salutis*, in which salvation follows the act of faith, is reinforced in Beza's discussion of the role of law in conversion. The law, he teaches, reveals to people their sins and kindles within them 'the first poynt of repentance',[7] which is why 'the spirite of God *beginneth* by the preaching of the lawe'.[8] As Kendall points out, Beza's teaching at this point comes very close indeed to putting repentance before faith in the *ordo salutis*.

Scholasticism

In opposition to this interpretation of Beza Robert Letham, Richard Muller and Paul Helm contend that the differences

---

[4] Kendall, *Calvin and English Calvinism*, p. 33.
[5] Kendall, *Calvin and English Calvinism*, p. 33.
[6] Kendall, *Calvin and English Calvinism*, p. 34. This is not to suggest, says Kendall, that Beza thinks Christians take the initiative in their salvation. Rather, faith is ultimately grounded in God's 'enabling grace'.
[7] *Questions and Answers*, 54a, cited Kendall, *Calvin and English Calvinism*, p. 37.
[8] *Q.A.*, 53a, cited by Kendall, *Calvin and English Calvinism*, p. 37 (italics Kendall's).

between Calvin and Beza have been exaggerated, and that in fact there is far greater continuity between their doctrinal systems than is often recognised. On the matter of scholasticism[9] it is conceded that Beza, especially in his later years, employed the methods of scholasticism far more than Calvin, but at the same time, it is said that greater recognition should be given to the fact that Calvin himself, despite his stated misgivings about scholastic methodologies, was not averse to utilising Aristotelian categories when the occasion warranted it.[10] As Letham puts it, 'to say that a particular writer was influenced by scholasticism is not so significant a statement as has often been thought, since the vast bulk of the academic curriculum in the sixteenth century was governed by Aristotelianism'.[11]

Muller, who describes scholasticism in terms of a developing academic methodology that had its roots in the Middle Ages, the Renaissance and the Reformation, makes the same point more forcefully.[12] Some distinction must be made, he claims, between the non-pejorative identification of 'scholasticism' as a method and the highly pejorative use of the term 'scholasticism', characteristic of polemic in the Reformation and post-Reformation eras to indicate a theology overburdened with its own logic and speculation. Thus it is, he argues, that Calvin accuses his adversaries of

---

[9] Brian Armstrong identifies a number of tendencies in Protestant scholasticism: the use of syllogistic reasoning; a heavy dependence on the philosophy and methodology of Aristotle; a stress on the role of reason and logic in religion; an interest in speculative, metaphysical thought; a view of scripture as containing a set of propositions so as to provide an inerrant base for philosophy; faith being reduced to one doctrine among many rather than being given a central place. Cf. *Calvinism and the Amyraut Heresy: Protestant Scholasticism and Humanism in Seventeenth-Century France* (Madison, 1969), p. 32, cited by Robert Letham in 'Theodore Beza: A Reassessment', *Scottish Journal of Theology* 40, (1987), p. 25, Richard Muller in *Christ and the Decree: Christology and Predestination in Reformed Theology from Calvin to Perkins* (Grand Rapids: Baker Book House, 1986), p. 11, and Jinkins in 'Beza: Continuity and Regression', pp. 144–5.

[10] Letham, 'Beza: A Reassessment', p. 27; Jinkins, 'Beza: Continuity and Regression', p. 144.

[11] Letham, 'Beza: A Reassessment', p. 27.

[12] Muller, 'Calvin and the "Calvinists"', pp. 371f.

being scholastic (in the pejorative sense) while his own writings show evidence of scholastic method. When this is understood, then the difference between Beza and Calvin is seen not in terms of a difference of method but in terms of a difference of stage in the development of the single method. The fact that Beza's writings are characterised by a more stringent rationalism and speculative metaphysic than those of Calvin does not mean that reason has been given equal standing with faith in theology or that the authority of revelation has been lessened.

Muller's point here is well made and certainly worth noting. It does, however, raise an important question: Even if it is the case that Calvin himself was not averse to employing the tools of medieval scholasticism, was a point reached by succeeding Reformers whereby the scholastic method became so rationalistic and speculative that instead of being a servant of church doctrine it became its master? This possibly takes us to the heart of the difference between Calvin and Beza. Whereas Calvin's writings exhibit a subordination of everything – including whatever interpretive methods were at his disposal – to the reality of God's self-disclosure in Christ as testified to in holy scripture, Beza's writings reflect a hardening of the scholastic method and its speculative metaphysic to the point where it becomes in itself the dominant feature. The *Tabula* from Beza's *Summa totius Christianismi*, which we must remember was one of his earlier works, produced four years *before* Calvin's final edition of the *Institutio*, and which seeks to provide 'a description and distribution of the causes of election and reprobation', is a good example of this. It begins not with a trinitarian God whose will is revealed in Christ, but with a God 'whose ways are past finding out' and whose purpose is 'eternal and immutable', preceding in order all causes, including the decree to elect some people to glory.[13]

---

[13] Cf. the *Tabula* diagram reprinted in J. B. Torrance's article, 'The Concept of Federal Theology – Was Calvin a Federal Theologian?', in *Calvinus Sacrae Scripturae Professor*, ed. W. H. Neuser (Grand Rapids, Michigan: Eerdmans, 1994), p. 39.

Of this contrast between Calvin and Beza, David Weir
writes:

> Beza affirmed everything that Calvin taught. For Beza,
> however, the *methodology* of defending Calvin's
> doctrine was different. First, in the *Tabula* ... Beza
> organised his material in a different manner than
> Calvin did in his *Institutes*. Calvin organised his
> *Institutes* essentially along the lines of the creed: God
> the Father, God the Son, God the Holy Spirit, and the
> Holy Catholic Church. Beza's table is a much more
> rational and logical exposition of subject-matter. One
> looks at the layout and connecting lines of the *Tabula*
> and thinks: '*If* there is a God, and that God is
> sovereign, *then* he must control everything that
> happens in the world. The central doctrine of
> Christianity is salvation, and then reprobation.
> *Therefore*, God has decreed to save some and to damn
> others.'[14]

Predestination and limited atonement

As to Kendall's claim that Beza's theology was dominated
by the doctrine of predestination, Letham rejoins that this
is overstated. 'Those works in which Beza used predestination as a governing principle', he says, 'were written in a
polemical context.'[15] His non-polemical works, including
his sermons, letters and some of his larger works, contain
no significant references to the doctrine. Moreover, insofar
as Beza did stress the doctrine of predestination, he was in
good company, for Reformers such as Zwingli and Bucer
were 'formidable predestinarians' also. Letham concludes
that 'in writing that double predestination was the theatre
of God's self-manifestation whereby he demonstrates his
justice towards the reprobate and his mercy towards the
elect, Beza was not saying anything with which Calvin

[14] Weir, *Origins of Federal Theology*, p. 72.
[15] Letham, 'Beza: A Reassessment', p. 27.

would have disagreed. Both made the will of God the sole cause of election and reprobation.'[16] The real difference between Beza and Calvin, he suggests, was the former's espousal of supralapsarianism, and the degree to which he made it the apex of his teaching on predestination. Whereas Calvin said that people are chosen by divine grace from a 'corrupt mass', Beza maintained that the elect – and the reprobate – are predestined from a mass 'yet unshapen'. That is to say, the divine decrees of election and reprobation precede and have priority over the decree of both creation and the Fall.

According to this line of thinking, God, having decreed two classes of people – the elect and the reprobate – each with a different end, then decrees the means by which those ends will be met. Accordingly, the Fall is deemed to be divinely ordained, for people cannot be saved unless mercy is shown nor can they be damned unless they sin. Salvation for the elect comes through Christ – a fact upon which Letham bases his claim that Beza views the doctrine of election christologically.

He goes on to concur with Kendall that the natural consequence of Beza's rigorous predestinarianism was a doctrine of limited atonement: Christ is the 'onely mediator between God *and his elect* eternally ordained'.[17] Thus while Calvin gave priority to the universal promise of the gospel over the particularity of God's intention, Letham suggests, Beza was not prepared to tolerate anything that might appear to compromise the hiddenness of God's purpose.

Saving faith and sanctification

This, however, raises the now familiar problem concerning the grounds of assurance of salvation: If the mind of God cannot be known because his eternal counsel is hidden from mere mortals, and if Christ died for the elect only, then, as Kendall observes, this makes trusting Christ's

---

[16] Letham, 'Beza: A Reassessment', p. 28.
[17] Beza, *Briefe and Pithie*, 3–4.

death presumptuous, for people could be putting their trust in One who unbeknownst to them did not die for them and therefore be damned. Beza was aware of this problem, Kendall suggests, so he placed the ground of assurance not in Christ but in the effects or fruits of saving faith in the believer. 'While Calvin thinks looking to ourselves leads to anxiety, or sure damnation, Beza thinks otherwise. Sanctification, or good works, is the infallible proof of saving faith.'[18]

But by making sanctification the grounds of Christian assurance, Kendall continues, Beza directs the believer's attention not to Christ, as Calvin did, but to human faith, making faith an act of the will, albeit one that is enabled by grace. This in turn leads him to depict conversion in terms of two works of grace: a 'first grace' (faith) and a 'second grace' (sanctification). The first grace is rendered void if it is not ratified by the second. 'But,' says Kendall, 'by making the knowledge of saving faith subject to the second grace (sanctification) he reverses the order Calvin intends. For Calvin insists we cannot truly repent until we are first assured of God's grace. Beza delays assurance until the "effects" are there; thus a change of life precedes the assurance that we have faith indeed.'[19]

Letham strongly disagrees with Kendall on this point. While Beza, he says, does direct our attention towards the believer's sanctification, he does not do so on the basis that it is the ground of assurance in itself. Rather, it is a crucial first step that leads the elect not only to God's written word but also to Christ himself. 'In the *Confessio Christianae fidei*,' he points out, 'Beza insists that it is through Christ's righteousness that we are made certain of salvation, since whatever is in Christ is imputed to us.'[20] This imputation and certainty is the work of the Spirit, who unites the elect to Christ by faith, using the word and sacraments as means. In this context, Letham continues, Beza's understanding of faith is not merely one of intellectual assent.

[18] Kendall, *Calvin and English Calvinism*, p. 33.
[19] Kendall, *Calvin and English Calvinism*, p. 35.
[20] *Confessio*, pp. 21–2, cited in Letham, 'Beza: A Reassessment', p. 34.

Rather, it is the knowledge of certainty and assurance. 'It is a "certain knowledge" engraved on the hearts of the elect by the Holy Spirit, by which we are made certain of our election.'[21]

At the same time, Letham proceeds to say, for Beza faith is more than knowledge, for knowledge leads to trust which is directly correlative in his writings with union with Christ:

> In the order of causes we are united to Christ before we apprehend Christ.[22] Thus our union with Christ has a logical priority over our reception of his benefits: wisdom, justification, sanctification and redemption.[23] Thus in the *Confessio Christianae fidei* the knowledge of faith by which we are made certain of our election precedes and gives rise to our application of the promise of salvation in Christ to ourselves.[24]

While Letham agrees with Kendall that Beza talks about faith as an act, it must be remembered he says, that so too does Calvin, although not as much.[25] Kendall is wrong to imagine that Beza views faith simply as an act and so is an incipient voluntarist, for he refers to faith in a variety of ways – he locates it in the heart (*cor*), the mind (*mens*), the soul (*animus*), as well as in the will (*voluntas*). Moreover, he says, Beza also follows Calvin in placing faith before repentance. Repentance is regarded as an effect of faith.[26] Paraphrasing Beza's thoughts on the matter, Letham writes:

---

[21] *Confessio*, p. 19, cited in Letham, 'Beza: A Reassessment', p. 36.

[22] *Confessio*, p. 21, cited in Letham, 'Beza: A Reassessment', p. 36.

[23] *Tractatonium* 1:684, cited in Letham, 'Beza: A Reassessment', p. 36.

[24] *Confessio*, p. 19, cited in Letham, 'Beza: A Reassessment', p. 36.

[25] Letham detects a hardened rationalism in Beza's writings towards the end of his life. In the 1589 edition of his annotated *Novum Testamentum* he tends to emphasise faith as an act more than in earlier editions. Cf. 'Beza: A Reassessment', p. 38.

[26] In support of this interpretation of Beza, Letham notes that whereas in his chart at the start of the first edition of the *Summa totius Christianismi* faith is placed after conversion, in subsequent editions they are placed side by side. Repentance is viewed as an effect of faith, not the foundation for faith. Cf. 'Beza: A Reassessment', p. 37.

No one is regenerate unless he is in Christ. No one is in Christ unless by faith.[27] Therefore Beza acknowledges what came to be known as a distinction between legal repentance (which precedes faith and is not saving but purely preparatory) and evangelical repentance (or repentance proper, which follows faith), although even here he provides further nuances which allow him to place gospel before law.[28]

Letham concludes his call for a reappraisal of Beza with the following words:

> Certainly, Beza gave a warmer welcome to scholastic methodology than Calvin. His prominent supralapsarianism may be symptomatic of that. He firmly defends limited atonement which Calvin, whatever his views on the question, did not do. However, his overall thought on predestination and on its relationship to Christology, his formulations on faith and assurance in connection with election, sanctification and the Spirit, all undermine the idea of a deep-seated departure from his predecessor.[29]

Calvin and Beza: Some concluding comments

While the degree of theological continuity between Calvin and Beza will be the subject of ongoing debate, we are able to draw one or two tentative conclusions, which pertain to our own subject matter. First, there does appear to be a fundamental difference in emphasis between the two men on the subject of soteriology. Jinkins gets to the heart of the matter when he writes:

---

[27] *Tractationum* 1:327–8; *Theses*, p. 103, Letham, 'Beza: A Reassessment', p. 38.

[28] Letham, 'Beza: A Reassessment', p. 38. Insofar as Beza validates this distinction between legal and evangelical repentance he differs from Calvin, who was highly critical of the Roman sacrament of penance, which implied a soteriology defined in contractual rather than covenantal terms, and a notion of 'legal repentance' that made repentance a condition of forgiveness.

[29] Letham, 'Beza: A Reassessment', pp. 39–40.

Calvin understood reconciliation primarily as that which took place in Christ, in the person of the God-man, who does not simply acquire a package of salvific benefits which can be applied to the elect, but assumes the sickness-unto-death of humanity, healing humanity in his own flesh. Calvin's was the soteriology of the 'wonderful exchange', a thoroughly ontological understanding of salvation, in which the Triune God was understood to have stood-in for humanity. This is rather a different picture of salvation from the scholastic image of salvation as a collection of benefits purchased by the merits of Christ and applied to the elect believer by gracious means, an image derived largely from Latin theology.[30]

In other words, Calvin's soteriology, in contrast to Beza's, stresses the ontological over the mechanical. It focuses not upon the reception of benefits but upon one's union with the One whose grace triumphs over sin and in whom sinners are reconciled to God.[31] This is a major point of difference between the two men. Letham's call for a reappraisal of Beza fails to address this vital point.[32]

Second, Letham's attempt to downplay the dominance (in position and effects) of the doctrine of predestination in Beza's writings is not convincing. It is clear, for example, that in his occasional paper, the *Tabula*, which was written in 1555 as a summary of Christian theology in its essentials, Beza makes the doctrine of predestination the pivotal principle around which all other dogmas are organised. And, as Jinkins points out, even in

---

[30] Jinkins, 'Beza: Continuity and Regression', pp. 142–3.

[31] Jinkins says that 'unlike Calvin, one does not sense that atonement is essentially a filial matter for Beza' and conjectures that 'perhaps this grows from Beza's corresponding lack of emphasis upon the universal fatherhood of God, as fatherly creator of all things' ('Beza: Continuity and Regression', p. 151). On this point, see also J. B. Torrance's, 'Interpreting the Word by the Light of Christ or the Light of Nature? Calvin, Calvinism, and Barth', in *Calviniana: Ideas and Influence of Jean Calvin* (Sixteenth-Century Essays and Studies, Vol. 10), ed. R. V. Schnucker (Missouri: Sixteenth-Century Journal Publishers, 1988), p. 265.

[32] The same criticism can be levelled at Helm and Muller.

his later and more comprehensive work, *Confessio*, he 'places predestination, in the first point in his discussion of the unity and triunity of God, and in the second point in the development of his doctrine of God as Father, so that predestination precedes his development both of Christology and soteriology, allowing, in effect, predestination to dominate his subsequent theological discourse'.[33]

The effects of this placement are felt throughout Beza's entire doctrinal system. As we have seen, by making election logically prior to grace, not only does a Christology arise which casts Christ in the role of Redeemer of the elect only, but also the grounds of assurance are located outside the person and work of Christ. Beza's teaching generates introspection on the part of the believer that Calvin, with his more objective christo-logical focus, did not permit to the same extent. With Beza, justification and sanctification are conceived in mechanical rather than ontological terms.[34] Accordingly, the notion of the priesthood of Christ is underdeveloped, both in terms of what he accomplished for all humanity in his vicarious life, death and resurrection, and in terms of his ongoing role as Intercessor and Advocate. In sum, his doctrinal system, dominated as it is by his doctrine of predestination, tends to render the justice of God essential but the love of God arbitrary, yields a theory of limited atonement which is divorced from the doctrine of the incarnation, and fosters an unhealthy introspection as the search for the signs of election is redirected away from Christ to the life of the individual believer.

---

[33] Jinkins, 'Beza: Continuity and Regression', p. 149.

[34] Whereas Calvin grounded justification and sanctification in the hypostatic union, Beza's *Tabula* portrays justification and sanctification in terms of being the result of one's effectual calling, conversion and faith. Through faith the believer is justified by the imputation of Christ's right-eousness, and sanctification begins. Beza thus lays the groundwork for Calvinism's tendency to insist first on judicial justification and justifying faith and then on that basis to speak of sanctification as something which follows that judicial act.

The Rise of Federal Theology

The origins of federal theology

If the latter half of the sixteenth century marks the growing influence of Beza on the shaping of Reformed dogmatics, it also marks the rise of the so-called 'federal theology', which, as J. B. Torrance points out, 'was to become the criterion of orthodoxy in the Calvinist, Puritan world on both sides of the Atlantic'.[35] Federal theology was that form of theology which gave central place to the concept of 'covenant' (*foedus*), and distinguished different covenants in God's relation to the world. The prevalence of the concept lay in the fact that it was both biblical and at the forefront of Scottish and English socio-political thought in the early seventeenth century. With the break-up of feudalism, the intensifying struggle for freedom and the first stirrings of democracy, people made 'bands', 'pacts', 'contracts' and 'covenants' with one another and with God. In Scotland the attempt of Charles I to impose uniformity of worship through the introduction of Archbishop William Laud's liturgy in 1637 provoked the response of the National Covenant in 1638. The Solemn League and Covenant of 1643 followed this. The next hundred years was a time when churches, congregations and individuals, swept along by the emerging socio-political philosophy of 'social contract' illuminated by the 'light of reason' and sanctioned by 'revelation', were making covenants with God. It was a time when many puritans were leaving for the 'free world' to escape the 'tyranny' of British kings, feudal overlords and an ecclesiastical episcopacy to pursue freedom in both political and religious life.

Theologically, the concept of covenant grew in prominence, first on the continent and then in Britain.[36] In tracing

---

[35] Torrance, 'Concept of Federal Theology', p. 16.

[36] Cf. Weir, *Origins of Federal Theology*. Weir argues convincingly that the lively sixteenth-century predestinarian debates involving (among others) Albert Pighius, John Calvin, Jerome Bolsec, Sebastian Castellio and Theodore Beza had a direct influence on the rise of federal theology, insofar as it constituted the backdrop against which 'Zacharias Ursinus, a new convert from Lutheranism to the Reformed faith, first proposed, in

the idea of covenant in Scotland, G. D. Henderson notes that Olevianus, one of the joint-authors of the *Heidelberg Catechism*, made a distinction in his 1581 Commentary on Galatians between *foedus legale* and *foedus gratiae*.[37] Olevianus had from an early date influenced Scotland, notes Henderson, for Robert Howie, who was to succeed Andrew Melville as Principal of Marischal College in Aberdeen, studied under him at Herborn and closely followed his teaching. Indeed, Melville himself placed considerable emphasis upon the concept of covenant, as did Robert Rollock of the University of Edinburgh, who was also influenced by Olevianus.

Rollock especially is a pivotal figure, for he was the first theologian on the Scottish scene to make explicit use of the concept of a 'covenant of works' (*foedus operum*) and to enlarge upon the contrast between the covenants, thus foreshadowing later federalist doctrine. He taught that all of God's dealings with humankind take the form of a covenant. Further, when God makes a covenant with humankind it generally involves a conditional promise. In particular there are two covenants: the covenant of works and the covenant of grace. The covenant of works, which may also be called a legal or natural covenant, is founded in nature, and in the law of God. It is applicable to all people. Unlike the covenant of grace, which applies to the elect, and is grounded in the person and work of Christ, it requires no mediator between God and humankind.

The weaknesses of federal theology

In his essay, 'Covenant or Contract?: A Study of the Theological Background of Worship in Seventeenth-

---

1561 and 1562, the idea of a prelapsarian *foedus naturale* with Adam' (*Origins of Federal Theology*, p. 87). Cf. also, W. Klempa, 'The Concept of Covenant in Sixteenth- and Seventeenth-Century Continental and British Reformed Theology', in *Major Themes in the Reformed Tradition*, ed. D. K. McKim (Grand Rapids, Michigan: Eerdmans, 1992), pp. 94–107.

[37] G. D. Henderson, 'The Idea of Covenant in Scotland', *Evangelical Quarterly* 27 (1955), p. 8. On the teaching of Olevianus, cf. also, Weir, *Origins of Federal Theology*, pp. 133f.

Century Scotland',[38] J. B. Torrance identifies five weaknesses in federal theology, which we shall summarise and briefly consider in turn, noting as we proceed a series of criticisms made of Torrance's analysis by D. Macleod:

Confusion between covenant and contract

The first weakness is that 'the whole federal scheme is built upon the deep-seated *confusion between a covenant and a contract*, a failure to recognise that the God and Father of our Lord Jesus Christ is a Covenant-God and not a contract-God'.[39] While in the Bible a covenant is always associated with promises, obligations and warnings, the *obligations* of grace are never regarded as *conditions* of grace. But in the sixteenth and seventeenth centuries, the words 'covenant' and 'contract' were almost used interchangeably. Nearly all the definitions of a covenant at that time were cast in contractual terms,[40] leading 'to a notion of conditional grace which inverts the evangelical order of forgiveness and repentance, so that we hesitate in the name of Christ to proclaim absolution and free forgiveness of sins, or hesitate to believe that we are truly forgiven'.[41]

Taking a contrary position, Macleod argues that Torrance's criticism is 'blunted' by the fact that 'the Hebrew *berith* frequently means a contract'.[42] Macleod's

---

[38] J. B. Torrance, 'Covenant or Contract?: A Study of the Theological Background of Worship in Seventeenth-Century Scotland', *Scottish Journal of Theology* 23 (1970), pp. 51–76.

[39] Torrance, 'Covenant or Contract?', p. 66. Cf. also, Klempa, 'Concept of Covenant', pp. 104–5.

[40] Torrance cites Ursinus, who wrote: 'A covenant in general signifieth a mutual contract or agreement of two parties joined in the covenant, whereby is made a bond or obligation on certain conditions for the performance of giving or taking something with the addition of outward signs and tokens' (*The Summe of Christian Religion*, trans. D. H. Parry (Oxford, 1601), p. 218, quoted by J. Murray, *The Covenant of Grace* (London: Tyndale Press, 1954). Also, notes Torrance, 'Samuel Rutherford in his Catechism describes the Covenant of Grace as "a contract of marriage" between Christ and the believer, and then goes on to speak of the conditions of the contract' (Torrance, 'Covenant or Contract?', p. 66).

[41] Torrance, 'Covenant or Contract?', p. 66.

[42] D. Macleod, 'Covenant Theology', in *Dictionary of Scottish Church History and Theology*, eds N. M. de S. Cameron, D. F. Wright, D. C. Lochman, D. E. Meek (Downers Grove, Illinois: Intervarsity Press, 1993), p. 217.

criticism however, appears to lack substance. It may be the case that *berith* can be used in contractual contexts, but it is clearly not used in that way when referring to God's relation to Israel in the Pentateuch, as is clear by its tight connection with the concept of *hesedh*, God's steadfast love. The predominant use of the term, especially as it is used in relation to the covenant at Sinai, is associated with the unconditioned, gracious, divine decision in Israel's favour. As the prophets constantly remind Israel, their covenant relationship with God is grounded ultimately in the faithfulness of God that persists in spite of Israel's persistent disobedience.[43] The imperatives of grace that are such an integral part of the covenant relationship are not conditions upon which the covenant stands or falls. Accordingly, Torrance's point is valid.

Dichotomy between nature and grace

The second weakness, Torrance asserts, is that 'the federal scheme made a radical *dichotomy between the sphere of Nature and the sphere of Grace*, of natural law and the Gospel, so that the Mediatorial Work of Christ is limited to the covenant of grace and the Church, the sphere marked out by the covenant of grace'.[44] While all people are deemed to be in a contractual relationship with God through the obligations of natural law discernible in the orders of creation, only the elect are related to God through Christ as Mediator. Nature and grace are thereby separated from one another, which, says Torrance, 'amounts to a reversion to the pre-Reformation medieval view that *grace presupposes nature* and *grace perfects nature* – a departure from the great emphasis of the Reformation that nothing is prior to grace'.[45] The nature–grace model is the inevitable corollary of Beza and Perkins' double decree, he argues, and 'hence we can see why the Confession has so much to say about the believer (his effectual calling, justification, sanctification, etc.) but so

---

[43] Cf. G. A. F. Knight, *A Christian Theology of the Old Testament* (London: SCM Press, 1959), pp. 218f.

[44] Torrance, 'Covenant or Contract?', p. 67.

[45] Torrance, 'Covenant or Contract?', p. 67.

little about the world at large'.[46] Accordingly, this dualistic model fails to take adequate account of the New Testament doctrine of the headship of Christ over all creation and all nations as Mediator.

Paul Helm challenges Torrance on this point by asking, 'what does it mean for all to be under the Mediatorial Headship of Christ as Man?'[47] Christ can only be the Saviour, he says, of those who need salvation, the Mediator of those who need mediation. While scripture does indeed teach that Christ is the one Redeemer and Judge before whom every knee shall bow and every tongue confess, it is equally the case that Adam, before he fell, did not need redemption and so was not in that sense under the mediatorship of Christ. Moreover, 'how could events that occurred before the incarnation be under the mediatorial headship of Christ *as Man*?'[48]

Helm's reference here to the fact the Adam, before he fell, did not need redemption, appears to confuse the issue, because the simple fact of the matter is that Adam *did* fall. We cannot divide the one Adam into a 'pre-fall' and 'post-fall' Adam, and conclude from this that there are two categories of human beings, one that needs redemption, the other that doesn't. There is but *one Adam* – a fallen Adam in need of redemption – and there is but *one humanity* – a fallen humanity in need of redemption.

A further theological issue underlying Helm's disagreement with Torrance is that of the relationship between the doctrines of creation and redemption. Federal theology, with its two spheres of nature and grace, argues Torrance, separates creation and redemption, and tends to overlook the fact that Christ is portrayed in scripture as

---

[46] J. B. Torrance, 'Strengths and Weaknesses of the Westminster Theology', in *The Westminster Confession in the Church Today*, ed. A. I. C. Heron (Edinburgh: St Andrew Press, 1982), p. 50.

[47] P. Helm, 'Was Calvin a Federalist?', *Reformed Theological Journal* 10 (1994), p. 56.

[48] Helm, 'Was Calvin a Federalist?', p. 56. D. Macleod voices a similar criticism when he says 'that there is always something (sin) which is prior to grace; and always something (law) which is prior to sin. ... Men and women must be related to God as sinners before they can be reconciled to him through a gracious adoption' ('Covenant Theology', p. 217).

Creator as well as Redeemer. Helm agrees that Christ is portrayed in scripture as both Creator and Redeemer, but argues that Christ's work as one is distinct from his work as the other. 'Creation does not entail redemption', he says. Indeed, 'redemption is only needed because creation is abused by the Fall'.[49] In sum, Helm links the doctrines of redemption and the mediatorial role of Christ to the doctrine of the Fall rather than to the doctrine of creation, and accuses Torrance of so confusing the distinctions between creation and redemption that he presents them as one and the same thing.[50]

One is bound to ask, however, whether Helm has represented Torrance fairly on this matter. At no point does Torrance suggest that creation *is* redemption, for that would indeed constitute a denial of the reality of the Fall – a denial which he certainly does not make. The real difference between Torrance and Helm here would appear not to be a matter of the former blurring the distinctions between creation and redemption, but rather, of the latter being compelled by his a priori doctrines of predestination and limited atonement to interpret creation (universal in scope) and redemption (limited in scope) as parallel processes with links so tangential that they are virtually non-existent. Interestingly, this is precisely the problem that Torrance identifies in relation to federal theology of the seventeenth century, when he says that it 'did not do justice to the Pauline teaching of Ephesians and Colossians that God's concern is to reconcile and sum up *all things in Christ'*.[51]

Doctrine of limited atonement

The third weakness of the federal scheme identified by Torrance is that it 'thrust up the doctrine of a *limited*

---

[49] Helm, 'Was Calvin a Federalist?', p. 56.

[50] Helm writes: 'It does not follow that because Christ is presented as both Creator and Redeemer that creation is redemption, any more than because God is presented as both Father and Son that the Father is the Son' ('Was Calvin a Federalist?', p. 56).

[51] Torrance, 'Interpreting the Word', p. 264 (italics mine).

atonement, that Christ only died for the elect – a doctrine or conclusion unknown to Calvin'.[52] As we noted in the previous chapter, Helm contests the claim that Calvin did not teach a doctrine of limited atonement. Without repeating the detail of that debate, we simply reiterate the observation that Helm's views are based on a very narrow range of texts. We also raise the question as to whether Helm's argument does not so alter the euangélion that it ceases to be *good* news. In this regard, we note Torrance's point that one of the effects of a doctrine of limited atonement in the Church is that it

> ... bred a deep lack of assurance in that it left people tortured by the question, 'Am I one of the elect? Have I fulfilled the conditions of grace?' It also appealed to the motives of 'fear of hell and hope of heaven'... *It was such preaching that became preoccupied with sin and judgment and repentance and which laid such an emphasis on the element of self-examination in prayer*, with a loss of the notes of joy and peace and gratitude and praise for the forgiveness so freely given in Christ.[53]

Macleod responds by claiming that Torrance assumes a false antithesis between divine mercy and justice,[54] and is guilty of basing his argument on 'a confusion between love and forgiveness. The loving God proceeded not to forgiveness, but to atonement... Christ's death was not the ground of God loving us. But it was certainly the ground of his being reconciled to us.'[55]

The theological questions raised by such a statement are myriad. Indeed, it seems to drive a wedge between the act (death on the cross) and being of God (who is love), and defines the atonement in wholly extrinsic terms of what

---

[52] Torrance, 'Covenant or Contract?', p. 68.
[53] Torrance, 'Covenant or Contract?', p. 68.
[54] Macleod, 'Covenant Theology', p. 217. 'A merciful judge and a loving father', writes Macleod, 'may sometimes show his true disposition not by foregoing punishment but by imposing it reluctantly. Besides, the whole Gospel is about God's provision of a just mercy.'
[55] Macleod, 'Covenant Theology', p. 218.

transpired on the cross, thereby ceasing to take account of the significance of the incarnation and ascension of Christ.

Pelagian tendencies

This anxiety leads to the fourth weakness in federal theology identified by Torrance, namely, 'the whole focus of attention moves away from *what Christ has done for us* and for all men, to *what we have to do* IF we would be (or know that we are) in covenant with God'.[56] For preaching, this means that the emphasis falls less on the indicatives of grace and more on the imperatives of repentance, obedience and faith. For the sacraments of baptism and the Lord's Supper, this means they are viewed not so much as seals of grace as seals of believing faith, or seals of one's repentance.[57] They confirm the interest of believers in Christ, and mark out those who belong to him and oblige them to obedience. The Lord's Supper thus becomes a feast of the converted, of the penitent, rather than an eschatological banquet for all humankind.[58] It was this view, notes Torrance, which 'tragically started that kind of fencing the tables which has in effect kept multitudes of people from communicating. It also led to the introspective tradition of self-examination for evidences of election, with the resulting loss of joy and assurance.'[59]

Macleod counters this assertion by arguing that 'in covenant theology faith itself is a gift of God, granted to the people of Christ in accordance with the covenant of redemption: and the object of faith was emphatically not anything we do ourselves, but Christ crucified'.[60] While Macleod is certainly correct in this regard, he is missing the

---

[56] Torrance, 'Covenant or Contract?', p. 69.

[57] As George Gillespie, a federal theologian, said of the sacraments, they are not to be understood or used as 'converting ordinances' but only as 'confirming ordinances' – cf. *Aaron's Rod Blossoming, Or, the Divine Ordinances of Church Government Vindicated* (London, 1646), Chapters XII and XIII, cited by Torrance in *Scottish Theology*, p. 146.

[58] In this respect, it is interesting to note that in the *Westminster Confession*'s teaching on the Lord's Supper, no place is given to the proclamation of the Lord's death until he comes again.

[59] Torrance, 'Strengths and Weaknesses', pp. 47–8.

[60] Macleod, 'Covenant Theology', p. 217.

main point, which is that despite the desire among federal theologians to emphasise grace, their doctrine of limited atonement and their failure to account properly for the vicarious humanity and priesthood of Christ, especially in relation to his redemptive work in heaven, effectively gave rise to a deep-seated anxiety among Christians, which manifested itself in the form of Pelagian tendencies in the Church.

False distinction between visible and invisible Church

The fifth and final weakness of the federal scheme according to Torrance is that it generated 'an unhappy if not false distinction between the visible and invisible Church, which lost sight of the passionate emphasis of the *Scots Confession* and the older Scottish tradition on the view that there is only One Church, the Body of Christ. In the federal scheme, the invisible Church comprises the elect, known only to God, whereas the visible Church is the sphere of the penitent, who have made their "external covenant".'[61]

The Influence of William Perkins and the Puritan Tradition

The priority of the double decree and the influence of Theodore Beza

While Robert Rollock foreshadowed federalist doctrine in Scotland, it was the English Puritan, William Perkins, who established it firmly in England. Such was his influence on English theology, Kendall notes, that by the end of the sixteenth century he had replaced the combined names of Calvin and Beza as one of the most popular authors of religious works in England.[62] The most systematic treatment of his theology is to be found in *A Golden Chaine Concerning the Order of the Causes of Salvation and Damnation, According to God's Word*, the dominant feature

---

[61] Torrance, 'Covenant or Contract?', p. 70.
[62] Kendall, *Calvin and English Calvinism*, pp. 52–3

of which is the doctrine of double predestination. Perkins claims in this work to be defending '(as they call it) the Calvinists' doctrine', but, significantly, in the title of his work he claims the support not of Calvin himself but of Beza.[63] As we have seen already, of course, it is a matter of some debate as to the extent to which Beza was faithful to the direction of Reformed thought established by Calvin.

Perkins was not an academic theologian concerned with devising a theological system. He was first and foremost a churchman, whose ultimate concern was a pastoral one of answering the basic question of Christian assurance: How may one know that one is truly a child of God?[64] Because his doctrine of predestination precluded him from finding the answer to this question in the person and work of Christ, he looked elsewhere, and found his answer in the human conscience, which, he maintained, was unaffected by the Fall. The conscience, in which the image of God resides, he alleged, is 'part of the understanding of al reasonable creatures, determining of their particular actions, either with them or against them'.[65] The soul consists of two faculties, understanding and will, the former being the realm of reason and conscience, the latter being the realm of affections. Inasmuch as the word of God binds the conscience, 'every

---

[63] It was not only Beza who influenced Perkins greatly. Tracing the history of federal theology in Elizabethan England, Michael McGiffert notes the influence of Dudley Fenner. Cf. 'Grace and Works: The Rise and Division of Covenant Divinity in Elizabethan Puritanism', *Harvard Theological Review* 75 (1982), pp. 463–502. Perkins' theology might best be described as a blend of Beza's predestinarian system and the federal theology of Elizabethan England.

[64] Cf. Perkins' 1592 work, *A Case of Conscience, the Greatest that ever was: how a man may know whether he be the childe of God, or no,* cited by Kendall, *Calvin and English Calvinism,* p. 54.

[65] *Workes,* i.510, Kendall, *Calvin and English Calvinism,* p. 56. Insofar as Perkins believed that the natural conscience was unaffected by the Fall (and therefore not in need of reconstitution by grace), he effectively reverted to the pre-Reformational medieval view that *grace presupposes nature* and *grace perfects nature.* As we saw in the previous chapter, Calvin's view was that the corruption of human nature is such as to require *total* renewal of heart and mind, which includes the conscience (Cf. *In.* II.3.1–5).

man to whome the Gospell is revealed, is bound to beleeve his owne election, justification, sanctification in, and by Christ'.[66] As Kendall points out, however, Perkins' treatment of the conscience clashes with his doctrine of predestination, for, since all people are not similarly predestined to eternal life, obviously some are bound to believe what is not true – that is to say, their conscience will deceive them.[67] Perkins attempts to resolve this problem by making a series of distinctions between the visible Church (which includes 'true beleevers and hypocrites, Elect and Reprobate, good and bad'[68]) and the invisible Church (consisting of the Elect only), between effectual and ineffectual calling, and between temporary faith and saving faith. Under this series of distinctions it is entirely possible to conceive of someone, through an ineffectual calling, having a temporary faith, being a member of the visible Church (or Church Militant), and resembling true Christians in every way, but still not being among the elect or being included in the invisible Church (or Church Triumphant). However, while this might, in theory at least, offer an explanation as to why some people are deceived by their conscience, it does not address the basic problem of assurance. In fact, if anything, it accentuates it and, as Kendall astutely observes, forces Perkins to make the ultimate ground of assurance not the conscience at all but rather the doing of good works.[69]

Moreover, Kendall discerns in Perkins' teaching on the subject of faith a vacillation between Beza and Calvin. He wants to hold together Calvin's concept of faith (as a persuasion, assurance, or apprehension) and Beza's concept of faith (as that by which we apply or appropriate the benefits of Christ), but in the end it is Beza's concept of faith which predominates, for it is not possible to make

[66] *Workes*, i.517, Kendall, *Calvin and English Calvinism*, p. 57.
[67] *Workes*, i.517, Kendall, *Calvin and English Calvinism*, p. 57.
[68] *Workes*, i.310, Kendall, *Calvin and English Calvinism*, p. 59.
[69] Kendall cites *Workes*, iii.32, where Perkins notes the Spirit's charge that, 'by keeping a continuall course in good works', we may have 'the most evident tokens of election' (cf. *Calvin and English Calvinism*, p. 75).

faith a persuasion within the context of a doctrine of limited atonement.[70] This is why he seeks to ground assurance in the conscience, and defines justifying faith in terms of that 'whereby a man is perswaded in his conscience'.[71] As Kendall paraphrases it, 'the will to believe in and of itself cannot deliver the immediate assurance but the conscience can do it, by reflecting upon itself'.[72]

The influence of federal theology

In *A Golden Chain* the distinctions that Perkins makes between temporary faith and saving faith, and true calling and ineffectual calling, are placed within an overarching two-covenant framework defined in contractual terms. 'God's covenant', Perkins argues, 'is his contract with man concerning the obtaining of life eternal upon a certain condition.'[73] The covenant of works is expressed in moral law,[74] and propounds the bare justice of God, without mercy. It applies to all people. In the covenant of grace, justice gives way to mercy for the elect. It is conditional upon the elect receiving Christ by faith and repenting of their sins.[75]

---

[70] Kendall, *Calvin and English Calvinism*, pp. 62–3.
[71] *Workes*, iii.29, Kendall, *Calvin and English Calvinism*, p. 63.
[72] *Workes*, iii.29, Kendall, *Calvin and English Calvinism*, p. 63.
[73] *Golden Chain*, Chapter XIX, in *The Work of William Perkins*, ed. I. Breward (Abingdon, Berks: Sutton Courtenay Press, 1970), p. 211.
[74] Interestingly, Perkins talks about a *covenant of works* (grounded in Mosaic law) rather than a *covenant of nature* (grounded in God's original relation with Adam), which, on face value, would seem to set him apart from the two-covenant framework of federal theology. However, as J. B. Torrance points out, federal theology held that 'when God created man (Adam), he created him the child of nature who could discern the law of nature (the Decalogue) by the light of reason, and then made a mutual covenant or contract with him (*foedus, mutua pactio*) that, if he obeyed, God would give him eternal life, but if he disobeyed, he would be eternally punished' ('Concept of Federal Theology', p. 22). This description of federal theology does fit with Perkins' teaching, for, as we have seen, he taught that through the conscience (which was unaffected by the Fall) every person is able to discern God's law. Thus, while the concept of a *foedus naturale* does not appear in Perkins' works as such, his overall theological system resonates closely with an emerging federal theology in which the concept was used far more explicitly.
[75] *Golden Chain*, Chapter XXXI, in *William Perkins*, p. 213.

J. B. Torrance argues that the contractual nature of Perkins' covenant of grace paves the way 'for a concept of repentance as a condition of grace – "legal repentance", which Calvin so vigorously attacked in the *Institutes* 3.3 in his distinction between "legal" and "evangelical repentance", and his rejection of the medieval sacrament of penance – the Western *ordo salutis* that made repentance (*contritio, confessio, satisfactio* – the *merita poenitentiae*) the condition of forgiveness'.[76] Paul Helm takes issue with Torrance on this point. He says 'it is only the covenant of works (as Perkins understands it) in which the language of conditionality enters. This is borne out by the fact that when Perkins discusses the covenant of grace (Ch. 31) the language of conditionality is completely absent.'[77]

That both Torrance and Helm are able to cite numerous references from Perkins' works to support their respective interpretations of his teaching suggests a tension in Perkins' treatment of the covenant of grace – a tension identified by Michael McGiffert.[78] In the same section of *A Golden Chain* that Perkins describes the covenant of grace in terms of being conditional upon the exercise of faith and repentance,[79] he appears to hedge by saying that the covenant 'hath partly the nature or properties of a testament or will' in relation to which 'we do not so much offer or promise any great matter to God as in a manner only receive'. Indeed, he goes even further and warns against interpreting the notion of 'mutual consent' in terms of a 'bare agreement', for it signifies the spiritual union of 'the whole person of every faithful man' with 'the whole person of our Saviour Christ' as 'members of his mystical body'.[80]

[76] Torrance, 'Concept of Federal Theology', p. 25.
[77] Helm, 'Was Calvin a Federalist?', p. 49.
[78] McGiffert, 'Grace and Works', p. 498.
[79] McGiffert also refers to Perkins' *Exposition of the Symbol* (*Works*, 164) where the covenant of grace is called 'nothing else but a compact made between God and man touching reconciliation and life everlasting in Christ'.
[80] *Golden Chain, Works*, 1.77, 78, cited in McGiffert, 'Grace and Works', p. 500. This is made even clearer in a key passage in which, addressing the question of how Christ saves, Perkins says that two things precede the believer's act of faith: first, 'Christ with his merits is given unto the

The language of necessity and an instrumentalist view of the incarnation

Central to Perkins' understanding of the covenant of grace is his doctrine of the person and work of Christ, in which he emphasises the incarnation, the titles of Christ (including his threefold office), and Christ's 'twofold estate'.[81] One of the more striking features of Perkins' teaching here, especially in relation to the mediatorship of Christ, is the language of necessity, although, as Richard Muller points out, he does not understand necessity in terms of an external imposition upon God to act in a certain way, but rather as a necessity determined by the divine will for salvation. Thus, Perkins believes, it was necessary that Christ should be God, it was necessary that he be a man, it was necessary that the Redeemer suffer and die, and by his blood pay the price for sin, it was necessary for him to assume human nature for the completion of the work of salvation in self-sacrifice.[82] Accordingly, Perkins regards 'the result of the hypostatic union', as 'the perfection and enrichment of the human nature *to the end that it might be the means* by which the Godhead works man's redemption'.[83]

The important thing to note here is that the language of necessity appears to dictate a very instrumentalist view of the incarnation – as the means to an end. Although Perkins refers extensively in his teaching to the humanity of Christ and his 'humiliation', he tends to regard them in

---

believer' and, second, the believer is brought into union with Christ 'by the bond of the spirit, and this is a mystical union but a true union, whereby he that is given unto Christ is made one with him' (*Exposition upon the Epistle of Jude, Works,* 3.594, cited in McGiffert, 'Grace and Works', p. 499).

[81] Cf. Perkins, *Exposition of the Symbol,* 165, cited in Muller, *Christ and the Decree,* p. 142.

[82] Cf. Muller, *Christ and the Decree,* pp. 144–5. The language of necessity also features strongly in Perkins' teaching on God's eternal decree, which he defines as 'that by which God in himself hath necessarily, and yet freely, from eternity determined all things' (*Golden Chain,* VI, in *William Perkins,* p. 183).

[83] *Exposition of the Symbol,* 181, cited by Muller, *Christ and the Decree,* p. 147 (italics mine).

terms of being part of the redemptive process by which God is pacified. He writes:

> It was necessary that Christ should be man. First that God might be pacified in that nature, whereby he was offended. Secondly, that he might undergo punishment due to sin, the which the Godhead could not, being void and free from all passion.[84]

Here the redemptive function of the incarnation is interpreted in terms of the need to pacify God rather than the rendering of faith and obedience on behalf of humankind and the healing and sanctification of fallen humanity in the humanity of the Saviour.[85] The Mediator's abasement or humiliation is merely 'for the sake of his priestly office and the satisfaction of man's sin'.[86] The three successive degrees of his humiliation (execution, burial and descent into Hell) reflect the three degrees of his subsequent exaltation (resurrection, ascension and the seating of Christ at the right hand of the Father).

Perkins' influence

In sum, while Perkins does acknowledge an ontological dimension to his soteriology (in the hypostatic union), the acknowledgement is made only insofar as it serves a doctrine of the atonement conceived primarily in judicial rather than filial terms, and deemed to be limited rather than universal in scope. This constitutes a major irreconcilable difference between Perkins and Calvin, thereby undermining Muller's call for a greater recognition of the continuity between these two Reformed scholars.

---

[84] *Golden Chain*, XV, in *William Perkins*, p. 199.
[85] Although Perkins does refer to the sanctification of human nature in the incarnation, he does so purely in terms of a means to an end, namely that Christ's humanity 'might be holy and be made fit to die for others' (*Golden Chain*, XVI, *William Perkins*, p. 200). The incarnation, together with the faith and obedience of Christ rendered in our place and on our behalf, are not regarded as having redemptive significance in and of themselves.
[86] Muller, *Christ and the Decree*, p. 148.

As to the influence of Perkins on the Westminster tradition, J. B. Torrance notes that he 'was the most widely read Puritan in the first half of the seventeenth century, doubtless read by all the Westminster divines'.[87] McGiffert says he 'gave greater prominence to covenant than any English theologian before him' and 'went far beyond his predecessors in taking covenant out of the schools and into the pulpit, where he energized it for evangelical and pastoral purposes'.[88] His major work of the 1590s, *A Golden Chain*, was foremost among the charter documents of English Calvinism.[89] He stands as a pivotal figure, not only in the propagation of federal theology in England, but also in ensuring that Calvinist theology would thereafter be based more on the doctrinal system of Theodore Beza than that of John Calvin.

The Westminster Documents

Fusion of religious concerns and political aspirations

In 1643 England and Scotland joined together in the Solemn League and Covenant, a military alliance underwritten by a commitment to religious reform. The English Parliament needed military support to continue its civil war against King Charles, while the Scots, having endured various royal attempts to impose Anglican liturgies and ecclesiastical government upon the Scottish Church, wanted the pledge of a religious settlement that would eliminate the episcopalian menace once and for all. The Stuart aim of universal episcopacy was displaced by a desire to see England now join with Scotland in a religious covenant to make the British Isles Presbyterian.

With this aim in mind, the episcopacy was abolished by parliamentary decree and the Westminster Assembly was

---

[87] Torrance, 'Concept of Federal Theology', p. 25.
[88] McGiffert,'Grace and Works', p. 499.
[89] M. McGiffert, 'The Perkinsian Moment of Federal Theology', *Calvin Theological Journal* 29 (1994), p. 118.

set up in 1643 to offer advice on the reformation of the Church in England in the hope of achieving unity and uniformity in relation to church government, liturgy and doctrine. In its composition it reflected that of the Parliament which appointed it, namely, a small number of Congregationalists and Episcopalians and a large number of Presbyterian Puritans. The Scots were invited to appoint non-voting assessors to the Assembly. Accordingly, a small but influential delegation were present, and were able to exercise considerable influence as advisors in the Presbyterian system which England was now considering.[90]

One of the most urgent tasks of the Assembly was to produce a *Directory of Public Worship* to replace the *English Book of Common Prayer* that Parliament had undertaken to set aside. As James McEwen notes, however, 'even this modest task was not achieved without considerable trouble, for the extremer Puritans objected not only to the old Prayer Book, but to any authoritative directions at all concerning worship which might hamper the free leading of the Spirit',[91] Despite these difficulties a *Directory* was produced which received Parliamentary sanction and was accepted by both the General Assembly and Parliament in Scotland – although there is little evidence of it having much influence on Scottish worship.

A year later the *Westminster Confession* and *Larger* and *Shorter Catechisms* were produced. The *Confession* achieved confessional status only in Scotland, where the General Assembly, after the collapse of Presbyterian Puritanism in England, continued to invest its hope in the establishment of one Presbyterian Church of the British Isles by laying aside Knox's Liturgy and Creed in favour of the new Westminster standards.

---

[90] Cf. Torrance, *Scottish Theology*, p. 126.
[91] J. S. McEwen, 'How the Confession Came to be Written', in *The Westminster Confession in the Church Today*, ed. A. I. C. Heron (Edinburgh: St Andrew Press, 1982), p. 14.

A case study in seventeenth-century Reformed doctrine: The *Westminster Confession of Faith*

Having considered the strong influence of Theodore Beza, William Perkins and federal theology on seventeenth-century Reformed doctrine, we must now examine the extent to which the Westminster documents exhibit this influence, noting as we begin, J. B. Torrance's claim that 'the *Westminster Confession* enshrines the "federal scheme", and is the first post-Reformation confession to do so'.[92] While the Westminster documents had relatively minor importance in England after the collapse of Presbyterian Puritanism, they continued to determine the course of Reformed theology through the Church of Scotland, whose General Assembly ratified them and continued to adhere to them even after the English collapse.[93]

As we proceed to look at the central tenets of the *Confession* and its accompanying *Catechisms* a comment needs to be made in relation to their overall style and tenor. The style is didactic rather than confessional, reflecting the constitutional background to the documents[94] and the twofold desire by their authors to give a rational explanation of Protestant theology[95] and practical instruction for the Christian life. Behind the second of these desires lay the powerful Puritan concern to apply the doctrines of grace to real life,[96] using the Bible as the basis for deriving precedents and principles.

Older confessions such as the *Scots Confession* were also grounded in scripture, but the authority of scripture was understood differently. In the *Westminster Confession* there

---

[92] Torrance, 'Strengths and Weaknesses', p. 48.
[93] McEwen, 'How the Confession', p. 16.
[94] Cf. Torrance, 'Strengths and Weaknesses', p. 43.
[95] Cf. Torrance, *Scottish Theology*, p. 127.
[96] In view of this desire for practicality it is noticeable, J. B. Torrance says, that the largest part of the *Confession* is devoted 'to the question as to HOW the benefits of the Covenant of Grace are applied to believers (IX–XVIII), followed by chapters on Law and Liberty (XIX–XX), worship and the Sabbath day (XXI) and Civil matters (XXIII–XXIV). Only then does the *Confession* turn to the doctrine of Church and sacraments (XXV–XXXI), leaving the "last things" to the last chapters (XXXII–XXXIII)' ('Strengths and Weaknesses', p. 44).

is a far greater stress on the infallibility of scripture and a corresponding tendency to extract passages and texts to support theological notions held on other grounds. In the *Scots Confession*, T. F. Torrance notes, biblical references are regarded 'as having an open-structured character, pointing away from themselves to divine truth which by its nature cannot be contained in finite forms of speech and thought, although it may be mediated through them'.[97]

With these general comments in mind, we are now ready to look at the Westminster documents in finer detail. We will concentrate on those chapters and areas of doctrine in which the influence of Beza, Perkins and the whole federal scheme is most evident, and where the contrast with the teaching of Calvin is therefore most pronounced.

Of God and the Holy Trinity[98]

The *Confession*'s doctrine of God is most notable for the way in which the orthodox trinitarian conception of God is nothing more than a two-sentence addendum to a long and rather abstract account of what God is in his infinite power and sovereign nature. J. MacPherson, in his 1881 publication of, and commentary on, the *Confession*, comments that the main emphasis is on the *unity of God* and his *attributes*, and the doctrine of the Trinity is merely another way of affirming the unity of God, albeit 'in full view of the personal distinctions which are recognised in it'.[99] In other words, the doctrine of the Trinity, rather than providing the basis for the *Confession*'s doctrine of God, is merely acknowledged in terms of affirming a doctrine of God already developed upon other grounds. MacPherson makes a telling comment that the *Confession*'s doctrine of God constitutes a fitting 'prelude to the chapter on the Divine Decrees'.[100] Talked about in this way, the doctrine of God is subordinated to the doctrine of divine decrees,

---

[97] Torrance, *Scottish Theology*, p. 130.
[98] *Westminster Confession*, chapter 2.
[99] J. MacPherson, *The Confession of Faith* (Edinburgh: T&T Clark, 1881), pp. 44–5.
[100] MacPherson, *Confession of Faith*, p. 44.

which explains its strong emphasis upon God's sovereignty and freedom.[101] The portrayal of God, not primarily as Father, but as Creator, Lawgiver and Judge, had massive repercussions, T. F. Torrance claims, especially when harnessed to 'a federalised and logicalised system of Calvinism'.[102] It deprived the *Confession* of a proper trinitarian and christological structure – thereby affecting people's understanding of the ultimate character of God – and led to a soteriology that was at odds with Calvin, the Church Fathers and the biblical witness alike.

Of God's eternal decree[103]

Although the Westminster documents embody federal Calvinism, it is, nevertheless, a moderate form of that theology, as evidenced by their treatment of the doctrine of predestination. Not only does the *Confession* avoid the term 'reprobation' altogether, but, as David Fergusson points out, 'the language of the Westminster theology (especially the *Larger Catechism*) oscillates freely between decree (singular) and decrees (plural), and it maintains that "this high mystery of predestination" is a doctrine becoming of "humility, diligence and abundant consolation"'.[104] Moreover, as Charles Bell says of the *Confession*'s teaching, while 'election to life is entirely lodged in God and his decree', foreordination to death, 'while lodged in the divine sovereignty, is nevertheless, due to the sin and guilt of man'.[105]

The *Confession*'s doctrine of limited atonement, therefore, tends to be implied in its references to the redemption of the elect, rather than explicitly taught through a formal

---

[101] C. G. McCrie, in his *The Confessions of the Church of Scotland* (pp. 59ff.), comments on the very frequent occurrence in the *Confession* of the phrase *'It pleased God ... according to the counsel of His own will'* in its exposition of the decrees, of creation, of providence, the covenants, revelation, redemption, effectual calling, etc. (cited by Torrance, 'Strengths and Weaknesses', p. 51).

[102] Torrance, *Scottish Theology*, p. 131.

[103] *Westminster Confession*, chapter 3.

[104] D. A. S. Fergusson, 'Predestination: A Scottish Perspective', *Scottish Journal of Theology* 46 (1993), p. 465.

[105] Bell, *Calvin and Scottish Theology*, p. 125. Cf. *Westminster Confession*, 3.7.

exposition of a doctrine of a double decree. Christ redeems the elect, and only the elect.[106] The *Confession* fails to follow Calvin in making a distinction between universal atonement and salvation for the elect.

In conjunction with its emphasis on the divine decree the *Confession* portrays election as being prior to grace. Insofar as it does this it reveals the influence of a theological tradition that owes more to Theodore Beza and William Perkins than it does to the line of Reformed thought established by Calvin, Knox and Craig. Of the doctrine of divine decrees underpinning the whole scheme of creation and redemption in the *Confession*, J. B. Torrance makes the following comment:

> This is clearly a move away from the *Scots Confession*, where election is placed after the Article on the Mediator, in the context of Christology. It is also a move away from Calvin who expounds election at the end of Book Three of the *Institutes* as a corollary to grace, after he has expounded all he has to say about the work of the Father, Son and Holy Spirit, and after his exposition of Incarnation and Atonement.[107]

Of God's covenant with man, saving faith and repentance unto life[108]

As we have already mentioned, the Westminster documents embrace the twofold covenant scheme of federal theology. Whereas they deem the covenant of works to have been made with all humanity through Adam, the covenant of grace is regarded as being limited to the elect.[109] Both covenants have conditions attached to them. When the first covenant was breached by the Fall, 'the Lord was pleased to make a second, commonly called the Covenant of Grace whereby he *freely offered* to sinners life and

[106] Cf. *Westminster Confession*, 3.6.
[107] Torrance, 'Strengths and Weaknesses', p. 46.
[108] *Westminster Confession*, chapters 7, 14, and 15.
[109] Cf. *Larger Catechism*, Q.31 (*School of Faith*, p. 190), and *Westminster Confession*, 7.5.

salvation by Jesus Christ, *requiring of them faith in him, that they may be saved'.*[110] Thus, while the *offer* of salvation is free, its *efficacy* is conditional upon faith.

As we noted in Chapter Two, while Calvin teaches that one must be among the elect to be saved, the basis of this salvation is not the saving faith of the elect themselves but rather the intercessory work of the ascended Christ. While true or saving faith is limited to the elect, as opposed to the temporary faith which may exist among the reprobate, such faith in Calvin's thinking never constitutes the conditional ground upon which salvation rests. This does not diminish the importance of faith in his doctrine. It merely anchors human faith in the vicarious faith and faithfulness of Christ, the Representative and Advocate of humankind, before the Father.

The issue here is well summed up by T. F. Torrance in an article on the biblical conception of faith:

> The whole of salvation depends upon the faithfulness of God who does not grow weary of being faithful. It is God's faithfulness that undergirds our feeble and faltering faith and enfolds it in his own. In Christ Jesus we are in fact unable to disentangle our faith from the faithfulness of God, for it belongs to our faith to be implicated in the faithfulness of God incarnated among us in Jesus Christ.[111]

In his commentary on the *Confession*, MacPherson seeks to qualify its notion of conditionality by arguing that, there is no inconsistency between the freeness with which the benefits of the covenant of grace are offered and the appointment of certain conditions:

> This grace and this freeness are attributed to a covenant into which only those ordained to life

---

[110] *Westminster Confession*, 8.3 (italics mine).
[111] T. F. Torrance, 'One Aspect of the Biblical Conception of Faith', *The Expository Times* 68 (1957), p. 114. Cf. also, Douglas Campbell's excellent exposition of justification by faith in *The Rhetoric of Righteousness in Romans 3:21–26* (Sheffield: JSOT Press, 1992).

enter, and that through the exercise of faith. The nature of this condition as pertaining to a covenant of grace is very clearly apprehended by Rollock as comprising faith with Christ and Christ with faith.[112]

MacPherson's appeal to the teaching of Rollock appears on the surface justifiable. For Rollock did indeed seek to describe faith in terms of God's grace, rather than a human work. As Charles Bell says of him, he 'frequently refers to the "grace of faith" and describes it as an "infused habit". Faith, he states, is wrought in us by God's Spirit and is a "supernatural ability".'[113] 'However,' as Bell also goes on to say of Rollock, 'because he views faith as the *condition* which man must fulfil in his covenant with God, he vacillates between faith as God's gift to us and an active view of faith as that which we accomplish.'[114] There exists, therefore, a tension in his writings between the passive reception of God's grace and Spirit and the active embrace and apprehension of Christ and his benefits.

However, as long as this tension or vacillation exists, the 'deepseated confusion between a covenant and a contract', which J. B. Torrance has identified in federal theology, continues to exert its influence.[115] As Torrance has pointed out many times in his writings, the divine *diatheke* (covenant) in the Bible is a covenant of grace unconditioned by anything in humankind.[116] While this divine covenant demands a response from humankind, the Bible never views that response in contractual terms. Rather, as Torrance puts it, the *'indicatives of grace are always prior to the imperatives* of law and human obligation. "I have loved you, I have redeemed you ... therefore, keep my commandments".'[117]

[112] MacPherson, *Confession of Faith*, p. 68.
[113] Bell, *Calvin and Scottish Theology*, p. 55.
[114] Bell, *Calvin and Scottish Theology*, p. 55 (italics mine).
[115] Torrance, 'Covenant or Contract?', p. 66.
[116] In the Bible the *diatheke*, which is a *unilateral* covenant, is quite distinct from the *suntheke*, which is a *bilateral* covenant. Cf. Torrance, 'Covenant or Contract?', pp. 54–5.
[117] Torrance, 'Covenant or Contract?', p. 56.

The Westminster documents effectively reverse this order, despite their strenuous attempts to give priority to grace. Kendall notes that while the Westminster divines do not explicitly state that repentance is the condition of the new covenant, that it is regarded as such is clear from the whole tenor of the Westminster documents.[118] The *Larger Catechism* states that 'repentance toward God, and faith toward our Lord Jesus Christ' is required of us that we may escape God's wrath and curse, which is due to us for our transgression of the law.[119] And the *Confession* defines saving faith in terms of that which yields obedience to the commands, 'trembling at the threatenings, and embracing the promises of God'. It then goes on to say that 'the principal acts of saving faith are accepting, receiving, and resting upon Christ alone'.[120] Moreover, it describes repentance in terms of that act by which people 'shall find mercy'.[121] This infers, as MacPherson correctly sums up the *Confession*'s teaching on the matter, that 'God refuses forgiveness to all who refuse to confess their sin.'[122] 'While the predestinarian structures of Westminster theology are undeniable – making salvation utterly the gift of God – its doctrine of faith', concludes Kendall, 'none the less tends to put the responsibility for salvation right back on to man'.[123] As we shall see, this situation has a flow-on effect in relation to the doctrine of assurance.

Of Christ the Mediator[124]

While the Westminster documents give proper attention both to the hypostatic union of Christ and to his perfect obedience and sacrifice on behalf of the elect, it is depicted in terms of satisfying the justice of the Father and the purchase of reconciliation.[125] This implies, as T. F. Torrance attests,

---

118 Kendall, *Calvin and English Calvinism*, p. 205.
119 *Larger Catechism*, Q.153 (*School of Faith*, p. 222).
120 *Westminster Confession*, 14.2.
121 *Westminster Confession*, 15.6.
122 MacPherson, *Confession of Faith*, p. 104.
123 Kendall, *Calvin and English Calvinism*, p. 206.
124 *Westminster Confession*, chapter 8.
125 *Westminster Confession*, 8.5.

a transactional notion of atoning satisfaction in fulfilment of a divine requirement, on the ground of which the Father was induced to reconcile us, and was as it were 'bought off'. At this important point the *Westminster Confession* departed from the teaching of the New Testament in which there is no suggestion that reconciliation was bought *from* God; and it also departed from the teaching of Calvin about 'the love of God the Father which goes before and anticipates our reconciliation in Christ'.[126]

Of justification and sanctification[127]

The pragmatism of the Puritan tradition and its associated emphasis on personal experience is evident in the *Confession*'s teaching on justification and sanctification. As J. B. Torrance observes, in the chapter on sanctification, summarised in the *Shorter Catechism*,[128] the concern is entirely with sanctification *in us*, with not a single reference to Christ as the One who assumed our humanity and sanctified it *for us* by his life in the Spirit.[129]

Nor does the *Confession* take the line of Calvin and Scots Reformation theology in which justification and union with Christ are held inseparably together. Instead, justification is construed mainly in terms of a forensic 'imputation', and union with Christ is understood as a 'judicial union', which must be cultivated and deepened in a spiritual and sanctifying way through the help of 'indwelling grace'. Because justification is deemed not to be effective until such time as the Holy Spirit actually 'applies' Christ to each of the elect,[130] there is a significant shift in emphasis from what has already taken place in the person and work of Christ to what must take place in the life of the believer.

---

[126] Torrance, *Scottish Theology*, p. 139. Cf. *In.* II.16.3–4.
[127] *Westminster Confession*, chapters 11 and 13.
[128] Cf. *Shorter Catechism*, Q.35.
[129] Torrance, 'Strengths and Weaknesses', p. 44.
[130] Cf. *Westminster Confession*, 11.4.

Of assurance of grace and salvation[131]

The Westminster documents' conception of God's covenant relationship with humankind in contractual terms ultimately leads to a loss of assurance of grace and salvation. There are two striking features of the *Confession*'s teaching in this regard. First, it suggests that 'infallible assurance doth not so belong to the essence of faith'.[132] Second, it suggests that a true believer 'may wait long, and conflict with many difficulties, before he be a partaker of it'.[133] The qualifying assurance that true believers are 'never utterly destitute of that seed of God, and life of faith, that love of Christ and brethren and conscience of duty, out of which, by the operation of the Spirit, this assurance may in due time be revived',[134] does little to counterbalance the main thrust of the *Confession*'s teaching on the matter. As Kendall correctly concludes, according to this teaching it seems that a believer could die without assurance.[135]

As we saw in the previous chapter, while Calvin's teaching on election undermines his ability to give a total assurance of salvation, he at least exhorts people to look not to their consciences or to their good works but to Christ, who, as the 'pledge of God's love for us', is the sole basis of Christian assurance.

Of prayer[136]

The *Confession*'s lack of emphasis on one's participation in Christ is especially evident in its teaching on prayer which, as MacPherson correctly observes, describes prayer in terms of 'a duty and privilege' which 'is incumbent upon

---

[131] *Westminster Confession*, chapter 18.
[132] *Westminster Confession*, 18.3. While the *Confession* states that 'infallible assurance' does not belong to the essence of faith, the *Larger Catechism* asserts merely that 'assurance' is not of the essence of faith – cf. *Larger Catechism*, Q.81 (*School of Faith*, p. 201).
[133] *Westminster Confession*, 18.3.
[134] *Westminster Confession*, 18.4.
[135] Kendall, *Calvin and English Calvinism*, p. 203.
[136] Cf. *Westminster Confession*, chapter 21, which is titled 'Of Religious Worship and the Sabbath Day'.

all men'.[137] The primary emphasis here is on duty rather than joyful participation. In conjunction with this emphasis, missing entirely from the *Confession*'s teaching on prayer is any reference to the intercessions of the ascended Christ – that is to say, to the One who prays with us and for us. The mediatorial role of Christ in prayer is entirely absent.

The absence of Christ as Mediator in the activity of prayer is also evident in the teaching of the *Larger Catechism*. While it acknowledges the role of the Spirit in helping Christians to pray,[138] and instructs them to pray in the name of Christ,[139] they are nevertheless instructed to pray 'with an awful apprehension of the majesty of God, and a deep sense of [their] unworthiness, necessities, and sins'.[140] The mediatorial role of Christ is acknowledged only in terms of his providing the elect with access to God's presence,[141] but not in terms of his continuing to intercede for all sinners or represent them in his own humanity before the Father. Having had access to God opened up for them by Christ the Mediator, the responsibility now falls upon the elect to fulfil the duty of prayer, albeit helped in 'the right performance of that duty' by the work of the Holy Spirit. As the *Catechism* puts it, 'We do not know what to pray for as we ought, but the Spirit helps our infirmities, by enabling us to understand both for whom, and what, and how prayer is to be made; and by working and quickening in our hearts (although not in all persons, nor at all times, in the same measure) those apprehensions, affections, and graces which are requisites for the *right performance of that duty*.'[142]

---

[137] MacPherson, *Confession of Faith*, p. 127. The *Westminster Confession*, 21.3, defines prayer in the following terms: 'Prayer, with thanksgiving, being one special part of religious worship, is by God required of all men; and that it may be accepted, it is to be made in the name of the Son, by the help of his Spirit, according to his will, with understanding, reverence, humility, fervency, faith, love, and perseverance; and, if vocal, in a known tongue.'
[138] *Larger Catechism*, Q.182 (*School of Faith*, p. 230).
[139] *Larger Catechism*, Q.180 and 181, (*School of Faith*, pp. 229–30).
[140] *Larger Catechism*, Q.185 (*School of Faith*, p. 230).
[141] *Larger Catechism*, Q.181 (*School of Faith*, p. 230).
[142] *Larger Catechism*, Q.182 (*School of Faith*, p. 230) (italics mine).

There is a sharp contrast with the teaching of Calvin at this point. For, as we have already seen, Calvin's doctrine of prayer stresses the intercessory role of Christ. Under his section on 'Prayer in the name of Jesus' he says that 'as soon as God's dread majesty comes to mind, we cannot tremble and be driven far away by the recognition of our unworthiness, *until Christ comes forward as intermediary, to change the throne of dreadful glory into the throne of grace*'.[143] Christ is the eternal and abiding Mediator and Advocate, the One who 'appears in our name and bears us upon his shoulder and hold us upon his breast so that we are heard in his person'.[144] The Church's intercessions, therefore, 'all depend solely upon *Christ's intercession*'. So, Calvin exhorts, 'let it remain an established principle that we should direct all intercessions of the whole church to that *sole intercession*'.[145]

If the *Confession*'s doctrine of prayer lacks a proper Christology, so too does it lack the pneumatology that is such a prominent feature of Calvin's teaching. We cannot understand the priesthood of Christ without simul-taneously understanding the ministry of the Spirit, through which the Church is lifted up in worship into the life of praise and communion that Christ shares with the Father.

Of the sacraments[146]

Just as the language of participation, borne of a proper pneumatology, is missing from the *Confession*'s doctrine of prayer, so too is it missing from its teaching on the sacra-ments. While the respective definitions of the word 'sacrament' are similar,[147] insofar as they both define it in terms of a two-dimensional act – the act of God and the act of human response – the way in which those definitions are elaborated upon in relation to baptism and the Lord's

---

[143] *In.* III.20.17 (italics mine).
[144] *In.* III.20.18.
[145] *In.* III.20.19 (italics mine).
[146] *Westminster Confession*, chapters 27, 28 and 29.
[147] Cf. *In.* IV.14.1 and *Larger Catechism*, Q.162 (*School of Faith*, p. 224).

Supper varies significantly. Calvin introduces a third dimension in referring to the crucified and risen Christ, and therefore to the new humanity in him, in which the Church is by grace given to share. It is his new humanity, risen from the dead and eternally in union with God, which is the *substance* or the *matter* of the sacraments.[148]

In relation to baptism, the *Larger Catechism* describes it in terms of *cleansing*, or of being washed with water. In and through this act of cleansing, baptism is a sign and seal of 'ingrafting into Christ', of 'remission of sins by His blood' and of 'regeneration by His Spirit'.[149] By way of contrast, Calvin says it is not only the message of *cleansing* which is sealed in baptism; it is also the message of *sanctification*.[150]

The implications of this become clear when we compare Calvin's rationale for the practice of infant baptism with that of the *Confession*. For Calvin, the baptism of infants is grounded in the conviction that in Christ they have already been sanctified, that in their stead and for their sake he might achieve perfect obedience and impart to them his holiness.[151]

By way of contrast, in the *Larger Catechism* the practice of infant baptism is justified solely upon the grounds that children of believers are regarded as being 'within the covenant'.[152] Calvin's understanding of the human condition being sanctified in the humanity of the Saviour is entirely absent.

The same contrast is evident in the Reformed teaching on the Lord's Supper. Whereas Calvin teaches that 'Christ is truly shown to us through the symbols of bread and wine, his very body and blood *in which he has fulfilled all obedience to obtain righteousness for us*',[153] the *Larger Catechism* refers not to his life (and hence his vicarious obedience) but only to his (sacrificial) death. The

---

[148] *In.* IV.14.16.
[149] Cf. *Larger Catechism*, Q.165 (*School of Faith*, p. 225).
[150] *In.*IV.15.2.
[151] *In.* IV.16.18.
[152] *Larger Catechism*, Q.166 (*School of Faith*, p. 225).
[153] *In.* IV.17.11 (italics mine).

sacrament, it teaches, is that which has been appointed by Christ so that '*His death is showed forth*; and those who worthily communicate feed upon His body and blood, to their spiritual nourishment and growth in grace; have their union and communion with him confirmed'.[154] Calvin's notion of the wonderful exchange is missing, thereby undermining his strongly eucharistic theology and making the sacrament peripheral to church life.

What becomes evident from this kind of comparison is that the real difference between Calvin and the Westminster documents lies not so much in what the latter teach but, rather, in what they *omit* from their teaching. This includes a proper pneumatology and a Christology that recognises the place of the human obedience of Christ in the doctrine of atonement. As we have seen, these failures result in an overly forensic interpretation of the atonement that ultimately undermines both the conception of *union with Christ*, which permeates Calvin's theology, and the sense of *participation* through word, sacrament and the activity of prayer in the life of Christ as the Second Adam. It is precisely because these elements are missing from the Westminster tradition that it is unable to assure believers of their salvation in Christ.

The Legacy of the Westminster Tradition

In politics

As we have already noted, federal Calvinism arose in the midst of considerable social and political upheaval. In this context, J. B. Torrance highlights the significance of the concept of 'covenant' – conceived in terms of social contract – and the nature–grace model on the development of civil law and the rise of democracy in Western civilis-ation. Civil law was regarded as enshrining natural law (*foedus naturale*) discerned by reason. Hence the tendency for political thinking in the West to be controlled not by the

---

[154] *Larger Catechism*, Q.168 (*School of Faith*, p. 226).

gospel, but by an abstract notion of natural law and civil rights, with an appeal to the 'light of nature' and the 'kindly light of reason'. The problem is, he goes on to say, that despite all the appeal to the objectivity of reason, there has in fact never been a consensus on what constitutes natural law and the orders of creation. So it was, that in the United States, for example,

> ... where the Northern theologians believed that all men are equal with equal rights, their Southern counterparts ... taught that God has created us with ethnic diversities – some black, some white, some masters, some slaves ... In terms of different concepts of natural law, each side exegeted the Old Testament differently, and found sanctions either for preserving the status quo (slavery) or for political renewal, for the emancipation of slaves, with equal rights for all.[155]

The same nature–grace model of federal Calvinism and the anthropology which accompanies it is discernible, argues Torrance, in many different political contexts around the globe. At the same time as it has given rise to modern democracy and a concern for human rights, it has also been used to generate romantic loyalty to one's nation and race (*Volk*) in Nazi Germany, to justify apartheid in South Africa, and to give divine sanction to political agendas in Northern Ireland. He puts the question:

> Must we not ask ourselves, Why is it that in Lutheran Germany in the 1930s, in Calvinist South Africa and Puritan Northern Ireland, political situations have arisen where we see the weaknesses in the dualism of the Law-Grace, Nature-Grace model of very different forms of Western theology – Catholic, Lutheran and Reformed? Do we not see a *status confessionis* in each situation, where, as Barth and Barmen have taught us, there is need to discover the Headship of Christ in every area of life, and unpack the anthropological,

---

[155] Torrance, 'Interpreting the Word', p. 262.

political and social implications of the incarnation? The question thus raised for us, as Barth raised it in his day, is this: Is our anthropology built merely on a concept of natural law (however we may interpret it), or is it based on our understanding of the incarnation?[156]

In theology and worship

The failure of the Westminster tradition to give adequate attention to the vicarious humanity and priesthood of Christ had a number of profound and far-reaching consequences. As the atoning significance of the incarnation and ascension faded into the background, salvation was increasingly interpreted in forensic, instrumentalist terms, grace was increasingly portrayed in conditional or contractual categories, preaching was increasingly marked by a 'legal' strain, and Christian life and worship was increasingly cast in a Pelagian mould. These developments manifested themselves in a number of ways in Puritan and Calvinistic church life.

Decline in the use of set liturgies and prayers

J. B. Torrance argues that in seventeenth-century worship in the Church of Scotland there was a 'revolt from any kind of required liturgical form in the interest of freedom in worship – with an emphasis on "free prayer" and the "freedom of the Spirit"'.[157] A struggle ensued in the higher courts of the Church, he says, between those who sought to preserve the older forms of worship and those of Puritan leaning who regarded liturgical form as loss of freedom, and 'protest' and 'dissent' as 'the marks of godliness of those who were

---

[156] Torrance, 'Interpreting the Word', pp. 263–4.
[157] Torrance, 'Covenant or Contract?', p. 71. Cf., too, Maxwell (*Outline of Christian Worship*, p. 133), who cites J. Moffatt's observation that 'the reaction against liturgies was partly due to an honourable but exaggerated devotion to freedom and spirit in worship, as though this was incompatible with the use of any forms of prayer, and partly due to the fact that, as in the case of Scotland, the King sought to impose a new liturgy upon it, and thereby created a distaste for liturgies in general'.

determined to stand fast in what they believed to be the liberty of the Gospel'.[158] One by one 'the older Scottish practices were discontinued largely in concession to Puritan pressures, both at Westminster Assembly and afterwards'.[159] He further suggests that while these changes represented a genuine plea for the liberty of the spirit, they 'were as much influenced by the emerging philosophy of self-determination, a concept of freedom which was interpreted to mean that we worship God as we please, when we please, and with whom we please, according to one's individual conscience and personal interpretations of Holy Scripture'.[160]

The movement away from the use of set liturgies was consistent with the Puritan conviction that God should be worshipped and obeyed according to the 'purity' of the Bible. In conjunction with this basic principle, Patrick Collinson identifies as the touchstones of Puritan worship the qualities of simplicity, sincerity, purity, directness and brevity.[161] For Puritans, the liturgical part of the service was always subordinate to the ministry of the word. Indeed, he argues, 'one of their more serious objections to the Prayer Book was that it reversed these priorities'.[162]

One of the consequences of the Puritan attempt to model worship more closely on biblical criteria was a preference for free or extempore prayer over the 'stinted forms' of the establishment.[163] Horton Davies identifies five chief

---

[158] Torrance, 'Covenant or Contract?', p. 73

[159] Torrance, 'Covenant or Contract?', p. 72. These changes included the dropping of the Apostles' Creed from the baptismal service, the omission of the Lord's Prayer from public worship (as another form of imposed prayer), the discontinuation of daily services, the replacement of read prayers by 'conceived' prayers, the omission of the reading of scripture unless accompanied by a lecture, and the exclusion of the offering from the actual service of worship.

[160] Torrance, 'Covenant or Contract?', p. 73.

[161] P. Collinson, *The Elizabethan Puritan Movement* (London: Jonathan Cape, 1967), p. 358.

[162] Collinson, *Elizabethan Puritan Movement*, p. 358.

[163] On the matter of extempore prayer, Patrick Collinson, warns against overstating the situation. Puritan worship was indeed characterised by a greater emphasis on freedom of prayer, he says, but not necessarily by spontaneity, for 'utterance in prayer was reserved almost exclusively to the minister, popular participation in responses and the Litany was excluded, and psalm-singing was the only element of the service in which the people actively joined' (Collinson, *Elizabethan Puritan Movement*, p. 359).

arguments advanced by the Puritans against set prayers:[164] (a) Their constant use deprived both minister and people of the desire to devise prayers for themselves; (b) They could not meet the varying needs of different congregations and occasions; (c) A liturgy was an abridgement of Christian liberty in that its prescription persuaded the people that it was an absolute necessity, thus equating a human composition with divine revelation, and leading to uncharitable censures on the churches that did not use one; (d) Liturgical prayers led to hypocrisy, mere lip-service; and (e) Those ministers who did not affirm the *Book of Common Prayer* were unjustly deprived of their livings in universities and parishes. The situation came to a head at the Savoy Conference in 1661, where Richard Baxter, together with other representatives of those who sought compensation within the established Church, laid before the bishops a full statement of the Puritan case. Baxter seized the opportunity to draw up an alternative service book 'with forms taken out of the word of God', and produced the *Reformed Liturgy*.

While the bishops refused to countenance such an alternative form of service, the mere fact that Baxter sought to gain approval for his *Reformed Liturgy* shows that the Puritan preference for extempore prayer did not necessarily imply universal opposition to liturgies as such. Davies notes that moderate Puritans, made up mainly of Presbyterians, did not cease to hope that a prayer book more in accordance with scriptural directions might be produced which would prove more acceptable to the established Church.[165]

One question which arises from the general movement away from the use of set liturgies and prayers in Reformed worship in the seventeenth and eighteenth centuries is, How well did the tradition of extempore prayer preserve the notion of the mediatorial role of Christ in prayer?

---

[164] H. Davies, *Worship and Theology in England (Vol. 2): From Andrewes to Baxter and Fox, 1603–1690* (Princeton: Princeton University Press, 1975), pp. 192–3.
[165] H. Davies, *The Worship of the English Puritans* (Westminster: Dacre Press, 1948), p. 115.

Gordon Wakefield, in his study of Puritan devotion, cites a selection of passages from the works of John Owen, Richard Sibbes, John Preston and Thomas Goodwin to substantiate his claim that the Puritans had a strong appreciation of the mediatorial role of both Christ and the Spirit in prayer:[166] 'The Puritans', he says, 'found themselves confronted by two verses from the eighth chapter of Romans to which they gave full weight. The one declares that Christ ever lives to make intercession for us, the other that we have also an Intercessor within – "The Spirit itself maketh intercession for us".'[167] That is to say, 'it is by the strength and assistance of the Holy Spirit that we are enabled, albeit groaningly, to approach God through Christ. The Spirit brings us to Christ, and Christ to God.'[168]

However, while all the passages cited by Wakefield do support his claim, they also show that, as with the doctrine of the atonement, the Puritan understanding of the priesthood of Christ in prayer tended to be framed in *mechanical* rather than *ontological* terms. Christ is deemed to be the mediator of prayer, not because in him the human condition has been assumed and sanctified, and continues to be represented before the Father, but because of what he has accomplished through his blood on the cross, because he alone is righteous, because he alone is able to protect the elect from the consuming fire of God, and because it is through his intercessions that their justification is made actual and continual. Similarly, the Spirit is deemed to be the One who works in the elect, stirring them to pray and making them able to pray, rather than the One through whom the human condition has been vicariously assumed, healed and sanctified in Christ, so that, re-created and reconstituted in the depths of their being, those who are united to Christ by the Spirit might share in his praise and communion with the Father. In other words, the Puritan notions of the priesthood of Christ and the activity of the

---

[166] G. S. Wakefield, *Puritan Devotion: Its Place in the Development of Christian Piety* (London: Epworth, 1957), pp. 77–82.
[167] Wakefield, *Puritan Devotion*, p. 80.
[168] Wakefield, *Puritan Devotion*, p. 80.

Spirit tend to be portrayed in pragmatic or utilitarian terms – they are the means by which prayer is effected – with the result that the Pelagianism which pervades seventeenth-century Puritanism is never quite overcome.

This claim finds support from J. B. Torrance, who argues that while the Westminster tradition perpetuated the Reformed emphasis on the threefold office of Christ, and in accordance with this perpetuation recognised the *continuing* office of Christ in terms of him being King and Prophet,[169] it failed to do the same in relation to his being our High Priest. While the priesthood of Christ was expounded in terms of his once and for all work on the cross, it was not expounded in terms of his continuing role as our Intercessor, Advocate and Leader of the Church's worship.

As a general rule it appears that seventeenth- and eighteenth-century Reformed worship was characterised by the loss of the doctrine of the continuing priesthood of Christ. Torrance attributes this loss largely to 'the severe polarisation between what Christ *did for us then*, once and for all, and *what we must do now*, in obedience, penitence and faith', which has 'the effect of eclipsing what Jesus Christ is doing *now* as the leader of our worship in His continuing Ministry of drawing men to Himself and uniting us to Himself in His communion with the Father'.[170] 'These two sharply contrasted poles', he continues, 'were held together in federal theology by the concept of covenant. But where the shift of emphasis moved more and more to the subjective pole, the objective pole of the Gospel steadily receded. The objective pole no doubt was acknowledged as an article of orthodox belief, but the real interest became the anthropocentric one – what we do!'[171]

---

[169] Of these two offices Torrance writes: 'The seventeenth century certainly emphasised that Christ is the *One King* and Head of His Church – the Crown Rights of the Redeemer – against the papacy, Erastianism and divine right of kings ... Christ was likewise the *One Prophet* in the Church, whose voice is heard in the preaching of the Word and in the councils of the Church' ('Covenant or Contract?', p. 74).

[170] Torrance, 'Covenant or Contract?', p. 74.

[171] Torrance, 'Covenant or Contract?', p. 74.

Interestingly, the concentration on the death of Christ rather than his continuing life, and the consequent polarisation between what Christ did for us then, once and for all, and what we must do now, in faith, can be attributed not only to the combined impact of Theodore Beza, federal theology and Puritanism on seventeenth-century Reformed thinking, but to Calvin also. As we saw in the previous chapter, it was Calvin's reaction against the notions of priesthood and sacrifice in the Roman Mass that largely accounted for his failure to integrate properly the Church's offering of praise and thanksgiving with Christ's eternal self-offering. This flaw in Calvin's eucharistic theology influenced the subsequent shape of Reformed worship and prayer just as much as the theology of the atonement which emerged in the seventeenth century.

Ecclesiastical discipline

In his seminal work on the worship of English Puritans, Horton Davies notes that one of the controlling principles of Puritanism was that God must not only be worshipped and obeyed according to the 'purity' of his holy word, he must also be served with a 'purity' of life.[172] Hence the heavy emphasis on ecclesiastical discipline and the Puritan devotion to the duty of exercising ecclesiastical censures, which covered all manner of sins from the display of 'strong and violent passions' to 'idleness, tatling, and being busie-bodies in other men's matters'.[173]

The reproof, punishment, confession and absolution of penitents were standard practice north of the border too, where, as we have already noted, ecclesiastical discipline was regarded as a mark of the true Church. However, as W. D. Maxwell points out, whereas in John Knox's day it was exercised in private, from the seventeenth to the mid-eighteenth century it was exercised publicly, 'in the face of

---

[172] Davies, *English Puritans*, pp. 232f.
[173] Examples taken from Stephen Ford's 1675 publication, *A Gospel–Church: or, God's Holy Temple opened*, p. 343, cited by Davies, *English Puritans*, p. 234. 'Even such peccadilloes as gossiping or occasional laziness', he says, 'were actually punishable by excommunication.'

the congregation', on Sunday mornings.[174] 'After the Reformation,' he writes, 'private and priestly confession and discipline were replaced by discipline exercised by the courts of the Church, and it was an unbelievably exacting tyranny... designed remorselessly to scrutinize and dictate moral behaviour down to the most minute detail, with the threat of excommunication... to enforce control and punishment.'[175]

Conclusion

In our consideration of the Westminster tradition we have identified the influences of Calvin's Genevan successor, Theodore Beza, federal Calvinism and the Puritan William Perkins. The elevation of the doctrine of predestination to a pre-eminent position in Calvinist dogmatics, combined with the pervasive influence of federal theology, produced a doctrine of atonement in which Calvin's emphases upon the filial and ontological aspects of redemption were completely overshadowed by the judicial and instrumental. Not only was election made logically prior to grace, thereby resulting in a disjunction between divine justice (shown to the reprobate) and mercy (to the elect), but the atonement was deemed to be limited in scope, insofar as Christ's mediatorial role was regarded as being restricted to the elect. Moreover, as Calvinism interpreted Christ's mediatorial role solely in terms of his work on the cross, the atoning significance of the incarnation and ascension was overlooked, and the atonement was interpreted in terms of an act which is external to the believer and which is of a purely forensic nature – that is, in terms of Christ paying the penalty of sin on the cross, of settling debts before a divine Judge.

---

[174] Maxwell, *History of Worship*, p. 145.
[175] Maxwell, *History of Worship*, p. 147. Maxwell also notes that sins and scandals were seldom confessed voluntarily, which meant that the whole system of ecclesiastical discipline was built up on informing and spying upon one's neighbour. 'It was', he writes, 'a grievously mischievous and poisonous system sustained by spying and informing by petty autocrats and malicious neighbours' (p. 148).

The Westminster tradition's failure to give adequate recognition to the vicarious humanity and priesthood of Christ, when harnessed to an overriding concern for practical instruction, meant that the emphasis moved away from what God has done *for us and for all humankind in Christ* to what *we* must do to know that we are among the elect and in covenant with Christ. Rather than upholding the line of Calvin, Knox and Craig in which justification and union with Christ were viewed in conjunction with one another, the *Confession* treated them separately, describing justification in terms of a forensic 'imputation' of Christ's righteousness, and union with Christ as a 'judicial union', which must be cultivated and deepened in a spiritual and sanctifying way through the help of 'indwelling grace'. Furthermore, as justification was wrenched from its grounding in humankind's union with Christ (in the incarnation) so it was deemed to be effective only at such time as the Holy Spirit actually 'applied' Christ to each of the elect, thereby reinforcing the shift in emphasis from what has already taken place in the person and work of Christ to what must take place in the life of the believer.

Significantly, this introspective focus on the individual believer became a feature of Reformed piety and worship as well as Calvinistic doctrine. Many congregations rejected set liturgical prayer in favour of 'free prayer', preferring to worship in the 'freedom of the Spirit'. At the same time, worship became inherently non-eucharistic, and ecclesiastical discipline, interpreted along narrowly moralistic lines and exercised in public, became a prominent feature of church life, together with the exhortation to self-examination, the heavy emphasis upon the individual conscience, and the ecclesial practice of fencing the Lord's Table. While there is some evidence that the Puritan tradition did recognise the priesthood of Christ in relation to prayer, it tended to be framed in mechanical rather than ontological terms. Christ was deemed to be the mediator of prayer, not because in him our humanity has been assumed and healed, and continues to be represented before the Father, but because of what he has accomplished on the cross and because it is through his intercessions that justification for the elect is made actual and continual.

In sum, in both doctrine and patterns of worship the Westminster tradition, which dominated church life in Scotland for the better part of two hundred years, constituted a marked departure from the teaching and practice of Calvin and the early Scottish Reformers.

4
John McLeod Campbell and the Reconception of Prayer through a Revised Doctrine of the Atonement

McLeod Campbell: Rethinking the Atonement, Reconceiving Prayer

In his book, *The Atonement and the Sacraments*, Robert Paul claims that the penal theory of the atonement, as it had been expressed for 150 years in federal Calvinism, 'had outlived its usefulness and outstayed its welcome', and 'by the middle of the nineteenth century the time was ripe for a complete revision of the doctrine'.[1] He goes on to say that this revision effectively began in 1856 with the publication of John McLeod Campbell's book, *The Nature of the Atonement*, which heralded the arrival of a new era of thinking in relation to the subject. Citing R. S. Franks' assessment of Campbell's work 'as the most systematic and masterly volume produced by a British theologian on the work of Christ during the nineteenth century', Paul says that 'Campbell liberated theology from the old categories in which it conventionally thought of the atoning work of Christ.'[2]

If Campbell's work constituted a break from Calvinism in relation to the doctrine of the atonement, so too did it constitute a break in relation to the understanding of the Christian life and, in particular, the nature of prayer. With this general comment in mind we must now acquaint ourselves more fully with Campbell's teaching.

---

[1] R. S. Paul, *The Atonement and the Sacraments: The Relation of the Atonement to the Sacraments of Baptism and the Lord's Supper* (London: Hodder and Stoughton, 1961), p. 140.

[2] Paul, *Atonement and Sacraments*, p. 142.

The authority of the *Westminster Confession*

In 1831 John McLeod Campbell was deposed from parish ministry for teaching the doctrine of universal atonement and pardon, as also the doctrine that assurance is of the essence of faith and necessary for salvation.[3] Although his teaching was condemned for being unbiblical, it was the fact that his statements contradicted the *Westminster Confession* that caused the real offence and provided the grounds for the charge of heresy.[4] That this was the case is indicative of the extent to which the *Confession* had come to dominate the Reformed ecclesiastical landscape. It is significant that the Moderates and Evangelicals combined to condemn Campbell. While the former did not share the latter's zealous defence of the Calvinistic tradition, George Tuttle notes that 'they still clung to the *Confession* as a symbol protecting the church's establishment'.[5] The *Confession*, especially in the hands of the Evangelicals, tended to be used as a tool for measuring the orthodoxy of doctrinal statements and for handling any apparent threat to the establishment.[6] Accordingly, Campbell's plea for his doctrinal views to be judged on scriptural grounds alone fell on deaf ears.[7]

Theological conviction borne of pastoral experience and the teaching of scripture

Campbell's teaching of the two doctrines for which he was placed on trial – the doctrines of 'universal atonement' and 'assurance of faith' – stemmed from his experience as pastor and preacher. One of the first things he discovered in the course of his parish ministry in Row was a prevailing lack of assurance of the love of God, accompanied by a lack

---

[3] Cf. Lusk, *Proceedings I*, cited by Bell, *Calvin and Scottish Theology*, p. 181.
[4] Cf. G. M. Tuttle, *So Rich a Soil: John McLeod Campbell on Christian Atonement* (Edinburgh: Handsel Press, 1986), pp. 44–45, citing *Proceedings I*, xxiii, xxiv and xxix.
[5] Tuttle, *So Rich a Soil*, p. 34.
[6] Tuttle, *So Rich a Soil*, p. 35.
[7] Cf. Tuttle, *So Rich a Soil*, pp. 44–5.

of joy in Christian life and worship. He noticed that initially when he preached, his congregation heard only a demand on them to be what they were not. 'They did not question Christ's power to save,' he says, 'neither did they doubt the freeness of the Gospel or Christ's willingness to save them' – but they did hold doubts with regard to whether or not they themselves would be included among the beneficiaries of his divine power and will.[8] The corollary of this doubt was a belief that there must be something which they must do in order 'to make Christ their own – a condition proposed to them, the consciousness of compliance with which would introduce them to the enjoyment of salvation'.[9] 'In other words,' as J. B. Torrance sums up, 'deep in their thinking was a *doctrine of conditional grace*',[10] perpetuated by a preaching tradition that placed the law ahead of the gospel, and made repentance logically prior to forgiveness.

The other Calvinistic doctrine which Campbell identified as having a devastating effect on people's assurance and joy was the *doctrine of election*, according to which only some people were chosen to be saved, namely, those for whom Christ died – the elect. As he observed people anxiously engaged in self-examination to see if they could discern the fruits of faith and election – 'evidences' of the work of the Spirit – he increasingly felt a conflict between the authorised teaching of the Church and the message of the gospel. This compelled him to examine both the extent and the nature of the atonement. Of this examination he wrote:

> It soon appeared to me manifest that unless Christ had died *for all*, and unless the Gospel announced him as the *gift of God to every human being*, so that there remained nothing to be done to give the individual a

[8] Cf. J. McLeod Campbell, *Reminiscences and Reflections: Referring to his Early Ministry in the Parish of Row, 1825–31*, ed. D. Campbell (London: Macmillan and Co., 1873), p. 132.

[9] Campbell, *Reminiscences and Reflections*, p. 132.

[10] J. B. Torrance, New Introduction to McLeod Campbell's *The Nature of the Atonement*, 1856 (Edinburgh: Handsel Press, 1996), p. 3.

title to rejoice in Christ as his own Saviour, there was no foundation in the record of God for the Assurance which I demanded, and which I saw to be essential to true holiness. The next step therefore was my teaching, as the subject matter of the Gospel, Universal Atonement and Pardon through the blood of Christ.[11]

Christology and the character of God

Implicit in the above statement are two things worth noting about Campbell's approach that immediately set him on a collision course with the federal Calvinism of his day. First, his determination to begin with a study of the person and work of Christ; and second, to give proper consideration to the mind and character of God. *Christology* rather than an abstract doctrine of a double decree was the basis for his doctrine of God.

At stake in Campbell's discussion about the character of God is the nature of the relationship between divine love and divine justice. In *The Nature of the Atonement*, he is critical of two of the most influential Puritan writers, John Owen and Jonathan Edwards,[12] for setting forth justice (for all people) as a necessary attribute of God while mercy and love (for the elect) are but arbitrary.[13]

The net effect of this disjunction between love and justice, he says, is that the atonement thus presented, '*ceases to reveal* that *God is love*'.[14] Not only does this distort the biblical witness to God's character, it also has significant

[11] Campbell, *Reminiscences and Reflections*, p. 24.
[12] Campbell has been criticised for his tendency to group Owen and Edwards (and others such as Thomas Chalmers) together, thereby ignoring their distinct contexts and different concerns and influences. This criticism is valid, although as Leanne Van Dyk points out, 'a complete comparison was not his intent. Historical sensitivity and conceptual accuracy was not the main concern. Rather, he wished to make a point about atonement options in the Reformed tradition and chose ... representative, although diverse, voices to represent a particular view' (*The Desire of Divine Love: John McLeod Campbell's Doctrine of the Atonement* (New York: Peter Lang Publishing, 1995), p. 101).
[13] Campbell, *Nature of the Atonement*, p. 73.
[14] Campbell, *Nature of the Atonement*, p. 73.

pastoral and doctrinal ramifications. If God's love and mercy are arbitrary, he asks, 'is it fair to ask men to put their trust in that God of whom we cannot tell whether He loves them or does not? in that Saviour of whom we cannot tell them whether He died for them or did not?'[15] Moreover, if justice rather than love is God's necessary attribute then one's relationship with God is ultimately defined in judicial rather than filial terms, and one's attention 'is fixed upon the obedience of Christ as the *fulfilling of a law*, and the *life of sonship* in which this fulfilment has taken place, *is left out of view*'.[16]

The atoning significance of the incarnation, understood retrospectively and prospectively

It is Campbell's determination to interpret the atonement in filial rather than judicial terms which leads him to ground his thinking in the doctrine of the incarnation. It is in the incarnation, he says, that 'we realise the divine mind in Christ as perfect Sonship towards God and perfect Brotherhood towards men'.[17] We recognise in the incarnation the filial resolve of God being fulfilled in a twofold movement of divine grace, as Christ deals with us on behalf of God, and with God on our behalf.[18]

It is Christ's dealing with humankind on behalf of God and his dealing with God on behalf of humankind that Campbell describes as constituting the *retrospective* aspect of the atonement[19] – God's dealing with every human being's guilty past by penetrating into the depths of human sin and guilt and undoing them. But this cannot be understood apart from the *prospective* aspect[20] – God's bringing people to share in Christ's sonship, lifting them from imprisonment in their mortal existence into the new life of the risen Jesus.

[15] Campbell, *Nature of the Atonement*, p. 75.
[16] Campbell, *Nature of the Atonement*, p. 77.
[17] Campbell, *Nature of the Atonement*, p. 19.
[18] Cf. Bell, *Calvin and Scottish Theology*, p. 184.
[19] Cf. Campbell, *Nature of the Atonement*, chapter 6.
[20] Cf. Campbell, *Nature of the Atonement*, chapter 7.

Traditional doctrines of atonement, he argues, have limited themselves to the retrospective aspect, interpreting the sufferings of Christ in terms of penal substitution, and interpreting the incarnation in terms of the necessary means towards atonement (for the sins of the elect). But when the atonement is understood prospectively as well, then it must be viewed in terms of securing the ends of the incarnation, namely, the Father's filial purposes for all humankind. 'This does not mean', says T. F. Torrance of Campbell's thinking here, 'that there was no penal element in the substitutionary sacrifice, but that it is of a fuller and profounder kind than can ever be expressed in terms of legal and logical equivalents as in the notion of "penal substitution".'[21]

At the heart of Campbell's thinking on this matter lies a concentrated focus on one's union with Christ – a union which is the fruit of the incarnation. As Michael Jinkins says of Campbell in this regard, he not only understood the love of God to be unlimited in scope, and therefore the atonement to be unlimited in extent, he also 'understood our union with Christ to be that which Christ did in uniting himself with all humanity in the incarnation, and not an event in the individual's religious experience'.[22] Not that religious experience – or a true 'religion of the heart', Campbell says, following Edwards – is unimportant. It is simply that salvation depends upon the inner ontological relation between the incarnation and the atonement, for it is in and through that ontological union that Christ has engaged in atoning expiation with the roots of sin and guilt in our fallen human existence, thereby dealing with original sin, and has brought his holiness to bear on our Adamic existence in such a way that the righteousness of God might be fulfilled in us.[23]

While Campbell taught a doctrine of universal atonement, this does not mean that he was a universalist in regard to the doctrine of salvation. Although the atonement is universal, he maintained, salvation is not, for God allows humanity the

---

[21] Torrance, *Scottish Theology*, pp. 308–9.

[22] M. Jinkins, *A Comparative Study in the Theology of Atonement in Jonathan Edwards and John McLeod Campell: Atonement and the Character of God* (San Francisco: Mellen Research University Press, 1993), p. 7.

[23] Cf. Torrance, *Scottish Theology*, p. 313.

freedom to reject God's grace, and the Bible teaches that some people do indeed use their freedom to choose 'the path of destruction'. God's love is not coercive. Accordingly, there is a judgement which love cannot, and will not, keep back; or more positively stated, as George Tuttle puts it, 'there is a judgement which love must exercise'.[24]

Faith and the 'perfect repentance' of Christ

The distinction between atonement and salvation in Campbell's teaching raises a question about the nature of faith: Is salvation conditional upon faith, understood as that act which constitutes the believer's personal response to the atonement wrought for all people in Christ? Further, if the answer to that question is Yes, then is not the believer's own assurance of salvation, deemed by Campbell to be of the essence of faith, subject yet again to the vagaries of faith rather than the person and work of Christ?

To understand Campbell's response to this question we must refer to his teaching on the perfect repentance of Christ. Campbell saw that in Christ's life of filial obedience he not only rendered a proper response of faith and obedience on behalf of all sinners, he also submitted to the judgement of God – vicariously confessing their sin, as their Great High Priest and Intercessor, and submitted for them (not for himself) to the verdict of guilty, in offering his life in death on the cross.[25] As J. B. Torrance puts it: 'Christ has once and for all made the perfect Response of vicarious evangelical repentance to the Father's love and the Father's judgment for us, and now by the Spirit unites us with himself that we might live a life of love and intercession and daily penitence before the Cross.'[26]

---

[24] Cf. Tuttle, *So Rich a Soil*, p. 31.

[25] Cf. Campbell, *Nature of the Atonement*, pp. 207–8

[26] Torrance, 'The Vicarious Humanity of Christ', in *The Incarnation*, ed. T. F. Torrance (Edinburgh: Handsel Press, 1981), p. 143. Cf., too, Daniel Thimell's very good exposition of Campbell's teaching on Christ's vicarious response, in 'Christ in our Place in the Theology of John McLeod Campbell', in *Christ in our Place: The Humanity of God in Christ for the Reconciliation of the World*, eds T. A. Hart and D. P. Thimell (Exeter: Paternoster Press, 1989), pp. 182–206.

Faith, then, for Campbell, is neither the condition of God's love and forgiveness nor a solely human response made out of one's own spiritual resources. Rather, it is a personal Amen made in response to the Amen of Jesus Christ as one is brought by the Spirit to participate in the Son's life with the Father and share in his ministry. Faith is a product of one's being in union with Christ through the Spirit. It is participation in the faith of Christ. So that, although believing is that which Christians do, it is so, as J. B. Torrance says, 'only in the sense of participating in what Christ has done and is doing'.[27] What is evident here is an inner relation between justification and faith, which is reminiscent of Calvin and the early Scottish Reformers. This inner relation is a feature of Campbell's teaching to which T. F. Torrance draws attention when he says that for Campbell justification is not just a non-imputation of sin in which we believe. Rather, 'justification is bound up with a feeding upon Christ, a participation in his human right-eousness, so that to be justified by faith is to be justified in him whom we believe, not by an act of our faith as such'.[28]

Did Christ vicariously confess our sins?

From the beginning, McLeod Campbell's teaching on the perfect repentance of Christ has drawn criticism,[29] the essence of which is best summed up in a single question posed by P. T. Forsyth: 'How could Christ in any real sense confess a sin ... with whose guilt he had nothing in common?'[30]

Forsyth's solution to the problem was to say that Christ confessed not human sin, but rather 'God's holiness in

---

[27] J. B. Torrance, 'The Contribution of McLeod Campbell to Scottish Theology', *Scottish Journal of Theology* 26 (1973), p. 310.
[28] Torrance, *Theology in Reconciliation*, p. 141.
[29] Cf. S. Lidgett, *The Spiritual Principle of the Atonement* (Charles H. Kelly, 1898), pp. 177–8, cited by Paul in *Atonement and Sacraments*, p. 148; P. T. Forsyth, *The Work of Christ* (London: Hodder and Stoughton, 1910, reprinted by Independent Press, 1938), p. 148; T. Smail, 'Can one Man Die for the People?', in Atonement Today, ed. J. Goldingay (London: SPCK, 1995), p. 86.
[30] Forsyth, *Work of Christ*, p. 148.

reacting mortally against human sin, in cursing human sin, in judging it to its very death.'[31] Christ's confession was rendered not as man but as God, for a confession of holiness 'can only be made by God, the Holy'.[32] Arguing in the same vein, the answer that Tom Smail offers is that in his life and death on the cross Christ was fulfilling and renewing the covenant that humankind had broken.[33] 'Christ entered in love into the sinful situation that was beyond our coping and the fallen nature that was beyond our curing, to execute his transformational justice upon it, so that in the very act by which the old humanity went down to death there was a new creation of a new humanity that was in right relation to God.'[34]

In responding to the criticisms made by Forsyth and Smail, two points need to be made. First, it is noticeable that neither of them refers to the nature of priesthood in the Old Testament. It is a significant omission, for, as J. B. Torrance has pointed out numerous times in his writings, the notion of vicarious confession is grounded in the actions of the priesthood on the Day of Atonement in ancient Israel.[35] A crucial moment in the cultic ritual was when the high priest, as the divinely appointed representative of the people, took an animal for sacrifice, laid his hands on it and *vicariously confessed* the sins of all Israel in an act of penitence, acknowledging the just judgements of God.

Thus understood, the vicarious confession of the high priest was an essential part of the renewal of the covenant in ancient Israel. Moreover, the notion of vicarious confession is carried through to the epistle to the Hebrews in the New Testament, where in its application to the person and work of Christ it is intensified and deepened. There, confession is not in word or feeling or ritual act but in the actualised relations between God and humankind as the divine holiness in Christ is brought to bear upon the

---

[31] Forsyth, *Work of Christ*, p. 150.
[32] Forsyth, *Work of Christ*, pp. 151–2.
[33] Smail, 'Can one Man Die?', p. 87.
[34] Smail, 'Can one Man Die?', pp. 89–90.
[35] Cf. Torrance, *Worship, Community and the Triune God of Grace*, pp. 47–8.

human condition at its deepest level. In Christ that human condition is opened up and offered to God in such a way that there results a clean conscience, a holy unity in knowing and living with God. Repentance is actualised in the submission of the sinner to the divine judgement and pardon – something that Christ the High Priest does in sinners' stead on their behalf.

This does not undermine the fact that sin is a personal matter and can only be dealt with personally. Indeed, it is precisely because sin *is* a personal matter, and in particular is a personal affront against God, that it can be forgiven only by a personal act on the part of God that establishes full personal fellowship between God and humankind. This act, the book of Hebrews maintains, has been achieved in and through Christ. In his sinless humanity the estranged and guilt-ridden mind and will of fallen humanity has been assumed, 'converted' and offered back to the Father in a perfect sacrifice and in the sanctity of prayer and praise and worship. 'It is at the point of vicarious repentance', argues T. F. Torrance, 'that we really face up to the radical notion of the priesthood of Christ, priest in our place, in vicarious sorrow and anguish, in vicarious trust and faith, in vicarious worship and thanksgiving.'[36]

The second point, which follows on from the first, stems from the biblical concept of *metanoia* – which is variously translated as 'repentance', 'conversion' and 'transform-ation'. That which is alienated from God cannot transform or convert itself.[37] When the apostle Paul, in Romans 12:2, speaks of being 'transformed by the renewing of your minds', he is not referring to the ability of the human mind to renew itself. He is referring to the renewal of the mind that takes place *in Christ*, the Second Adam. It is in his life of vicarious obedience and faith alone that the alienated

---

[36] Torrance, unpublished lecture notes on 'The Priestly Aspect of Atonement'.

[37] Cf. Jesus' reply to Peter's confession of Jesus as the Son of the living God, in Matthew 16:13–20: 'Blessed are you, Simon son of Jonah! *For flesh and blood has not revealed this to you, but my Father in heaven*' (italics mine). It is as people's minds are reconciled to God through Christ that they are enabled to confess the truth about God and about themselves.

human mind – the seat of all sin – has been brought back into harmony with God's will and transformed at its deepest level. It is in and through his life that proper repentance – the kind of repentance that ordinary human beings can never offer – has already been made on their behalf. As Trevor Hart puts it, 'The oft made complaint that the notion of a sinless Christ "repenting" for others is meaningless fails to see that for Campbell Christ's sinlessness, far from disqualifying him from such "repentance", is actually that which *enables* him to confess the sins of the race, and that this "repentance" culminates precisely in a oneness of mind with the divine judgment on sin, and a submission to the sentence of death.'[38]

We conclude from this discussion that McLeod Campbell's views are consistent with the biblical tradition. The vicarious confession of sins is portrayed in both the Old Testament and the epistle to the Hebrews as an integral part of covenant renewal and fulfilment. Moreover, it is fundamental to the notion of 'evangelical repentance' as expounded by Calvin, which, as J. B. Torrance notes, 'takes the form "Christ has borne your sin on the Cross, therefore repent!" '[39] Repentance is not something which sinners do out of their own moral awareness, inner strength and spiritual resolve; it is something which they do within the context of Christ's vicarious repentance, as they are led by the Spirit to say Amen to his Amen to the Father on their behalf.

Prayer as the utterance of participation

According to Michael Jinkins, 'few dogmatic theologians have worked out with such care a theology of prayer as McLeod Campbell has'.[40] This statement is not made

---

[38] T. Hart, 'Anselm of Canterbury and J. McLeod Campbell: Where Opposites Meet?', *Evangelical Quarterly* 62 (1990), p. 329. Cf. too, Karl Barth, 'Very God and Very Man', *Church Dogmatics* (Vol. II, Part 1): *The Doctrine of the Word of God*, eds G. W. Bromiley and T. F. Torrance, trans. G. T. Thomson and H. Knight (Edinburgh: T&T Clark, 1956), pp. 155–8.

[39] Torrance, New Introduction, *Nature of the Atonement*, p. 12.

[40] M. Jinkins, *Love is of the Essence: An Introduction to the Theology of John McLeod Campbell* (Edinburgh: St Andrew Press, 1993), p. 18.

lightly. Campbell's first book, *Christ the Bread of Life*,[41] while serving the primary purpose of offering a Reformed response to the Roman doctrine of transubstantiation, in fact constitutes a fine body of teaching on the nature of Christian prayer and worship, aspects of which are subsequently dealt with more systematically in *The Nature of the Atonement*.

One of the distinguishing features of *Christ the Bread of Life* to which Campbell's son, Donald, draws attention in the *Memorials of John McLeod Campbell*,[42] is that Campbell is as critical of the Protestant understanding of worship and prayer as much as he is of Rome's.[43] A wrong conception of justification of faith cannot fail to introduce wrong conceptions of prayer and worship, whether that is in the Protestant or Roman tradition. On the one hand, Campbell is critical of the Roman tendency to ground the doctrine of justification in the event of the Mass rather than in the person of Christ, thereby providing a 'material substitute' for Christ. On the other hand, he is critical of the Protestant tendency to deal with the doctrines of justification and sanctification in abstraction from the reality of our union with and life in Christ, thereby providing an 'intellectual substitute' for Christ.[44]

We noted in the previous chapter the tendency in the Westminster tradition to separate the doctrines of justification and sanctification, interpreting the former in terms of the atoning work of Christ on the cross and the latter in terms of a subsequent regenerating work of the Spirit in us. Campbell is critical of this separation, observing with regret that 'two things have been spoken of where there is but one thing, laborious efforts at harmony made where

[41] J. McLeod Campbell, *Christ the Bread of Life: An Attempt to Give a Profitable Direction to the Present Occupation of Thought with Romanism*, second edn (London: Macmillan and Co., 1869), first published in 1851.

[42] *Memorials of John McLeod Campbell: Being Selections from his Correspondence*, ed. D. Campbell, Vol. 1 (London: Macmillan and Co., 1877).

[43] *Memorials of John McLeod Campbell*, p. 212.

[44] Cf. Campbell, *Christ the Bread of Life*, pp. 138–9.

identity should be recognised, and a complexity to the spirit has been introduced instead of the simplicity that is in Christ'.[45]

In holding the two doctrines together, thereby recognising the sanctifying work of the Spirit in Christ's assumption of our human nature, Campbell shows a clear affinity with the teaching of Calvin and the early Scottish Reformers. He regards as 'superficial and inadequate' those views of the atonement that fail to 'apprehend the nature of the condemnation of sin in the flesh which is in the sacrifice of Christ'.[46] It leads to all kinds of errors, not least of which is the linking of divine favour with the work of Christ (on the cross) rather than with the life of Christ (in the incarnation). This in turn teaches us 'to expect participation in that favour, not in receiving Christ's life to be our life, but in having his work imputed to us',[47] and ultimately portrays the activity of prayer, not as an 'utterance of participation' in the life of Christ in accordance with the mind of Christ, but as something which *we* do, all the while praying in the name of Christ and pleading his merits in the hope of being answered.[48]

Campbell anchors his highly participatory view of prayer in a rich definition of Christian worship. For him, worship is nothing less than 'Eternal Life', which comes to

---

[45] Campbell, *Christ the Bread of Life*, p. 103.

[46] Campbell, *Christ the Bread of Life*, p. 117. On this subject of the condemnation (and not merely the forgiveness) of sin in the sacrifice of Christ, see also a tract by Campbell entitled 'The Ministry of Reconciliation', published in 1830 by John Lindsay and Co. of Edinburgh, included in *Tracts on McLeod etc.*, where he writes: 'Christ has, indeed, put away sin through the sacrifice of himself. But this means something very different from some mere compact, by which God, on account of Christ's sacrifice, consents to overlook the sins of men, connected or unconnected with him. Christ put away sin, in putting away his flesh. He offered up our sins in his own body on the tree, just by offering up that body. For he was made sin for us. And the nature being fallen, he really assumed it, just that *in it* he might put it away spotless through the Eternal Spirit, in the suffering of the curse, and by that meritorious act of obedience unto the death, purchase for it a new constitution from the grave above all fall and curse. He was made sin, just that by the perfection of a holy sacrifice elicited from it, he might put it away in death.'

[47] Campbell, *Christ the Bread of Life*, p. 128.

[48] Cf. Campbell, *Christ the Bread of Life*, pp. 133–5.

us through the Son, ascending from us through the Son, as the Son in us honours the Father:

> In such worship there is a continual living presentation of Christ to the Father – a continual drawing upon the delight of the Father in the Son – the outgoing of a confidence that, whatever is asked in Christ's name – in the light of His name – in the faith of the Father's acknowledgment of that name – will be received. The praises rendered – the desires cherished – the prayers offered – are all within the circle of the life of Christ, and ascend with the assurance of partaking in the favour which pertains to that life – which rests upon Him who is that life.[49]

Deeply imbedded in this description of Christian worship, and worthy of note, is a strong appreciation of the continuous nature of Christ's offering to the Father. His offering is not confined to the offering of his life at Calvary two thousand years ago. Rather, it is deemed to continue in heaven. Christ is the one, true worshipper in whom, with whom and through whom, and by the Spirit, the Church's own meagre offerings of praise and thanksgiving are joined, perfected and offered to the Father. In highlighting this important aspect of Christian worship McLeod Campbell goes beyond Calvin, the Scottish Reformers and the Westminster tradition, who, as we have seen in the two previous chapters, failed to develop a proper under-standing of the nature of Christ's *eternal* offering and its implications for worship and prayer.

Within McLeod Campbell's definition of worship the Eucharist has a crucial function, both because it has been ordained by Christ, and because it brings to a concentrated focus the reality of the Church's abiding in Christ:

> Our ordinary feeding upon Christ has its ever-varying aspect determined by the special demands of faith which successively arise in God's ordering of our

---

[49] Campbell, *Christ the Bread of Life*, pp. 130–1.

circumstances, but at the Communion Table we are, as it were, upon the mount of the Lord, above the region in which the daily battle of the life of faith has to be fought: though in the light in which the excellence of that conflict and its high issues are clearly seen and calmly realised, as they cannot be in the fight itself. With all its elements present to our spirits we seal our faith by that special act of personal appropriation of the unsearchable riches which we have in Christ of which eating the bread and drinking the wine, the symbols of the Lord's body and blood, is the divinely chosen form of expression.[50]

From the above descriptions of prayer, worship and the Eucharist it becomes clear that for McLeod Campbell 'feeding upon Christ, and worshipping God through Christ' are integrally related.[51] 'What we receive from God, in Christ, as Eternal Life, is what, being fed upon, and so becoming our actual life, we offer to God in worship. Our life ascends to God in worship. And it is its being the Divine nature – its being the Eternal Life, that is the secret of the acceptableness of the worship, and of the sureness of the response to it.'[52]

The atoning significance of prayer

While *Christ the Bread of Life* constitutes a fine exposition on what it means to feed on Christ and abide in him, it is in *The Nature of the Atonement* that Campbell explores further the link between atonement and prayer. In particular, he continues his reflections upon the mediatorial role of Christ, focusing on his intercessory role. These reflections are brought together in a chapter entitled, 'The Intercession which was an Element in the Atonement Considered as Prayer'. In that chapter, Campbell is critical of the tendency to interpret Christ's work in a rather mechanical way as the

---

[50] Campbell, *Christ the Bread of Life*, pp. 146–7.
[51] Cf. Campbell, *Christ the Bread of Life*, p. 50.
[52] Campbell, *Christ the Bread of Life*, p. 51.

acting out of a prearranged redemptive plan. Such an interpretation undermines both the totality of Christ's identification with the sinful condition that all people share, and the truly human basis for his response rendered to God on their behalf. His perfect response and intercession was made not in some kind of docetic fashion as though his humanity was merely the vehicle for his divine action. Rather, it was integrally related to his humanity – it was a genuinely human response. When this is understood then, as Campbell puts it, 'faith must make us present to the work of our redemption in its *progress* as well as in its *result*, so that the love which is working for us – the difficulties which that love encounters – the way in which it deals with them – the salvation which it accomplishes – all may shed their light on our spirits and be to us the light of life'.[53]

That the gospel narrative gives attention to the progress of Christ's redemptive work as well as its result, suggests Campbell, is evident from the way in which 'the Son is represented as by prayer, and intense and earnest and agonising prayer, obtaining for us from the Father what the Father has infinitely desired to give – what he has given in giving Him to us as our Redeemer to whose intercession it is yielded'.[54] Here we have Christ's hope for humankind taking the form of intercession, 'the divine love in Christ pleading with the divine love in the Father, and thus obtaining for us that eternal life, which yet in giving the Son to be our Saviour the Father is truly said to have given'.[55]

'Proceeding this way', Campbell continues, 'the intercession of Christ has presented itself as a form which His love must naturally take ... With all the weight of all our need upon His Spirit – bearing our burden – that He should cast this burden upon the Father appeared the perfection of sonship towards the Father and brotherhood towards us.'[56] Thus understood, the mediatorial role of

[53] Campbell, *Nature of the Atonement*, p. 174 (italics mine).
[54] Campbell, *Nature of the Atonement*, p. 175.
[55] Campbell, *Nature of the Atonement*, p. 175.
[56] Campbell, *Nature of the Atonement*, pp. 175–6.

Christ is integrally linked to his life of prayer, and in particular to his intercessions, which, as the vehicle for his pleading with the Father on behalf of sinners, have redemptive significance. In the life of Christ we 'see that knowledge of the Father's will and confidence in His love supersede not prayer, but, on the contrary, only move to prayer, giving strength for it – making it the prayer of faith and hope and love – love perfected in thus flowing back to its own fountain'.[57] Campbell even goes so far as to describe Christ's intercession as 'the perfection of forgiving love'.[58] 'It is the cry of sonship in humanity bearing the burden of humanity, confessing its sin, asking for it the good of which the capacity still remained to it, which being responded to by the Father has revealed the Father's heart.'[59] In sum, the prayer life of Christ is an essential part of his redemptive activity.

When the nature of Christ's intercession is understood in these terms then we are better placed to understand the nature of the Christian prayer life as well. Campbell notes a tendency to interpret prayers in a rather deterministic manner, so that '"asking things according to the will of God" comes to sound like asking God to do what he intended to do'.[60] In response to this tendency, he argues:

> God is not revealed to our faith as a fate, neither is His will set before us as a decree of destiny. God is revealed to us as the living God, and His will as the desire and choice of a living heart, which presents to us not the image or picture of a predetermined course of events to the predestined flow of which our prayer is to be an Amen, but a moral and spiritual choice in relation to us His offspring, to which our prayer is to respond in what will be in us the cry of a moral and spiritual choice.[61]

---

[57] Campbell, *Nature of the Atonement*, p. 176.
[58] Campbell, *Nature of the Atonement*, p. 176.
[59] Campbell, *Nature of the Atonement*, p. 177.
[60] Campbell, *Nature of the Atonement*, p. 178.
[61] Campbell, *Nature of the Atonement*, p. 178.

It is this understanding of prayer as an active engagement through Christ in the will of a living God rather than mere contemplation of submission to the will of God, which also distinguishes prayer from meditation. In correspondence addressed to the Revd D. J. Vaughan in 1862, Campbell says that 'there may be as real communion in meditation as in prayer; there may be as much faith in expecting as in asking; but, in the knowledge of the *evil that is* and of the *good* which God *wills to be,* prayer according to that will of God seems to have a fixed place between *desire* and *hope'.*[62] In other words, prayer, as opposed to meditation, actively seeks the mind and will of God. In this regard, Campbell continues, how striking the mention that Christ' "continued all night in prayer" just before choosing from among his disciples the twelve to be apostles'.[63]

In light of all that has been said above, we can offer no better summary of Campbell's doctrine of prayer than that given by Michael Jinkins, who writes:

> Christ is the only true worshipper, according to Campbell, perfectly praying to God in our humanity on our behalf. The way to true prayer is to pray 'in the name of Christ,' with 'the mind of Christ.' In other words, we only pray truly when our prayers participate in the prayer which Christ continually offers to God on our behalf. To pray in the name of Jesus is to pray after Christ, or in accordance with the mind of Christ, trusting the Spirit of God to join our prayer to Christ's own, and to open our ears to Christ's prayer for us, to what it is that Christ wants us to pray. The essential quality of this prayer (and this is the key to understanding the true nature of prayer) is the utter dependence upon God, the Father, which we have seen in the self-giving of Christ.[64]

Campbell's teaching on prayer makes it clear that when prayer is understood in terms of participation in the

---

[62] *Memorials of John McLeod Campbell,* Vol. 2, p. 37.
[63] *Memorials of John McLeod Campbell,* Vol. 2, p. 37.
[64] Jinkins, *Love is of the Essence,* pp. 19–20.

prayer-life of Christ, then instruction in prayer focuses first of all not on *how* people should pray, but on *to whom, in whom, with whom* and *through whom* they pray. In this regard, we cannot separate the activity of prayer from the person and work of Christ, understood retrospectively and prospectively, for it is in him, with him and through him (by the power of the Spirit) that the Church's prayers (and its worship) ascend to the Father.

McLeod Campbell in continuity with John Calvin and the early Scottish Reformers

While McLeod Campbell scarcely mentions John Calvin in *The Nature of the Atonement*, and despite a difference in terminology and imagery in their respective writings, there are nevertheless, as Leanne Van Dyk has rightly observed,[65] significant areas of conceptual similarity and continuity between the two men. In the light of this study we can identify the following lines of continuity which serve to place Campbell firmly in that stream of Reformed theology which is represented by Calvin, Knox and Craig:

1. A twofold methodological emphasis on the love of God (as the primary divine attribute and motivation for the atonement) and the person and work of Christ.
2. A portrayal of the priestly office of Christ in terms that maintain integral links between (a) its retrospective and prospective aspects,[66] (b) its God-humanward and human-Godward aspects,[67] (c) the atoning significance

---

[65] Cf. Van Dyk, *Desire of Divine Love*, Chapter 5, pp. 137–66.

[66] For both Calvin and Campbell, the doctrine of the ascension and in particular its emphasis upon the continual intercession of Christ before the Father, far from being an addendum to the priestly role of Christ, is central.

[67] Of equal importance to Christ the High Priest's representation of God to humankind, by which he reveals God's reconciling love to a sinful world, is his representation of humankind to God, by which he issues a faithful response to that love on behalf of the world, thereby effecting true and lasting reconciliation.

of the incarnation and the Cross,[68] (d) the passive and active obedience of Christ,[69] (e) atonement and worship.[70]

3. The concept of being in union with Christ as the basis for understanding the inner connection between the atonement (which includes the doctrines of justification and sanctification), faith, the Eucharist, worship and prayer.

4. The consequent portrayal of the Christian life – which includes the activity of prayer – in terms of *participation* (through the Spirit) in the life and 'sonship' of Christ.[71] Or, as T. F. Torrance puts it, the whole life of faith is nothing less than 'an abiding in and a living by Christ as he abides in and lives by the Father'.[72]

5. The belief that Christian assurance is of the essence of faith.

McLeod Campbell, William Milligan and Nineteenth-Century Liturgical Reform in the Church of Scotland

Although McLeod Campbell was deposed from parish ministry in 1831, *The Nature of the Atonement*, which was published twenty-five years later, attracted a wide

---

[68] When the redemptive significance of the incarnation is downplayed then 'penal substitutionary' theories of the atonement tend to dominate, casting the atonement in instrumentalist and extrinsic terms – the error of federal Calvinism and the Westminster tradition which Calvin failed to foresee and Campbell fought so hard to overcome.

[69] Christ the High Priest's self-offering is conceived by Calvin and Campbell not merely in terms of his passive acceptance of the sacrificial death that awaited him on the cross, but in terms of his actively seeking the Father's will through prayer and the offering of his whole life in faithful obedience to that will.

[70] As High Priest Christ is not only the Mediator of at-one-ment with God. He is also the Mediator of worship and prayer. The two roles are integrally related.

[71] As Calvin himself says, 'Christ plays the priestly role, not only to render the Father favourable and propitious toward us by an eternal law of reconciliation, *but also to receive us as his companions* in this great office. For we who are defiled in ourselves, yet are *priests in him* ...' (*In.* II.15.6 – italics mine).

[72] Torrance, 'Mind of Christ', p. 142.

readership and was highly regarded as a theological work. Of its significance, Douglas Murray, citing John McIntyre, has observed that 'by linking the atonement to the incarnation and to the sonship and priesthood of Christ, Campbell broke through the theology of the *Westminster Confession* and "set going a ferment of dissatisfaction with the stereotyped theology associated with inflexibilities of old style Calvinism, and a concern for the faithful presentation of the character of God and of his work in the life and death of Jesus Christ"'.[73]

In 1865, nine years after *The Nature of the Atonement* was published, and in keeping with the growing spirit of reform in Scotland, the Church Service Society was formed. Its declared object was 'the study of the liturgies – ancient and modern – of the Christian Church, with a view to the preparation and ultimate publication of certain forms of prayer for public worship, and services for the administration of the Sacraments, the celebration of marriage, the burial of the dead, &c'.[74] The main way of pursuing this aim was through the publication of a service book, *Euchologion*, the first edition of which appeared in 1867. It played a significant role in the reformation of worship in the Scottish Church. However, as Douglas Murray points out, behind the scenes there was a tension between two parties in the Church Service Society, one of which (known as the broad churchmen) did not want to see dogma unduly reflected in worship and objected to the *Euchologion*'s doctrinal tone and expression. The other

---

[73] J. McIntyre, *Prophet of Penitence: Our Contemporary Ancestor*, a lecture delivered in Rhu Church, 24 February 1972, to commemorate the centenary of the death of John McLeod Campbell, cited by D. M. Murray, 'The Scottish Church Society, 1892–1914: A Study of the High Church Movement in the Church of Scotland' (PhD thesis, Cambridge University, 1975), p. 38.

[74] G. W. Sprott, 'Introduction' to the 1905 edition of *Euchologion* (Edinburgh and London: William Blackwood and Sons), p. xviii. For a detailed coverage of the background influences to the formation of the Church Service Society, cf. Kenneth Hughes' PhD thesis, 'Holy Communion in the Church of Scotland in the Nineteenth Century' (Glasgow University, 1987), although the one glaring omission from Hughes' thesis is any reference to John McLeod Campbell.

party (known as the high churchmen) took the opposite view regarding the place of doctrine in worship.[75]

Given the irreconcilable nature of these contrasting views not too many years passed before the high churchmen 'came to realise that a separate society was needed to assert the place of catholic doctrine in the church's worship, and in other areas of the church's life'.[76] To this end, the Scottish Church Society was formed in 1892. Its general aim was 'to defend and advance Catholic doctrine as set forth in the Ancient Creeds and embodied in the Standards of the Church of Scotland; and generally to assert Scriptural principles in all matters relating to Church Order and Policy, Christian Work, and Spiritual Life, throughout Scotland'.[77] It saw itself as a kind of non-political theological think tank, whose doctrinal agenda would be complementary to the liturgical agenda of the Church Service Society. Indeed, there was open communication between the two bodies, and a number of men served on both.

The Society counted among its members a number of leading churchmen, including George Sprott, Thomas Leishman, James Cooper, John Macleod, J. M. Kirkpatrick and Henry J. Wotherspoon, but it was its first President, William Milligan, who really gave the Society theological legitimacy in the eyes of the Church. Professor of Divinity and Biblical Criticism in the University of Aberdeen and Moderator of the General Assembly in 1882, Milligan had established himself as a scholar and theologian of international repute through the publication of two major works, *The Resurrection of our Lord*[78] and *The Ascension and*

---

[75] Cf. 'Scottish Church Society', pp. 88–90, in which Murray refers to James Cooper's declaration that 'the Church Service Society was not likely to do much good work because its committee was paralysed by a "spirit of compromise"'.

[76] Murray, 'Scottish Church Society', p. 90

[77] *Scottish Church Society, Its Work, 1892–1925, and Its Claims*, Occasional Papers I (Edinburgh: Andrew Elliot, 1925), p. 3. 'Catholic doctrine' was deemed by members of the Society to be that deposit of faith that finds expression in the Catholic creeds of the Church, namely, the Nicene and Apostles' Creeds (Cf. Scottish Church Society, *The Catholic Faith*, Occasional Papers III (Edinburgh: Andrew Elliot, 1926), p. 13).

[78] W. Milligan, *The Resurrection of our Lord* (London: Macmillan and Co., 1890).

Heavenly Priesthood of our Lord.[79] It was from him that the Society took its theological bearings.[80]

One of Milligan's major contributions to nineteenth-century theology stemmed from his question, 'Are we to confine the thought of "offering" on the part of our Lord to His sacrificial death? Or are we so to extend the thought as to include in it a present and eternal offering to God of His life in heaven?'[81] The significance of this question is apparent when we recall, from Chapter Two, John Calvin's failure to, first, develop the idea of the Eucharist as an offering in a proper way and, second, depict the role of Christ in heaven as being not only one of intercession, but of offering too. This twofold failure was perpetuated by subsequent Scottish Reformers and the Westminster tradition, and had a profound influence upon the development of Reformed worship, especially in the Scottish Church. In this context, Milligan's question concerning the nature of Christ's offering, which begins to draw out the implications of McLeod Campbell's line of thinking, penetrated to the heart of Reformed theology and liturgical tradition.

Milligan responded to the question not only on exegetical grounds, but also on theological grounds, by exploring the inner connection between the ascension and the incarnation. The ascension, he said, 'was the completion of all that was involved in the incarnation'.[82] The object of the incarnation was not simply to prepare Christ for his sacrificial death. Rather, it had a far greater purpose, namely, of bringing humanity 'into a state of perfect union with the Father of our spirits, and so to introduce into our weak human nature the strength of the Divine nature, that not in name only, or outwardly, or by a

[79] W. Milligan, *The Ascension and Heavenly Priesthood of our Lord* (London: Macmillan and Co., 1892).
[80] Cf. Milligan's 1893 publication, *The Scottish Church Society: Some Account of its Aims* (Edinburgh: J. Gardner Hitt). For an excellent analysis of the development of Milligan's theology, cf. Hogan L. Yancey's 'The Development of the Theology of William Milligan (1821–1893)' (PhD thesis, University of Edinburgh, 1970).
[81] Milligan, *Ascension and Heavenly Priesthood*, p. 116.
[82] Milligan, *Ascension and Heavenly Priesthood*, p. 27.

figure, but in truth, inwardly and in reality, we might receive the right to become children of God'.[83] The incarnation by itself could not have effected this, says Milligan, because it could only identify the Redeemer with the essential elements of the human condition. The resurrection and ascension needed to follow, 'that the "quickening Spirit" of Jesus, thus set free, might enter into our spirits, and make us sharers of its victory'.[84]

This single movement of incarnation and ascension implies two things. First, Christ's offering of himself to the Father is an *eternal* offering.[85] Second, what he offered on the cross, and what he offers eternally, is his *life*.[86] Both William Milligan and his son George made this a focal point of their teaching. 'So long as we think of *death* as offering,' wrote the latter, 'we can speak only of the efficacy of the death stretching forward into the future. As soon as we substitute *life*, the true Biblical idea of offering, for death, the thought of the life offered (the life of one who dieth no more) involves in its own nature the element of *continuousness*.'[87] 'There is thus no inconsistency', he concludes, 'between proclaiming the continuousness of Christ's offering of Himself in heaven, and the fact that the offering begun upon the cross was then complete, and can never be repeated.'[88]

In associating sacrifice with the offering of life rather than the giving up of death William Milligan sought to rediscover the true meaning of sacrifice in the Old Testament and, at the same time, departed from the understanding of sacrifice as involving the death of Christ alone which had largely been assumed in Western theology from the time of the Middle Ages.

Once the biblical link between sacrifice and the offering of life is established in his work, Milligan immediately

---

[83] Milligan, *Ascension and Heavenly Priesthood*, p. 29.
[84] Milligan, *Ascension and Heavenly Priesthood*, p. 30.
[85] Milligan, *Ascension and Heavenly Priesthood*, p. 133.
[86] Milligan, *Ascension and Heavenly Priesthood*, p. 133.
[87] G. Milligan, *The Theology of the Epistle to the Hebrews* (Edinburgh: T&T Clark, 1899), p. 144 (italics mine).
[88] Milligan, *Theology of Hebrews* p. 144.

gives a christological focus to the discussion by pointing out that 'the idea of offering is associated in Scripture with our Lord's work in heaven',[89] and he proceeds to map out the implications of seeing Christ's heavenly role in terms of offering as well as intercession:

> The thought of Offering cannot give way to that of Intercession. The first is the foundation of the second, but the second is pervaded by the conception and spirit of the first. If we rightly interpret the words, Offering and Intercession imply one another. There is even a sense in which Intercession is Offering, and Offering Intercession.[90]

Milligan then identifies four characteristics of Christ's offering:

(a) Christ's offering of life 'possesses the power of a present offering, not merely of an offering made and accepted for us nineteen centuries ago, but of one which ascends even now for us before God, as much an offering as it ever was'.[91]

(b) Christ's offering of life possesses true unity and completeness. Insofar as we are in union with Christ, and our repentance, our cry for pardon, our acceptance of the penalty of sin, our new and higher life, are all *in* him also, so we realise that there is nothing we can add to what Christ has offered and continues to offer in our place and on our behalf. It is complete: 'Union on our part to Christ in all His fortunes penetrates the whole process of redemption; and our Lord's offering, while He takes us into it and along with it from the first, is complete as well as one.'[92]

(c) Christ's offering of life '"fulfils" those various offerings of the law by which it was foreshadowed'. In the life of

---

[89] Milligan, *Ascension and Heavenly Priesthood*, p. 120.
[90] Milligan, *Ascension and Heavenly Priesthood*, p. 126.
[91] Milligan, *Ascension and Heavenly Priesthood*, p. 143.
[92] Milligan, *Ascension and Heavenly Priesthood*, p. 146.

Christ '*now* offered to the Father we see not only the
perfected Sin and Trespass, but the perfected Burnt and
Peace offerings'.[93]

(d) Christ's offering of life 'embraces in its efficacy the
whole life of man. When as our High-priest and
Representative Jesus offers His life to God, that life
touches not only our individual acts of our life, it covers
every one of its departments.'[94] Moreover, as High
Priest Christ not only bears every aspect of our
lives before the Father, he also includes within his
offering the conquest that he has gained for us: 'As the
offering which He makes is His perfected human life,
our whole human life is brought within the scope of His
consecrating power, and every part of it is presented to
God as a trophy of His victory.'[95]

As something that is both continuous and inclusive,
Christ's priestly sacrifice is highly participatory, because it
involves his Church here on earth. William Milligan attributes this participatory dimension of Christ's sacrificial
offering to the power of the Spirit, actively present,
enabling Christ's priestly ministry to be fulfilled in and
through his Church, which is his Body. 'The Christian
Church does not simply live by Christ,' he writes. 'She lives
in Him, and He lives in Her. By the constant communication of His Spirit she is what she is.'[96]

As far as Milligan is concerned, it is in the Eucharist that
the Church's participation in the priestly ministry of Christ
is seen most clearly.[97] It is much more than a memorial of
the death of Christ two thousand years ago. Those who
gather at the Table 'do not simply remember what Jesus
did on earth. They bring to remembrance as a present fact
what He is doing in heaven. They commemorate, they hold
communion with, they accept, and at His Table are

[93] Milligan, *Ascension and Heavenly Priesthood*, pp. 146–8.
[94] Milligan, *Ascension and Heavenly Priesthood*, p. 148.
[95] Milligan, *Ascension and Heavenly Priesthood*, p. 149.
[96] Milligan, *Ascension and Heavenly Priesthood*, p. 243.
[97] Milligan, *Ascension and Heavenly Priesthood*, p. 266.

nourished by, a living Lord, – "in remembrance of *Me*," of Me, not as I was, but as I am, to the end of time.'[98]

What has been said about Christ's eternal priesthood and the Eucharist must also be said about his eternal priesthood and the activity of prayer. William Milligan points out that the book of Hebrews presents Christ's high-priestly work in heaven not only in terms of his offering, but also in terms of his intercession. 'Rightly conceived', he argues, 'the work of Intercession on the part of our heavenly High-priest seems to be that, having restored the broken covenant and brought His Israel into the most intimate union and communion with God, He would now, amidst all their remaining weaknesses, and the innumerable temptations that surround them, preserve them in it.'[99]

In expounding the nature of Christ's intercession and its relationship to his other high-priestly work, namely, his offering, Milligan warns against regarding intercession as Christ's only ongoing work, as though his offering was merely a past event. In conjunction with this warning, he observes that Christ's intercession is often deemed 'to refer to petitions which He offers up to His Father for those members of His Body who are still amidst the trials and temptations of their earthly pilgrimage'.[100] This popular view, he suggests, is deeply problematic because it drives a wedge between Christ's intercession (present) and his offering (past), thereby ignoring the continuousness of the offering. Furthermore, it tends to assume, one, that Christ's intercession is constituted by a series of petitions to the Father and, two, that in making these petitions the Redeemer prays to the Father in much the same way as the creature prays to the Creator.

Against this rather restrictive and misleading interpret-ation of Christ's intercession, Milligan notes that there is no evidence that the high priest of ancient Israel actually prayed or uttered a series of petitions when he entered the

[98] Milligan, *Ascension and Heavenly Priesthood*, p. 266.
[99] Milligan, *Ascension and Heavenly Priesthood*, p. 158.
[100] Milligan, *Ascension and Heavenly Priesthood*, p. 149.

veil on the Day of Atonement to intercede for the people. Instead, he 'simply completed the offering which he had begun immediately before; and, when the offering was complete, he came out to perform the ceremony of the two goats, in which the results of his offering were set forth'.[101] He concludes:

> In these circumstances, it may be a matter of regret that the English language seems to possess no better word than 'intercession' to express the action of our High-priest in heaven after He had presented His offering to the Father. For this, however, there is no help, and all that can be done is to impress upon the inquirer the fact that 'Intercession' is a much wider word than prayer. That prayer is included under the term is not for a moment to be denied, but we are not to limit it to prayer. We are to understand it of every act by which the Son, in dependence on the Father, in the Father's name, and with the perfect concurrence of the Father, takes His own with Him into the Father's presence, in order that whatever He Himself enjoys in the communications of His Father's love may become also theirs.[102]

In drawing attention to the intercessory role of Christ, Milligan takes care to relate it to the intercessory role of the Holy Spirit. There are, he says, two 'Advocates':

> The first Advocate is external, the second internal. The first takes all our necessities to the Father, that, as

---

[101] Milligan, *Ascension and Heavenly Priesthood*, p. 152.
[102] Milligan, *Ascension and Heavenly Priesthood*, p. 152. Milligan grounds his argument in a reflection upon John's Gospel, in which, he says, it may be observed that 'our Lord never uses of His own approach to the Father the word expressive of the manner in which the creature approaches God. He goes to Him, not as one between whom and God a gulf has to be bridged, or as if He were asking aid from an external source. He goes to Him in the full consciousness of mutual love; in that Divine fellowship in which He knows that the will of the Father is His will; and in which, therefore, He has only to utter the thoughts that belong in common to the ineffable unity of Their common life. But, so going, he prays' (*Ascension and Heavenly Priesthood*, p. 153).

Himself one with the Father, He may so 'make request' on our behalf that, out of the common love of the Father to the Son and the Son to the Father, these necessities may be supplied. The second brings the Redeemer in such a manner home into our hearts that, in the innermost depths of our nature, we see and judge and feel with Him; that His requests for us become our prayers for ourselves; and that the unity of Father, Son, and redeemed humanity is in Him completely realised.[103]

From the above it can be seen that, as with McLeod Campbell before him, one of the most striking features of Milligan's scholarship is the heavy emphasis placed upon the high priestly role of Christ both on earth and in heaven. The resonance of thought between the two men has been articulated well by Douglas Murray in the following terms:

Milligan emphasised, as did Campbell, the life of Christ as man in his offering to the Father on our behalf. Milligan rejected, as did Campbell, the view of penal substitution as an adequate view of the atonement. Christ is our representative as well as our substitute. He becomes what we are that in him we might become what he is. The essence of the atonement lay, not in his death considered as physical suffering, but in the surrender of his will to God. Milligan saw the incarnation, as did Campbell, not just as the divine means of dealing with sin, but as the first step in the attainment of a new relationship between men and God. Milligan thus saw the work of Christ as Priest in terms of the person and present life of Christ, who is now risen and ascended.'[104]

Moreover, says Murray, for both Milligan and Campbell the heavenly work of Christ as High Priest is not just one of intercession, but offering – an offering of life.[105]

---

[103] Milligan, *Ascension and Heavenly Priesthood*, pp. 159–60.
[104] Murray, 'Scottish Church Society', pp. 38–9.
[105] Murray, 'Scottish Church Society', pp. 42–3.

Following Milligan's lead the Scottish Church Society
maintained that the doctrines of union with Christ and the
priesthood of Christ were of central importance for the life
of the Church and underlay its worship. It regretted the
fact that 'the missing link in much that is called evangelical
religion is the link of vital union with the Second Adam,
including that bodily *nexus* with His glorified Humanity,
as signified and sealed in the sacraments, which Calvin
held as dear as life'.[106]

In conjunction with their emphasis upon the doctrines of
union with Christ and the priesthood of Christ, members
of the Scottish Church Society devoted a lot of time and
energy to the subject of holy communion. They regarded it
as the divinely ordered means by which the Church feeds
upon Christ, is joined to him, and worships God through
him. There was a strong feeling among members that the
sacrament had become peripheral to the life of the Church
in Scotland, and that its 'God-ward' aspect had been
almost totally lost.[107] Christ tended to be portrayed as the
Mediator of divine blessing rather than the Mediator of
prayer and worship, as the One whose death is remembered in the sacrament rather than the One into whose
living presence people are lifted in the Spirit, as the One
who receives offerings of praise rather than the One to
whose continual self-offering people are joined.

Milligan's lasting influence on the shape of Reformed
worship in Scotland can also be seen in the work of one of
his sons, Oswald, who, influenced by his father, made a
special study of worship[108] and served as the convener of
the Committee on Public Worship and Aids to Devotion. 'It
was this committee', Yancey observes, 'that prepared *The
Book of Common Order of the Church of Scotland*, published in
1940 and approved by the General Assembly the same
year.'[109]

[106] G. W. Sprott, *Aims of the Scottish Church Society*, p. 7, cited by Murray,
'Scottish Church Society', p. 19.
[107] Murray, 'Scottish Church Society', p. 265.
[108] Oswald wrote *The Ministry of Worship* (London: Oxford University
Press, 1941) – cited by Yancey, 'Development', p. 393.
[109] Yancey, 'Development', p. 393.

Conclusion

We have now come full circle in our consideration of the nature of Christ's priesthood in the activity of prayer. This book began with a discussion of the widespread practice in the early Church of directing liturgical prayer to the Father through Christ as the one Mediator between humankind and God. It traced the decline of that practice and its accompanying doctrine of the priesthood of Christ in the Middle Ages, its revival in the Genevan and Scottish Reformation, and its decline again in federal Calvinism and the Westminster tradition. We now note the renewed emphasis on the mediatorial role of Christ in prayer in the nineteenth century's reform process, spearheaded by William Milligan and a cluster of leading churchmen but owing a great deal to the groundbreaking theological work of John McLeod Campbell. His teaching of universal atonement and unconditional grace was characterised by a strong appreciation of the priesthood of Christ, not only in relation to the atonement itself – understood both retrospectively, in terms of God dealing with our guilty past, and prospectively, in terms of God bringing us to share in Christ's sonship – but also in relation to the ongoing life of worship and prayer.

Campbell's doctrine of the priesthood of Christ led him to describe prayer as an utterance of participation in the life of Christ in accordance with the mind of Christ, and to follow Knox in seeing an inextricable link between the activity of prayer and the celebration of the Eucharist, which brings to a concentrated focus the reality of abiding in Christ. As sinners feed on Christ at the Table, his life becomes theirs, their life ascends to the Father in worship through him, and they are drawn to seek his mind in prayer.

Viewed in this way, prayer is not a passive submission to the will of God, understood in some kind of deterministic fashion. It is the active seeking of the mind of Christ, a sharing in Christ's own life of prayer in the Spirit as he pleads with the Father on behalf of sinners. As we noted in relation to John Knox, it is essentially a redemptive activity, a trinitarian event, in which the Church prays to the Father through, with and in Christ, and in the Holy Spirit.

If this was the doctrinal position of McLeod Campbell, Milligan and others in the Scottish Church Society, the question that remains is, to what extent have these views been given liturgical expression in the life of the Church? It is to that question that we shall now turn as we compare specific eucharistic liturgies from the time of the Genevan Reformation through to the current day in the Church of Scotland.

The Priesthood of Christ and Eucharistic Prayer in the Reformed Tradition: A Liturgical Comparison, with Special Reference to the Church of Scotland

Thus far in our consideration of the theological significance of the doctrine of the priesthood of Christ, first in the early Church and then in the Reformed tradition, we have identified a deep-seated tension between Calvin and the early Scottish Reformers on the one hand, and the Westminster tradition on the other. We have seen how this tension erupted in the nineteenth century when John McLeod Campbell was placed on trial for heresy. The doctrine of atonement which he expounded, and which focused very strongly on the priesthood of Christ, was unacceptable to a Church that had come to take its theological bearings more from Theodore Beza, William Perkins and seventeenth-century federal Calvinism than from John Calvin, John Knox and John Craig. We have also noted that the second half of the nineteenth century was characterised by some liturgical reform in Scotland. This reform owed much to the efforts of the Church Service Society and the Scottish Church Society, and, in terms of its doctrinal base, owes much to the direct influence of William Milligan and the indirect influence of McLeod Campbell.

Throughout the preceding chapters we have sought to relate the doctrinal issues of atonement and the priesthood of Christ to the subject of prayer. However, because prayer is an activity before it is a matter of theological reflection we must move beyond a doctrinal discussion to examine the extent to which the priesthood of Christ has been enshrined in the Church's actual prayer life. The best way of doing this is by a comparative analysis of its eucharistic liturgies. These liturgies provide us with a useful compilation of prayers from which we can identify changes and emerging patterns. For the purposes of this book we will concentrate on the eucharistic liturgies from the time of the Genevan Reformation through to the current day in the Church of Scotland. It will become evident from the following analysis that our study of each liturgy is driven by three interrelated questions:

1. What are the main features of this liturgy, and what are the major differences between it and that which precedes it?
2. How do these features and differences relate to the doctrinal discussion of the preceding chapters?
3. To what extent does this liturgy reflect a proper understanding of the vicarious humanity and mediatorial role of Christ our High Priest in (a) the atonement, and (b) prayer?

German and Swiss Foundations

We begin our comparative analysis with two forerunners to the Genevan reformation of worship, Martin Bucer and Diebold Schwarz, who in many respects laid the foundations for the reform that followed.

Martin Bucer's Rite, 1537

Order of worship[1]

> *The Liturgy of the Word*
> Confession of Sins
> Scriptural words of pardon (1 Tim. 1)
> Absolution
> Psalm, hymn, or *Kyries* and *Gloria in Excelsis*
> Collect for Illumination
> Metrical Psalm
> Lection (Gospel)
> Sermon[2]

---

[1] Source: *Liturgies of the Western Church*, ed. B. Thompson (Philadelphia: Fortress Press, 1980), pp. 167–81.

[2] Near the end of the sermon, the minister explains the action of the Lord's Supper and exhorts the people to observe the same with right faith and true devotion – cf. *Liturgies of the Western Church*, p. 171.

The Liturgy of the Upper Room
Preparation of elements while Apostles' Creed sung
Intercessions and Consecration Prayer
Lord's Prayer
Exhortation[3]
Words of Institution
Fraction
Delivery
Communion, while psalm or hymn sung
Post-communion collect of Thanksgiving
Aaronic Blessing
Dismissal

Commentary

In the early part of the sixteenth century the German city of Strasbourg became a centre of Reformed liturgical development, due in large part to the influence of Martin Bucer, whose 1537 rite is the one from which the Calvinian and Scottish rites and services were later derived. However, liturgical reform in Strasbourg did not begin with Bucer. The first revision of the Latin Mass was carried out by Diebold Schwarz in 1524, and is worthy of mention because of the bridge that it represents between the Roman and Reformed liturgical traditions.[4] In translating the Mass into German, Schwarz, Maxwell notes, retained as many as possible of the old familiar things, although all that pertained to the Roman doctrine of sacrifice was expunged, either by slight omissions or by the paraphrasing of familiar words.[5]

There is much to admire in Schwarz's rite, the main features of which are worth highlighting here. First, in the

---

[3] If it has not been included within the sermon – cf. note 2 above.
[4] Cf. W. D. Maxwell, *The Liturgical Portions of the Genevan Service Book*, (Westminster: Faith Press, 1931), p. 26; also, Thompson's commentary on Schwarz's rite, *Liturgies of the Western Church*, pp. 159–60.
[5] Maxwell, *Outline of Christian Worship*, p. 88. Maxwell goes on to say that of all the changes, 'the most important and far reaching was the saying of the rite audibly, for this meant that, although the traditional ceremonial remained, the people were no longer dependent upon it for following the service. That, at one stroke, relegated the ceremonial to a subordinate place; and what had been of primary importance now became a mere enrichment of the rite' (*Outline of Christian Worship*, p. 89).

prayer of Confession, there is an acknowledgement both of sins that we commit and the sin into which we are born – 'in sin did our mother conceive us'.[6] In other words, sin does not constitute a mere catalogue of moral failures. It is a state of being, a fundamental orientation into which all people are born and from which they cannot escape. When sin is understood in this way then the atoning significance of the incarnation becomes even more pronounced. Christ did not merely forgive individuals for their moral failures. Rather, in his own humanity he healed and sanctified the sinful human condition which all persons share.

One of the abiding strengths of Schwarz's rite is that it not only recognises the true nature of sin; it also recognises the full extent of the atonement that has been wrought in the person and work of Christ. The words of Absolution which follow the second prayer of Confession are taken from 1 John 2:1–2, and exhibit a strong appreciation of the unconditional assurance of grace which stems from his atoning mediatorship:

> Brethren, if any man hath sinned, *we have an advocate* with the Father, Jesus Christ the righteous; and He is a propitiation for our sins; and not for ours only, but also *for the sins of the whole world*. Believe the Gospel, and live in peace.[7]

This assurance of atonement is powerfully reinforced in the prayer of Thanksgiving, wherein the priest leads the people in rejoicing:

> How great is Thy goodness, that Thou hast merited for us and for all ours not only the forgiveness of our sins, but by Thy grace hast given Thy Son Jesus Christ unto death for a propitiation. Wherefore, *we now have a great and unassailable safeguard in Thy grace, and know that we are Thy children, Thine heirs, and joint-heirs with Christ*.[8]

---

[6] Schwarz's rite, *Outline of Christian Worship*, p. 92.

[7] Schwarz's rite, *Outline of Christian Worship*, p. 92 (italics mine).

[8] Schwarz's rite, *Outline of Christian Worship*, pp. 95–6 (italics mine).

As a consequence of this emphatic assurance of divine grace and favour, the Exhortation which immediately precedes the liturgy of the Upper Room is refreshingly free of the excessive and morbid self-examination which came to characterise seventeenth-century Reformed liturgies. The priest merely says the following words:

> Dearly beloved, pray God the Father, through Jesus Christ our Lord, that He will send us the Holy Ghost, the Comforter, to make our bodies a living sacrifice, holy, acceptable unto God, which is our reasonable service.[9]

In conjunction with its embodiment of a strong theology of grace, Schwarz's rite is highly participatory. Congregational participation is effected through the service being conducted in the language of the people rather than in Latin, and through the utilisation of congregational responses, which give the liturgy an antiphonal character. The officiating priest faces the people rather than turning his back on them, thereby reinforcing the notion that God is in the midst of the people rather than at a distance. Overall, there is an overwhelming impression of worship as *participation* involving the *whole people of God*. Maxwell makes precisely this observation, citing two sixteenth-century accounts of the Schwarz liturgy in action, and summing up the sentiment of these accounts by noting 'how the worship has become again a corporate action in which the two characteristics of the early worship as recorded in Acts, fellowship and joy, are predominant'.[10] This assessment is supported by Thompson, who notes that 'the *Confiteor*, which Schwarz adapted from the local breviary and renamed "The Common Confession," became a congregational confession of sin and thus a manifestation of the priesthood of all believers'.[11]

One other feature of the liturgy worth noting concerns the prayer of Intercession. Instead of being a stand-alone

---

[9] Schwarz's rite, *Outline of Christian Worship*, p. 94.
[10] Maxwell, *Outline of Christian Worship*, p. 98.
[11] *Liturgies of the Western Church*, p. 159.

prayer, it is included within the prayer of Consecration and Thanksgiving. W. Perry, noting the same placement in the subsequent *Scottish Liturgy* of the Episcopal Church in Scotland, provides solid theological justification for such treatment:

> The Eucharist is the supreme opportunity for inter-cession; for there we are not only pleading the one Sacrifice, but are also doing this 'in remembrance,' not simply of His Death, but 'of *Me*,' of Me who 'am alive for evermore' as Priest and Intercessor. If this be so, the natural place for the intercession is the central part of the service, as close as may be to that divine 'remembrance' which every Eucharist enacts. Therefore, in the Scottish rite intercession immediately follows the Prayer of Consecration. It is no doubt dangerous to introduce unnecessarily questions of time into a service which brings us face to face with the eternal; but there is here involved something more than a mere matter of order or arrangement; for inter-cession in this place is the recognition and practice of the great truth, too commonly forgotten, that Christ our Lord is Priest as well as Victim, and with His perfect Intercession we would fain mingle ours. This idea would account for the fact that from the fourth century the great intercession has been connected with the consecration, and in most liturgies occurs just after it, as in the Scottish rite.[12]

In summary, Schwarz's rite constitutes a fine liturgy with a strong appreciation of the priesthood of Christ, understood both retrospectively and prospectively.

From 1525 Bucer's influence gradually increased until he became the ecclesiastical leader at Strasbourg. J. M. Barkley, following Maxwell, describes Bucer's theological position as 'a *via media* between Lutheranism and Zwinglianism' and sums up his influence upon public

---

[12] W. Perry, *The Scottish Liturgy: Its Value and History* (London: Mowbray and Co., n.d.), pp. 14–15.

worship in terms of a movement 'towards simplification and the laying of greater emphasis on the didactic element, so we have the introduction of the sermon'.[13] Under his influence a number of other changes were introduced, some of which, notes Maxwell, are to be welcomed, while others are to be deplored.[14] While greater variety was introduced into the choice of prayers, they were much longer and more didactic, tending to lead to a 'loss of simplicity and directness' – a tendency, Maxwell says, which marred the later prayers of the Reformed churches.[15] Most of the congregational responses, save the Amens, disappeared, and the worship lost its antiphonal character. While worship was enriched by the use of metrical psalms and hymns, many of the traditional features of corporate worship were omitted, including the *Gloria in Excelsis*, the *Kyries*, and the *Sursum Corda*. A general prayer of Thanksgiving for Christ's work and passion replaced the traditional Prefaces, *Sanctus* and *Benedictus qui venit*, leading Maxwell to note 'a general impoverishment and an unnecessary departure from a tradition almost as old as the Church itself; for however excellently conceived such a substitute might be, it lacked the dignity and beauty, the variety and comprehensiveness and devotional grace of the historic forms; and in the end it achieved no more than slight revision of them could have accomplished'.[16]

There were other changes, too, during this period. Maxwell notes the disappearance of the lections from worship, and the extension of the sermon to over an hour in length, the abolition of days commemorating the saints, and the dropping out of use of eucharistic vestments. Thompson

---

[13] J. M. Barkley, *The Worship of the Reformed Church: An Exposition and Critical Analysis of the Eucharistic, Baptismal, and Confirmation Rites in the Scottish, English–Welsh and Irish liturgies* (London: Lutterworth Press, 1966), p. 15.
[14] Maxwell, *Outline of Christian Worship*, p. 98.
[15] Maxwell also says of these long prayers that the 'laudable desire to make the worship completely intelligible to the worshippers and fully expressive of their needs' too often led instead to 'an undue focusing of attention upon the needs of man so that worship tended to lose its proper objectivity and focus' (*Outline of Christian Worship*, p. 99).
[16] Maxwell, *Outline of Christian Worship*, p. 100.

notes that under Bucer's influence, the word 'Mass' gave way to 'Lord's Supper', the 'altar' became 'altar-table' or simply 'table', the celebrant was no longer described as 'priest' but as 'parson' or 'minister', and traditional vestments were discarded in favour of some sort of black gown.[17] But perhaps even more important than all these changes to the *form* of worship, yet closely aligned to them, was the change to its theological *content*. In this regard, a comparison between Bucer's 1537 rite and Schwarz's 1524 rite reveals a number of interesting theological developments.

To begin with, Bucer's rite opens in the same manner as Schwarz's, with a confession of sins and an acknowledgement that sin is a state of being into which all people are born.[18] The main difference is found in the more explicit reference in Bucer's liturgy to the Ten Commandments, with the third and longest form of confession being based entirely upon them, each commandment supplying a paragraph of confession. Maxwell believes that this confession played a part in influencing Calvin to use the Decalogue as the first singing in his service.[19] While the use of the Ten Commandments in this manner gave appropriate liturgical expression to the Reformed conviction that God's law reveals to people their sin and moves them to seek grace,[20] it also had the damaging effect of placing the

---

[17] *Liturgies of the Western Church*, p. 160.

[18] Three forms of confession are offered. The first form says that 'we confess and acknowledge unto thee that we were *conceived in unrighteousness and are full of sin* and transgression in all our life'. The second form, which was that adopted by Calvin, says that 'we confess and acknowledge that we, alas, were *conceived and born in sin*, and are therefore inclined to all evil and slow to all good' (Bucer's rite, *Liturgies of the Western Church*, p. 168 – italics mine). The third form is constituted by a series of confessions based on the Ten Commandments.

[19] Maxwell, *Outline of Christian Worship*, p. 103. Maxwell notes that this *Confiteor* was the one translated by Calvin, and an enlarged version of it was subsequently used in Knox's Liturgy, 1556 onwards.

[20] Cf. *In*. II.7.6–9, where Calvin describes divine law in terms of that which shows the righteousness of God, and as a mirror discloses our sinfulness, leading us to seek God's grace. Cf. also, Thompson, who says of this third form of confession that 'Bucer used the law as Calvin also used it in worship: not to accuse sinners, but to bring the faithful to true piety by teaching them the divine will and exhorting them to obedience' (*Liturgies of the Western Church*, p. 164).

law before the gospel, thereby opening the door for an *ordo salutis* which, insofar as it viewed repentance as a *condition* of forgiveness, placed the imperatives of the law before the indicatives of grace and inverted the biblical *ordo salutis*.

As we have seen throughout this book, the effects of this inversion have been widespread. It radically undermined the basis of the assurance of faith and focused attention not on what *Christ has done for us* and for all humanity, but rather on *what we have to do* IF we would be in covenant with God. Increasingly, the atonement was interpreted in judicial rather than filial terms and disengaged from the doctrine of the incarnation.

The greater stress on the Ten Commandments at the beginning of Bucer's liturgy is accompanied by a higher priority given to the Exhortation at the centre of the service. Having said that, it should also be noted that Bucer's Exhortation is characterised more by a proclamation of the gospel and a theological rationale for the Lord's Supper than it is by a call for personal self-examination and an assessment of one's worthiness to receive the sacrament. Accordingly, it is not the content of the Exhortation that is the problem here but, rather, its potential for being reworked in such a way that a moralistic introspection would be imposed upon the Lord's Supper, thereby fundamentally altering its character.

These criticisms aside, Bucer's liturgy generally exhibits a very strong grasp of the principle of *sola gratia*, the priesthood of Christ, and the atoning significance of the incarnation. The first sign of this is found in the Absolution, drawn from 1 Timothy 1:15, which follows the Confession and which pronounces the forgiveness of sins unconditionally.[21]

The redemptive significance of the incarnation is evident in the Exhortation, wherein it is declared that the 'eternal Word

---

[21] The Absolution reads: 'This is a faithful saying, and worthy of all acceptance, that Christ Jesus is come into the world to save sinners. Let each make confession in his heart with St Paul in truth, and believe in Christ. So in His Name do I pronounce forgiveness unto you of all your sins, and I declare you to be loosed of them in earth so that ye may be loosed of them also in heaven and in all eternity' (Bucer's rite, *Outline of Christian Worship*, p. 103).

of God became flesh, so that there might be a *holy flesh and blood
... through whom our flesh and blood would be restored and
sanctified'.*[22] As we have already noted, the call for self-
examination, when it is issued, is not for the purpose of
assessing one's worthiness. Rather, it is to 'consider why the
Lord thus communicates Himself in holy, sanctifying
Communion in the holy Sacrament, namely, in order that He
may live in us increasingly, and that we may live in Him as our
Head, as we all there partake of the Bread'.[23] Attention is thus
directed towards the basis of one's union and communion
with Christ rather than oneself and one's merits. There is a
very clear sense here of the Christian life being one of union
and communion with Christ. This emphasis is accentuated in
the prayer of Consecration, wherein a prayer is offered that as
we partake of Christ's body and blood, then 'we may no more
live to ours sins and in depravity, but that *He may live in us, and
we in Him,* to a holy, blessed, and eternal life'.[24]

In summary, although Bucer's rite loses some of the
simplicity and elegance of Schwarz's, and becomes unne-
cessarily wordy and didactic in parts, it remains
nevertheless theologically sound, with a strong appreciation of the priesthood of Christ.

Calvin's Rite, Geneva, 1542

Order of worship[25]

The Liturgy of the Word
Scripture Sentence: Psalm 124:8[26]

---

[22] Bucer's rite, *Outline of Christian Worship*, p. 104 (italics mine).
[23] Bucer's rite, *Outline of Christian Worship*, p. 105.
[24] Bucer's rite, *Outline of Christian Worship*, p. 108 (italics mine).
[25] Source: *Liturgies of the Western Church*, pp. 197–210.
[26] Thompson comments: 'The liturgy ... began with the solemn declaration
of God's glory and man's frailty: "Our help is in the name of the Lord."
Directly, the minister led the people in the confession of sin, using a revised
form of Bucer's second *Confiteor*. In "well-ordered churches" confession was
the proper beginning of worship. It brought men to a "true estimation" of
themselves; and by the very acknowledgement of their wretchedness, they
paid testimony to "the goodness and mercy of our God". So the "gate of
prayer is opened" (*In.* III.4.10f)' (*Liturgies of the Western Church*, p. 190).

Confession of sins
Prayer for pardon[27]
Metrical Psalm
Collect for Illumination
Lection
Sermon

The Liturgy of the Upper Room
Intercessions
Lord's Prayer in long paraphrase
Preparation of elements while Apostles' Creed sung
Words of Institution
Exhortation
Fraction
Delivery
Communion, while psalm or scriptures read
Post-communion collect
Aaronic Blessing

Commentary

When Calvin came to Strasbourg he was greatly impressed by the worship that was established there. He adopted it almost word for word when he translated it from German into French.[28] In his preface to the third edition of his service book he described his ideal Sunday service. The description is worth quoting in part because it gives us a good insight into his theology of worship and prayer, which we discussed at greater length in Chapter Two:

[27] In Calvin's Strasbourg text of 1540, the confession of sins was followed by scriptural words of pardon and an Absolution. Thompson explains the difference between the two liturgies at this point: 'In Strassburg Calvin supplied an Absolution no less forthright than that of Bucer; but when he returned to Geneva, the people objected to this "novelty," illustrating their hostility by jumping up before the end of the Confession to forestall an Absolution' (*Liturgies of the Western Church*, p. 191).
[28] For a detailed exposition on Bucer's influence on Calvin, see Willem van't Spijker, 'Bucer's Influence on Calvin: Church and Community', in *Martin Bucer: Reforming Church and Community*, ed. D. F. Wright (Cambridge: Cambridge University Press, 1994), pp. 32–44.

We begin with the confession of our sins, adding readings from the Law and the Gospel (that is, sentences of remission) ... and after we are assured that as Jesus Christ has righteousness and life in Himself, and that He lives for the sake of the Father, so we are justified in Jesus Christ, and live in a new life by the same Jesus Christ ... and we continue with psalms, hymns of praise, the reading of the Gospel ... and ... quickened and stirred by the reading of the Gospel, and the confession of our faith (that is, Apostles' Creed) ... it follows that we must pray for the salvation of all men for the life of Christ should be greatly enkindled within us. Now the life of Christ consists in this, namely, to seek and to save that which is lost. Fittingly, then, we pray for the estates of men. And because we receive Jesus Christ truly in this Sacrament ... we worship Him in spirit and in truth; and receive the Eucharist with reverence, concluding the whole mystery with praise and thanksgiving. This then, is the whole order and reason for its administration in this manner; and it agrees also with its administration in the ancient Church of the apostles, of the martyrs, and of the holy fathers.[29]

Calvin's description of worship here has a strong christological focus. Christians have assurance of pardon not because of anything of merit that they find in themselves but because *in Christ* there is found righteousness and life, and *in him* they have been justified. The Church prays for the salvation of all peoples (not just the elect) because *in Christ* God's will to seek and save the lost has been revealed. Christ himself stands at the heart of the sacrament. It is he whom worshippers receive, it his life which is greatly enkindled within them, it is he whom they worship in spirit and in truth, and in him the mystery of salvation is held forth, bringing forth a response of awe and reverence together with praise and thanksgiving.

---

[29] Text 35, vol. xxxiv, pp. 194–6, cited by Maxwell in *Outline of Christian Worship*, p. 116.

A number of these features are enshrined in the long prayer of Intercession which, though verbose, contains some excellent clauses. The opening section of the prayer lays out the christological rationale for prayer. We pray because Christ and his apostles teach us to gather together in his name, with the promise that '*he will be in the midst of us*, and *will be our intercessor* ... to obtain all those things for which we agree to ask on earth'. Therefore, we 'do heartily beseech thee, our gracious God and Father, in the name of our *only Saviour and Mediator*, to grant us the free pardon of our offences through thine infinite mercy, and to *draw and lift up our thoughts and desires unto thee* in such wise that we may be able to call upon thee with all our heart'.[30]

Having acknowledged the intercessions of Christ as the basis for the Church's own intercessions, Calvin proceeds to pray for others. The scope of this prayer is set forth with the following words:

> We pray thee now, O most gracious and merciful Father, for *all men* everywhere. As it is thy will to be acknowledged the Saviour of the whole world, through the redemption wrought by thy Son Jesus Christ, grant that those who are still estranged from the knowledge of Him ... may be brought ... to the straight way of salvation.[31]

Following the intercessory section of Calvin's prayer, the celebrant prays to the Father for those 'who are gathered together in the name of thy Son Jesus', that they may approach the Lord's Table without hypocrisy, knowing 'what perdition is ours *by nature*', and in the hope that we may 'yield ourselves completely' to Christ, 'to the end that *he, dwelling in us,* may mortify our old Adam, renewing us for a better life'.[32] This sense of being in union with Christ and participating in his life is reinforced by the concluding section of the prayer, in which the minister makes the following plea on behalf of the people:

---

[30] *Liturgies of the Western Church*, p. 199 (italics mine).
[31] *Liturgies of the Western Church*, p. 199 (italics mine).
[32] *Liturgies of the Western Church*, p. 200 (italics mine).

In steadfast faith may we receive His body and blood,
yea *Christ Himself* entire, who being true God and true
man, is verily the holy bread of heaven which gives us
life. So may we *no longer live in ourselves, after our nature*
which is entirely corrupt and vicious, *but may He live in
us* and lead us to the life that is holy, blessed and
everlasting: whereby *we may truly become partakers* of
the new and eternal testament, the covenant of grace.[33]

There is a very real sense in the above words of the
sacrament being regarded as a converting rather than a
confirming ordinance. This is accentuated by the structure
of the main body of the prayer, which is less a prayer of
thanksgiving than it is a series of petitions for personal
transformation. These petitions beseech numerous things
of God, including: true knowledge of the state of one's
corrupt nature; a yielding of oneself completely to Christ; a
daily submission to God's majesty; a rendering of perfect
and due obedience; nourishment through God's goodness,
that one may receive at his hands all things necessary and
trust him more fully; a more affectionate knowledge of
God as our Father; pardon for one's innumerable offences;
divine aid to help one and sustain one's weakness; and
strength through the Spirit to withstand all temptations.[34]

Notably absent from Calvin's Great Prayer and from the
liturgy as a whole is a prayer of Consecration.[35] This
omission is partly due to the general reaction of the
Reformers against the Roman doctrine of transubstantiation
and the associated adoration of the consecrated host.
Calvin's own denunciation of the Roman Mass in this regard
was especially vehement.[36] However, we must not conclude
that his decision to omit the prayer of Consecration was
entirely reactionary. As we noted in Chapter Two, it also
stemmed from his theological conviction that the efficacy of
the sacrament is derived not from the consecration of the

---

[33] *Liturgies of the Western Church*, p. 202 (italics mine).
[34] *Liturgies of the Western Church*, pp. 201–2.
[35] While there was no consecration prayer in Calvin's Genevan service book, there was a short one in his earlier Strasbourg version.
[36] Cf. *In.* IV.17.35–37.

elements but rather from the preaching of the word.[37] Accordingly, in Calvin's worship service the prayer for illumination prior to the sermon effectively serves the same purpose as the traditional *epiclesis* or prayer of Consecration in the Latin Mass. Because Calvin understood God's presence in the sacrament in terms of the Church being lifted up by the Spirit into the presence of the Father through Christ the High Priest, he could not condone a consecration prayer that sought to 'bring down' the heavenly Christ and 'imprison' him in the material substances of bread and wine.

When it comes to the communion itself, Calvin retains the primitive and Catholic custom of the celebrant serving himself the elements before their distribution to the congregation. It had become the practice in some of the early Strasbourg rites for the priest's communion to follow that of the people to enable him to consume what remained of the elements after the people had communicated.[38] Theologically, however, there is no warrant for this departure. The custom of the celebrant receiving the elements first is consistent with the doctrine of the priesthood of Christ. For, by virtue of his eternal priesthood, Christ alone is the true Host at the Table, not the officiating minister, who stands in Christ's place merely as his 'ambassador'. Because Christ is both Priest and Host, the celebrant must first receive what the Host offers before he can serve others; and because the celebrant is Christ's ambassador at the Table, he must serve himself. As Maxwell observes, this practice has the advantage of the minister setting an 'example to Christ's flock of faithful people, first partaking of the sacred Elements himself, then giving of them to the people'.[39]

It is increasingly clear from the above analysis that Calvin's liturgical reforms were theologically driven. It was not change for change's sake, or a matter of merely discarding that which was found to be objectionable in the

[37] Cf. *In*. IV.17.39.
[38] Cf. Maxwell, *Genevan Service Book*, pp. 206–7.
[39] Maxwell, *Genevan Service Book*, p. 209.

236   PRAYER AND THE PRIESTHOOD OF CHRIST

Roman liturgy. A striking feature of Calvin's description of worship, cited above, is his linking of the administration of the sacrament to that of the 'ancient Church of the apostles, of the martyrs, and of the holy fathers' – Reformed worship, properly understood, is truly catholic. Maxwell comments:

> It was not the intention of the Reformers to depart from the central tradition of Christendom and innovate according to mere whim or mood. Rather they counted themselves as the faithful trustees of Catholic tradition, and if they simplified the Roman worship of their day, they did so with the intention of removing all mediaeval and sacerdotal accretions in order to achieve the simplicity and purity of the primitive rites.[40]

Taking an opposing stance to Maxwell, Yngve Brilioth argues that Calvin's 'Genevan rite came into being more under pressure of external circumstances than as the creative expression of a clearly defined view.'[41] He concludes that Zwingli's liturgy was 'immeasurably' superior to Calvin's 'meagre liturgy', which 'provided only a very defective expression for the deep and spiritual thoughts contained in his eucharistic teaching'.[42]

In the light of our own foregoing analysis of Calvin's liturgy, we cannot agree with Brilioth's harsh assessment, although neither must we underestimate the effects of the 'external circumstances' to which he alludes, namely the intensity of Calvin's hatred for the Catholic Mass, the influence of the rite already in use in Geneva, and the influence of Bucer in Strasbourg.

In conjunction with his strongly eucharistic theology, Calvin advocated a weekly celebration of the Eucharist. Although he was prevented from implementing this practice by the Genevan magistrates, he still retained the

---

[40] Maxwell, *Genevan Service Book*, pp. 34–5.
[41] Y. Brilioth, *Eucharistic Faith and Practice Evangelical and Catholic* (London: SPCK, 1956), p. 177.
[42] Brilioth, *Eucharistic Faith*, p. 178.

Eucharist as the norm of Sunday morning worship, even when the elements of bread and wine were of necessity not present. The only change that he made to the standard eucharistic service was to omit the Eucharistic Prayer and communion.

The unity of word and sacrament which Calvin sought to maintain by establishing the eucharistic service as the norm for Sunday worship, even on those Sundays when the sacrament was not celebrated, set him apart from Zwingli, for whom the preaching of the word, as the only means of grace, had pre-eminence. When Calvin returned to Geneva in 1541, he found that due to Zwingli's influence the Lord's Supper was generally regarded as a meal of remembrance rather than a means of grace, it was limited to four celebrations a year, and a vernacular prone or preaching service had become the established norm for Sunday worship.

The contrast between Calvin and Zwingli is worth noting because, when Calvin returned to Geneva in 1541, five years after Zwingli's death, the Zwinglian offices were still in use, which probably accounts for some of the bitter resistance to Calvin's proposal to celebrate communion more regularly. So persistent has the hold of Zwingli's liturgy been that H. G. Hageman makes the following observation:

> In the average Reformed or Presbyterian congregation today, customary liturgical practice is that of Zwingli in Zurich, not that of Calvin in Strasbourg. Visit such a congregation next Sunday and you will in most instances discover a Sunday preaching service in which the elements are more or less strung together without any structural relatedness. Four times a year a Communion service is added which, whatever the confessional standards may say, is generally thought of as an act of remembrance.[43]

A comparison between Calvin's Strasbourg rite of 1540 and his Genevan rite of 1542 reveals the latter to be more

[43] H. G. Hageman, *Pulpit and Table* (London: SCM Press, 1962), pp. 33–4.

meagre in structure, probably reflecting the insistence of the Genevan magistrates that the rite be as simple as possible.[44] While the changes made by Calvin to Bucer's rite were slight, it is interesting to note the introduction of the Decalogue in metre, a short Collect for grace to keep God's law, and the substitution of a prayer for pardon for the scriptural words of pardon and absolution following the confession of sins. Taken together, these changes indicate a stronger emphasis on God's law and a corresponding reduction in emphasis on the assurance of God's grace and favour, which have the unfortunate effect of undermining the strong theology of unconditional grace which is so clearly present in Calvin's long Eucharistic Prayer.

Scottish Developments

The *Book of Common Order* (*John Knox's Liturgy*)[45]

The first Reformed rite in English was based on Calvin's Genevan rite of 1542, and printed in Geneva in 1556 under the title, *The Forme of Prayers and Ministration of the Sacraments, &c., used in the Englishe Congregation at Geneua; and approued by the famous and godly man, Iohn Caluin*.[46] John Knox, who was a key figure in the rite's publication during his term as minister of a congregation of English exiles in Geneva, introduced the book to Scotland when he returned from exile in 1559. Once established on Scottish soil, it passed through over seventy editions, was known as the

---

[44] The Strasbourg rite is generally regarded as a better indication of Calvin's preferences. Cf. Maxwell, *Outline of Christian Worship*, p. 115.

[45] Church Service Society, *The Book of Common Order of the Church of Scotland, commonly known as John Knox's Liturgy, 1868* (Edinburgh and London: William Blackwood and Sons, 1901). It was originally published in one volume with the *Westminster Directory*.

[46] Maxwell notes extensive textual evidence which shows that *The Forme of Prayers* is derived directly from Calvin's service book, *La Forme des Prieres*. 'At the same time,' he says, '*The Forme of Prayers* is not a slavish translation, and evidence of an independent spirit is not lacking' (*Outline of Christian Worship*, p. 123).

Forme of Prayers, or the *Book of Common Order*, and was loosely designated as *John Knox's Liturgy*. Adopted by the General Assembly in 1564, it became the standard of worship in Scotland for over eighty years until it was supplanted in 1645 by the Westminster Assembly's *Directory for Public Worship*.

It was during this period that King Charles I and his archbishop, William Laud, sought to unite the churches of England and Scotland. To this end, after many years of careful preparation, the *Scottish Book of Common Prayer* was completed in 1637. Maxwell describes it as an 'excellent production'[47] and a 'noble liturgy, closely affiliated to the English rite of 1549'.[48] However, it was never judged upon its merits because the king's attempt to enforce its use without consulting the Scottish Church resulted in its instant rejection, and the whole country broke out in revolt. With the king's book repudiated, the *Book of Common Order* was restored.

Order of worship

1552	**1868**
The Liturgy of the Word	
Confession of sins[49]	Confession of sins[50]
Prayer for pardon	Prayer for pardon
Psalm in metre	Psalm in metre
Prayer for illumination	Prayer for illumination
Scripture lection	Scripture lection
Sermon	Sermon
The Liturgy of the Upper Room	
Collection of alms	Collection of alms
Prayer for the whole	Prayer for the whole

[47] Maxwell, *Outline of Christian Worship*, p. 128.
[48] Maxwell, *Outline of Christian Worship*, p. 154.
[49] Choice of two, the second one being a development and extension of Calvin's.
[50] Choice of four, the first one being the same as the first option in the 1552 edition.

estate of Christ's church (Intercessions)	estate of Christ's church (Intercessions)[51]
Lord's Prayer	Lord's Prayer
Apostles' Creed	Apostles' Creed
	Prayer of Approach
Words of Institution	Words of Institution
Exhortation[52]	Exhortation[53]
Eucharistic Prayer	Eucharistic Prayer[54]
Fraction	Fraction
Distribution[55]	Distribution[56]
Post-communion thanksgiving[57]	Post-communion thanksgiving[58]
Psalm 103 in metre	Psalm 103 in metre
Blessing	Blessing

Commentary

In his book, *The Faith of John Knox*, James McEwen claims that 'though Knox followed Calvin's doctrine of the sacraments, it was with some change of emphasis, and a very remarkable change of practice'.[59] Calvin's treatment of the sacraments, he argues, exhibits an inconsistency between his description of the Eucharist as a great mystery – a communion in the body and blood of Christ – and his description of it as a mere seal – a useful but not essential stimulus to faith.[60] This belief that the Eucharist is not

[51] Slightly reduced version of 1552 original.
[52] Slightly modified version of Calvin.
[53] Very similar to 1552 version.
[54] Same words as 1552 liturgy.
[55] During which, following a practice begun by Calvin at Geneva, passages of scripture are read concerning Christ's death 'so that our hearts and minds also may be fully fixed in the contemplation of the Lord's death, which is by this holy Sacrament represented' (Genevan Liturgy, *Genevan Service Book*, pp. 126–7).
[56] Same action as 1552 liturgy.
[57] Slight amplification of Calvin's post–communion prayer, which itself can be traced back to Bucer's liturgy.
[58] Same words as 1552 liturgy.
[59] McEwen, *Faith of John Knox*, p. 55.
[60] McEwen refers to Calvin's discourse on baptism, in which Calvin says that the efficacy of God's covenant promise does not depend on the rite of baptism itself (*In.* IV.15.22). Calvin makes this comment in the context of

absolutely essential to the life of the Church, McEwen observes, led Calvin to advise postponement of the sacrament in situations of persecution and disorganisation – that is, when orderly discipline was impossible.[61] Because sacraments belong to the full life of the organised Church, where the organised Church does not yet exist, individual piety will not be hurt by their absence.

By way of contrast, McEwen argues, for Knox there was no question of waiting for the establishment of an organised church before administering the sacrament. 'Wherever two or three could be gathered together, there Knox administered Communion, carefully noting the date and place of celebration as important and significant events. The inference is clear: the Sacrament had an importance and a vital quality to Knox that it apparently did not have to Calvin.'[62]

McEwen goes on to point out that Knox's attitude and practice were derived from his theological convictions, which are laid out in a little document prepared by him on the occasion of him being summoned to stand trial before the Council of the North during his ministry in the North of England. In a remarkable and striking way Knox refers the whole action of the sacrament to Christ. As McEwen puts it:

---

asserting that infants are not barred from the kingdom of heaven just because they happen to die before they have been baptised. He goes on to say that when we cannot receive the sacraments from the Church, 'the grace of God is not so bound up with them that we cannot obtain it by faith from the Word of the Lord'. McEwen interprets this statement to mean that for Calvin the sacraments become peripheral, and that 'it is the Word alone – not the unity of Word and Sacrament – that he regards as central in the Church's life'. Calvin's statement here, however, does not have to be interpreted in this way. Perhaps it is simply the case that while the *sign* and the *thing signified* are integrally related in his theology of the sacraments, he does not equate the two in such a way that the efficacy of the thing signified is regarded as being dependent upon the sign itself. Interpreted in this way, McEwen's contrast between Knox and Calvin appears to be overstated.

[61] McEwen gives the example of Calvin discouraging the persecuted Huguenots of France from seeking to institute the celebration of the sacraments on the grounds that 'the celebration of these could well wait until such time as they had the opportunity to organise their Church in an orderly manner' (*Faith of John Knox*, p. 53).

[62] McEwen, *Faith of John Knox*, p. 56.

There is nothing at all about what 'we' do, or what the Church does. The Sacrament is not looked on as a ministerial act, or a Churchly ordinance. It is, first and last, something that Christ does for us. 'The Lord Jesus, by earthly and visible things set before us, lifteth us up to heavenly and invisible things – He prepares His spiritual banquet – He witnesses that He Himself was the living bread – He sets forth the bread and wine to eat and drink – He giveth unto us Himself – and all this He does through the power of the Holy Ghost.'[63]

Immediately following this, McEwen notes, Knox writes something even more significant: 'Herewith, also, the Lord Jesus gathers us unto one visible body, so that we be members one of another, and make altogether one body, whereof Jesus Christ is the only Head.' McEwen concludes from these words that, in Knox's opinion, Christ does not merely gather and create the Church – he gathers and creates it *by this sacrament*, and *on this sacrament he founds it*.[64] McEwen identifies the same emphasis in the *Scots Confession*, which, he says, speaks of the dynamic presence of Christ 'with such earnestness that it passes over into something more than Calvin's Calvinism, and certainly more than the Calvinism of any of Calvin's successors elsewhere than in Scotland'.[65]

The grounds for assessing McEwen's thesis concerning the difference between Knox and Calvin must be sought elsewhere than in a comparison of their liturgies, for such a comparison reveals only the extent to which Knox has relied upon Calvin's liturgy for the drafting of his own. Indeed, Knox certainly followed Calvin rather than Zwingli in his understanding of the relationship between word and sacrament and, like Calvin, he made the eucharistic service the pattern for regular Sunday worship.

Knox's liturgy begins with the minister 'exhorting the people diligently to examine themselves' through the

---

[63] Knox, *Works*, III, pp. 73ff., cited by McEwen, *Faith of John Knox*, p. 56.
[64] McEwen, *Faith of John Knox*, pp. 56–7.
[65] McEwen, *Faith of John Knox*, p. 58.

Confiteor.[66] This tendency to begin worship with the confession of sins constitutes a real weakness in Reformed thinking as it focuses one's attention first on oneself and one's sins and only then on God and his glory. Far better that worship begin with an act of praise and adoration, setting forth the glory and majesty of the triune God by whose mercy sinners have been redeemed, which then reveals to them the real extent of their alienation, both from God and from each other. God's grace is not merely that which forgives people their sin; it is that which also *reveals* to them their sin.[67]

Like Bucer's and Calvin's rites, the first *Confiteor* in Knox's liturgy refers to the fact that we are 'conceived and born in sin', thereby acknowledging the ontological as well as moral dimension to the human state of alienation from God. The prayer concludes with an expression of confidence that God's 'Spirit doth assure our consciences that Thou art our merciful Father, and so lovest us Thy children through Him, that nothing is able to remove Thy heavenly grace and favour from us'. In both the 1552 original and subsequent versions a selection of *Confiteors* is provided, the tenor and structure remaining the same, and all concluding with a prayer for pardon.

In the Liturgy of the Upper Room, it is interesting to note the relocation of the Words of Institution. In Schwarz's liturgy, they are contained in the Eucharistic Prayer. In Bucer's liturgy, they are read out in narrative form immediately prior to the distribution of the elements and following the prayer of Consecration and a short Exhortation. Calvin's liturgy follows Bucer's in locating the Words of Institution towards the end of the liturgy, but it has the Exhortation following rather than preceding them. However, in Knox's liturgy, the change is more pronounced, for the Words of Institution are placed towards the beginning of the liturgy, *prior* to the Consecration prayer, so that they serve as a *warrant*

---

[66] Unlike Calvin, who at least began his service with a scripture sentence: Ps. 124:8.

[67] Cf. W. D. Maxwell, *Concerning Worship* (London: Oxford University Press, 1948), p. 31.

PRAYER AND THE PRIESTHOOD OF CHRIST

for what follows. While Maxwell is correct in observing that the use of the Words of Institution as a warrant is a quite catholic practice,[68] a question is raised about the theological appropriateness of such practice. By including the Words of Institution within the *anamnesis* section of the Eucharistic Prayer, the Words shed their didactic function and become more integrated into the act of worship. They also avoid giving rise to the inference that the Church is having communion simply because Jesus did it and told his followers to do it.

The lengthy Exhortation that immediately follows the Words of Institution, constitutes a strong call to self-examination, mindful of 'the danger great if we receive ... unworthily, for then we ... eat and drink our own damnation, not considering the Lord's body, we kindle God's wrath against us, and provoke Him to plague us with divers diseases and sundry kinds of death'.

As we discussed more fully in Chapter Two, McEwen relates this Exhortation to self-examination to the issue of ecclesiastical discipline. He notes the close link between the Lord's Supper and discipline in Knox's thinking, and argues that the discipline, which the Reformed Church insisted upon exercising, was an expression neither of legalism nor of over-scrupulous moralism. As we also noted at that time, his view that the aim of Knox's Exhortation is to prevent profanation of the sacrament rather than exclude sinners from the Table is supported by the declarations which follow the pronouncement of excommunication.

The main difference between the liturgies of Knox and Calvin is found in the Eucharistic Prayer. Knox's prayer, comments Maxwell, 'is not derived from any known source, and appears therefore to be wholly the work of the compilers themselves. It does not follow Calvin.'[69] Maxwell identifies the following components in the prayer: adoration, thanksgiving for creation and redemption, *anamnesis*, doxology. However, he incorrectly describes the

---

Maxwell, *Genevan Service Book*, pp. 128–9.
Maxwell, *Genevan Service Book*, p. 134.

prayer as a Prayer of Consecration. It is an incorrect description because, as Bard Thompson notes, '*The Forme of Prayers* made no provision for a consecration of the elements. The Word, which supplied validity and reality to the sacrament, was not addressed to the bread and wine, as if to change them; it was addressed to the people. So (said the appendix) that "Christe might witnes vnto owr faithe, as it were, with his owne mowthe," promising us the communion of his body and blood. Thus, the essential point was the lively preaching of the promises of Christ, which underlay the Lord's Supper.'[70] Knox clearly followed Calvin in this regard.

Structurally, Knox's prayer is considerably shorter and more direct because it deletes the long prayer of Intercession with which Calvin's prayer begins, and it substitutes a proper prayer of Thanksgiving for the much longer petitionary prayer of Calvin. As we noted above, Knox followed Calvin in omitting the *epiclesis* or prayer of Consecration from the prayer. Maxwell notes, however, that 'the lack of an *epiclesis* was soon generally felt, and though one does not appear in the texts until later, there is evidence that an *epiclesis* was comparatively early supplied in practice'.[71]

Knox's prayer of Thanksgiving, which can be divided into two main sections, is thoroughly christological. The first section gratefully calls to mind the work of God who, 'rich in mercy and infinite in goodness' has provided for our redemption *in his Son*, who received the 'punishment of our transgression', *by his death* made 'satisfaction' to God's justice, and *by his resurrection* destroyed the 'author of death'. The second section expresses awe at the length and breadth of God's mercy and grace, through which believers have been brought to the Table, which Christ

> ... hath left to be used in remembrance of His death, until His coming again, to declare and witness before

---

[70] *Liturgies of the Western Church*, p. 292.
[71] Maxwell, *Outline of Christian Worship*, p. 124.

the world, that *by Him alone* we have received liberty
and life, that *by Him alone* Thou dost acknowledge us
Thy children and heirs, that *by Him alone* we have
entrance to the throne of Thy grace, that *by Him alone*
we are possessed in our spiritual Kingdom, to eat and
drink at His Table, *with whom* we have our conversation presently in heaven, and *by whom* our bodies
shall be raised up again from the dust, and shall be
placed with Him in that endless joy.[72]

Two things are worth noting here. First, the above-
italicised words highlight the extent to which the
mediatorial role of Christ, retrospectively in the incarnation and prospectively in the ascension, is stressed in
Knox's prayer of Thanksgiving. Second, and in conjunction
with the first point, while the Eucharist is described in
terms of a 'remembrance' (*anamnesis*) meal, it is a meal in
which Christ himself is present – it is, after all, *his* Table –
drawing people by the Holy Spirit into union and
communion with himself, and through himself with the
Father. The eucharistic *anamnesis*, thus understood, is not
merely something which the Church does by way of
remembrance in consciousness, word and deed of the
historical self-offering of Jesus Christ once and for all on
the cross. It is something that is done in and through the
real presence of the risen and ascended High Priest, in
whose self-consecration and self-offering made on the
world's behalf the Church is given to participate through
the Holy Spirit. As T. F. Torrance puts it, 'when we in the
Eucharist remember his passion and plead his atoning
sacrifice, this is not a mere recollection of what he has done
for us once and for all on the Cross, but the setting forth of
a memorial or *anamnesis*, according to his command, which
through the Spirit is filled with the presence of Christ in the
indivisible unity of all his vicarious work and his glorified
Person'.[73] He also notes the immense significance of the

---

[72] *Book of Common Order*, pp. 124–5 (italics mine).
[73] Torrance, *Theology in Reconciliation*, p. 136.

Sursum Corda[74] in this regard,[75] and it is a matter of regret that it was omitted from these early Reformed liturgies.

In conjunction with this, Knox's liturgy could have benefited from a more explicit pneumatology, thereby strengthening the sense of being in union and communion with the risen and ascended Christ, and actively participating in his *koinonia* with the Father, rather than merely remembering his death and its benefits. This would have the added advantage of enhancing the tone of the liturgy, for its rather sombre tone would be lightened by a note of joy; the meal of remembrance would become also an eschatological banquet.

The remembrance of Jesus' death and its benefits is a prominent feature of the prayer of Thanksgiving. It is reinforced by the distribution of the elements, during which a portion of scripture is read, 'which doth lively set forth the *death* of Christ, to the intent that our eyes and senses may not only be occupied in these outward signs of bread and wine, which are called the visible word, but that our hearts and minds also may be fully fixed in the contemplation of the Lord's death, which is by this holy Sacrament represented'.[76] However, as we have already noted in relation to Knox's doctrine of prayer, when the traditional forensic language, which describes the redemptive purposes of Christ's death, is viewed in relation to his prior emphasis upon the mediatorial role of Christ as High Priest, then the atonement is to be understood not in terms of the man Jesus placating a wrathful God, but rather in terms of a propitiatory sacrifice in which God himself through the death of his Son draws near to humankind and draws humankind near to himself. So it is that in the Thanksgiving, thanks is rendered unto the Father, who is 'rich in mercie and infinite in goodness', for having 'prouided our redemption' in and through his Son who in his body received 'the ponishmentes of our transgression', by his death made 'satisfaction to thy iustice', and by his resurrection destroyed him 'that was auctor of death', thereby bringing

---

[74] The *Sursum Corda* ('Lift up your hearts') is the call to thanksgiving, leading to the prayer of Thanksgiving.
[75] Torrance, *Theology in Reconciliation*, p. 128.
[76] *Book of Common Order*, p. 125 (italics mine).

'agayne life to the world, frome which the whole offspring of Adame moste iustly was exiled'. The overwhelming impression created by this passage is not of an angry God who holds himself aloof, waiting to be placated, but rather, of a merciful God who suffers in and with Christ to reconcile the world to himself. Moreover, there is no suggestion that Christ, through his atoning death, has brought life only to the elect. Rather, he has brought life 'to the *world*'.

Following the communion itself, the liturgy concludes with a short prayer of Thanksgiving, which is very similar to Calvin's and Bucer's, and the singing of Psalm 103, or some other appropriate thanksgiving. Whereas the main focus of the pre-communion prayer of Thanksgiving is on the redemption which people have been granted in Christ, the primary focus of the post-communion prayer is on their inclusion in the 'fellowship and company' of Christ. The theological question that is posed here, however, is why this stress on belonging is delayed until the end of the service rather than being declared at the outset. If, through the mediatorial work of Christ and the work of the Spirit, one's belonging is already assured and the fellowship of the Church is already a reality, and the sacrament is a sign and seal of these existing facts, then is it not inappropriate to infer that it is only because one has received that one then can be referred to as 'belonging' and having 'fellowship'?[77]

Overall, despite these critical comments, there is much to commend Knox's liturgy. Maxwell describes it in terms of 'the Eucharist reduced to its simplest elements, but ... it is by no means an inadequate vehicle of devotion, and its composition is unmistakably catholic'.[78]

The Westminster Directory for Public Worship

The chief architects of the *Directory* were clergy of the Church of England, most of whom were of Presbyterian or Puritan persuasion, assisted by a small group of Independents and

---

[77] I owe this point to Alan Torrance's unpublished notes on eucharistic liturgies.
[78] Maxwell, *Outline of Christian Worship*, p. 124.

Scottish assessors. Understandably, given this mix of personnel, the *Directory* represents a compromise, and exhibits the influence of both the English *Book of Common Prayer* and the Scottish *Book of Common Order*. It was adopted by the General Assembly in 1645, and is still a standard of worship in the Church of Scotland, although from the outset its use was not made mandatory. While it contains no prayers as such, its directions concerning the order and content of worship are comprehensive and, as Maxwell points out, if followed in every detail, would easily fill 'three hours on ordinary Sundays and many more at the communion'.

Order of worship

> *Liturgy of the Word*
> Summons to worship
> Prayer of approach:
>> Adoration
>> Supplication for worthiness to stand before God
>> Prayer for illumination of holy scripture
> Scripture Lections:
>> A chapter from each Testament, interspersed by a metrical psalm
> Lecture
> Confession of sins
> Prayer for pardon
> Absolution for a sanctified life
> Sermon
> General Prayer:
>> Thanksgiving (especially for the gospel and redemption)
>> Supplications (related to the sermon)
>> Self-oblation and a petition that the spiritual sacrifice of worship be acceptable to God
>> General intercessions
>
> *Liturgy of the Upper Room*
> Offertory psalm and procession of the elements
> Exhortation
> Fencing of the tables

Words of institution
Prayer of Consecration:
  Prayer for access
  Thanksgiving for creation and providence,
  redemption, the word and sacraments
  Anamnesis
  Epiclesis
  Lord's Prayer
Fraction
Delivery and communion
Exhortation to live a worthy life
Post-communion prayer:
  Thanksgiving for benefits received in Communion
  Prayer for a worthy life
Metrical Psalm
Blessing

Commentary

Three things worked against the *Directory*'s use in the Church. First, the minuteness of detail and sheer length rendered the recommended Order of Worship impractical. Second, its use was never made compulsory, and at the Restoration Parliament annulled the Act by which it had been introduced. Third, the lack of a common mind in the Church – the *Directory* was issued in a period of ecclesiastical turmoil and division – meant that most ministers simply ignored it and continued in their ways.

The first thing to note about the *Directory* is the heavy emphasis placed upon the preaching of the word, which reflected a tendency in the sixteenth-century Reformed Church to view the Eucharist as a peripheral rather than central act of the Church. 'Out of twelve pages describing the normal Sunday service,' Gordon Donaldson observes, 'ten are taken up with "Public Prayer before the Sermon", "Of the Preaching of the Word" (designed to instruct the minister in the structure of his sermon) and "Of Prayer after Sermon".'[79]

---

[79] G. Donaldson, 'Covenant to Revolution', *Studies in the History of Worship in Scotland*, second edn, eds D. Forrester and D. Murray (Edinburgh: T&T Clark, 1996), p. 60.

The other striking feature of the recommended Order of
Worship, apart from its length, is the emphasis laid upon
the 'benefits' and 'merits' of Christ in the prayer of
Thanksgiving, about which the following words, or
something to their effect, are recommended:

> With humble and hearty acknowledgment of the
> greatness of our misery, from which neither man nor
> angel was able to deliver us, and of our great unwor-
> thiness of the least of all God's mercies: To give
> thanks to God for all His *benefits*, and especially for
> that great *benefit* of our redemption, the love of God
> the Father, the suffering and *merits* of the Lord Jesus
> Christ the Son of God, by which we are delivered; and
> for all the means of grace; and for this Sacrament in
> particular, by which Christ, and all His *benefits*, are
> applied and sealed up unto us, which, notwith-
> standing the denial of them unto others, are in great
> mercy continued unto us, after so much and long
> abuse of them all . . . [80]

The portrayal of redemption in the above prayer is that of
Christ, through his 'merits', purchasing salvation for the elect,
the 'benefits' of which may now may be 'applied' and 'sealed'
through the sacrament. It is a rather impersonal and transactional portrayal, likely reflecting Puritan influence and the
theological mindset forged by federal Calvinism.

However, because of the *Directory*'s limited use, of main
interest to us is not what the *Directory* contains, but what
kind of worship and public prayer emerged in its wake.
Having already touched upon this subject in Chapter Three,
we simply note here J. M. Barkley's description of this period
of liturgical history as a 'chaotic situation in which, broadly
speaking, "every man did that which was right in his own
eyes"'.[81] The strong suspicion of set liturgies was generated

---

[80] The Westminster Directory, 1644, cited in *Prayers of the Eucharist: Early
and Reformed*, eds R. C. D. Jasper and G. J. Cuming (London: Collins, 1975),
pp. 176–7 (italics mine).
[81] Barkley, *Worship of the Reformed Church*, p. 31.

not only by the Scottish reaction against Laud's liturgy but by the growing influence of English Puritanism, with its stress upon 'freedom' in worship. 'It was for a long time believed', writes James Moffatt, 'that spontaneous, unpremeditated prayer was more inspired than any carefully drawn up collect.'[82] Even the Lord's Prayer was tabooed.[83]

One of the regrettable consequences of this Puritan emphasis upon free prayer and free worship without any ritual was the failure to grasp the opportunity to focus on the Sole Priesthood of Christ as the true ground of a proper liturgical theology. As a result, worship became rather Pelagian, if not in theory then at least in practice, with the focus very much on what *we* must do to worship in an authentic manner. Maxwell notes many changes to the nature of worship and prayer during this period, which lasted until the mid-nineteenth century. While the details are beyond the scope of this book,[84] he provides us with a succinct picture of worship from the latter half of the seventeenth century:

> Communion was celebrated very infrequently, the structure of the ordinary services was bare in the extreme, sometimes reduced to the singing of a metrical psalm, followed by a long prayer, another psalm, the sermon, and a concluding prayer, after which another psalm was sung, followed by the benediction.[85]

The *Euchologion* and the *Prayers for Divine Service*

Despite some liturgical developments in the eighteenth

---

[82] J. Moffatt, *The Presbyterian Churches* (London: 1928), p. 149, cited by Maxwell in *Outline of Christian Worship*, p. 133.

[83] Wakefield notes that John Owen was vehemently against all liturgies, and John Bunyan once stated that even the Lord's Prayer can become blasphemous if uttered without Spirit or understanding (cf. Wakefield, *Puritan Devotion*, p. 69).

[84] A detailed description of the changes can be found in Maxwell's *Worship in the Church of Scotland*, chapters 4 and 5 and in Donaldson's 'Covenant to Revolution', pp. 59–72.

[85] Maxwell, *Outline of Christian Worship*, p. 132.

century,[86] liturgical revival in the fuller sense did not come until the second half of the nineteenth century. This was due in large part – as we noted in the previous chapter – to a reform movement that was fostered principally by the strong body of scholars who formed the Church Service Society in 1865, and two years later issued a service book, *Euchologion*. It passed through many editions, and played a significant role in the re-formation of worship in the Reformed tradition. We also noted in the previous chapter the doctrinal impact of the Scottish Church Society,[87] which, as Duncan Forrester notes, manifested itself in the Church Service Society becoming more high church as time went on and exerting considerable influence in the Committee on Public Worship and Aids to Devotion.[88] In 1923 the General Assembly of the Church of Scotland authorised the publication of its own service book, *Prayers for Divine Service*, the content of which was drawn largely from the *Euchologion*. Five years later, in 1928, the United Free Church of Scotland, on the eve of union with the Church of Scotland, published the *Book of Common Order* which, together with *Euchologion*, became the standard of worship in the reunited Church of Scotland. The *Prayers for Divine Service*, 1929, and the *Book of Common Order*, 1928, were replaced by the *Book of Common Order*, 1940, which attempted to combine the best features of its predecessors and included much of the material supplied in them.

[86] Cf. Henry Sefton's account of worship in eighteenth-century Scotland in 'Revolution to Disruption', in *Studies in the History of Worship in Scotland*, pp. 73–85.

[87] Societies similar to the Church Service Society were formed in the other two main Presbyterian Churches: The United Presbyterian Devotional Service Association was founded in 1882, and the Free Church followed in 1891 with the formation of the Public Worship Association – cf. D. M. Murray, 'Disruption to Union', in *Studies in the History of Worship in Scotland*, p. 97.

[88] D. Forrester, 'Worship since 1929', in *Studies in the History of Worship in Scotland*, p. 178.

Order of worship

Euchologion (6th edn), 1890	*Prayers for Divine Service*, 1929
Liturgy of the Word	
Psalm or hymn	Psalm (sung)
Scripture sentence and Call to Worship	Scripture sentence
Prayers of Invocation and Confession	Prayers of Invocation and Confession
Prayer for Pardon and Peace	Prayer for Pardon
Supplications	
Congregational Response: Psalm (said or sung), ascription of glory	Psalm (read or sung)
Lections, with *Te Deum Laudamus* hymn or psalm in between *Benedictus*	Lections, with hymn or psalm in between
Apostles' Creed	Apostles' Creed or Nicene Creed
Extended prayer of Intercession	Prayer of Intercession
Prayer of Thanksgiving	
Psalm, hymn or anthem	Hymn or psalm
Prayer for Illumination	Collect for Illumination
Sermon	Sermon
Ascription of praise	
Prayer after sermon	Post-sermon collect
Liturgy of the Upper Room	
Exhortation	
Collection of alms	Collection of alms
	Brief invitation to the Lord's Table
Psalm or hymn, while	Singing of Paraphrase

elements brought to Table	35, while elements brought to Table
Words of Institution	Words of Institution
Instructional address	
Nicene Creed[89]	
Prayer of access, including *Agnus Dei* and *Sursum Corda*	Prayer of access, concluding in *Sursum Corda*
Eucharistic Prayer, concluding in *Sanctus* and *Benedictus*	Eucharistic Prayer, concluding in *Sanctus* and *Benedictus*
Invocation	Consecration and Intercessions, concluding in *Agnus Dei*
Lord's Prayer	Lord's Prayer
Fraction	Fraction
Delivery	Delivery
Peace	Peace
Exhortation to thankfulness	Exhortation to thankfulness
Post-Communion Prayer: Thanks and self-dedication	Post-Communion Prayer: Thanks and self-dedication
Intercession for Church militant and thanks for Church triumphant	Intercessions (if not included with prayer of consecration)
Nunc Dimittis, Gloria in Excelsis or other hymn sung	Psalm 103:1–5 or other psalm sung
Benediction	Blessing

Commentary

The *Euchologion*[90]

The *Euchologion* provides Orders of Divine Service, morning

---

[89] The Nicene Creed has been substituted for the Apostles' Creed at this point in the service. The first edition of *Euchologion* followed the customary practice of reciting the latter.

[90] Our analysis of the communion liturgy here is based on the sixth edition of 1890, which gives us a good idea of the form and content of the communion

and evening, for each of the five Sundays of the month. The structure remains the same for all the morning services. On Communion Sundays the service is conducted as on other Sundays, but with the addition of the prescribed Order for the Celebration of the Lord's Supper. In this regard, Maxwell notes that the *Euchologion*'s chief defect was that in the sixth edition 'the structure of the ordinary morning worship was assimilated to the structure of Anglican Morning Prayer, instead of following the ancient Reformed Church norm of Ante-Communion'.[91] Maxwell's criticism here alludes to the point made in the previous chapter that the Church Service Society was more concerned about the pragmatics of reform than the theological reasons for reform. As the Preface to the first edition of the *Euchologion* states, one of its principal aims is to do nothing more than provide a resource for 'a worship more solemn, uniform, and devout, than ... our non-liturgical service sometimes is'.[92]

The shift away from the norm of Ante-Communion is significant, not only because it shifts the Eucharist from the centre to the periphery of Reformed worship, thereby changing the pattern of worship, but also because it undermines the strongly eucharistic theology established in the Reformed tradition by Calvin and the early Scottish Reformers. In particular, the doctrine of the priesthood of Christ, which is an integral part of eucharistic worship, is severely diminished, one of the results of which is a more Pelagian conception of worship and prayer, as is seen by the location of the prayers of Intercession before both the sermon and the liturgy of the Eucharist.

The insertion into the liturgy of an opening psalm or hymn and a prayer of Invocation is to be welcomed, insofar

---

service only two years before the formation of the Scottish Church Society. A comparison of various editions of the *Euchologion*, from the first edition in 1867 through to the eighth in 1905, shows that while there are significant changes and additions to the service book overall, including the provision of complete services for non-communion Sundays and prayers for many different occasions, the actual communion service itself remains substantially the same.

[91] Maxwell, *Outline of Christian Worship*, p. 134; cf. also Douglas Murray's summary of this controversial change in 'Disruption to Union', in *Studies in the History of Worship in Scotland*, p. 96.

[92] Church Service Society, *Euchologion* (Edinburgh and London: William Blackwood and Sons, 1867), pp. ix–x.

as these things focus the congregation's attention on God
rather than on the congregation itself, thereby helping to
rectify the rather introspective focus of earlier Reformed
liturgies. Three of the five prayers of Confession in the
sixth edition begin with words based on 1 John 1:8–9, 'If
we say we have no sin, we deceive ourselves, and the truth
is not in us. If we confess our sins, Thou art faithful and just
to forgive us our sins, and to cleanse us from all unrighteousness.' While this statement is biblical, when it is
detached from the assurance of Christ's advocacy and
atoning sacrifice which immediately follows it in 1 John,[93]
and which constituted the Absolution in Schwarz's liturgy,
all the emphasis goes on the 'If', thereby implying a
contractual rather than a covenantal understanding of
grace: *If* we confess our sins, then God will forgive us. That
this is the case is suggested by the confession that follows.
It tends to focus on those acts that separate people from
God, while the ontological dimension of sin goes
unacknowledged. Moreover, there is a corresponding
failure to acknowledge the healing and sanctification of
our sinful human condition in the person of Christ, which
in turn contributes to a withholding of an unconditional
assurance of divine pardon. There is, instead, only a prayer
for pardon and peace. Worshippers confess their sins not
because they have been forgiven and sanctified in Christ
but, rather, *in the hope* that they will be forgiven.
Forgiveness and reconciliation with God are held forth as
future possibilities rather than existing and unassailable
facts based on one's atonement in Christ and the assurance
of his advocacy on behalf of oneself and all sinners. In
accordance with this view, the prayer of Access, which
leads into the Eucharistic Prayer, implores God to grant
believers the assurance of mercy.[94]

Four out of the five prayers of Intercession begin with the
words, 'O God, who hast taught us to make supplications,

---

[93] The affirmation is found in 1 John 2:1–2, which reads: 'But if anyone
does sin, *we have an advocate* with the Father, Jesus Christ the righteous;
and *he is the atoning sacrifice* for our sins, and not for ours only but also *for
the sins of the whole world*' (italics mine).

[94] *Euchologion*, 1890, p. 295.

prayers, intercessions, and giving of thanks for all men, we humbly beseech Thee to receive these our prayers which we offer to Thy divine majesty.' Christ is portrayed in these words as the *exemplar* of prayer whose example the Church follows rather than the ascended High Priest in whose life of intercession the Church participates by the Spirit. This separation of *the Church*'s intercessions from those of *Christ* is further emphasised by the placement of the prayer very early on in the service, prior to the sermon, and far removed from the liturgy of the Eucharist where the priesthood of Christ is given its strongest emphasis.

The Exhortation with which the Liturgy of Holy Communion begins is a condensed, modified and toned-down version of that found in Knox's liturgy. Gone is the long declaration of excommunication of all blasphemers, idolators, murderers, adulterers, etc. from the Table, and in its place is a simple exhortation to examine one's conscience to 'know whether you truly repent of your sins, and whether, trusting in God's mercy, and seeking your whole salvation in Jesus Christ, you are resolved to follow holiness, and to live in peace and charity with all men'.[95] Interesting here is the explicit reference to the 'conscience', a reference which is lacking in Knox's liturgy, which simply exhorts people to 'examine themselves'. The reference is perhaps indicative of the legacy of Puritanism in Reformed theology, which we have already identified in our discussion of the theology of William Perkins, namely, a belief that the conscience was unaffected by the Fall and therefore has the capacity to convict us of our sin. The conscience is thus regarded as being part of the realm of nature (Adam) as opposed to the realm of grace (Christ).

One of the strengths of the *Euchologion* liturgy is to be found in the Address which follows the Words of Institution, and which provides the theological rationale for the sacrament.[96] Especially noteworthy is the uncompromising

---

[95] *Euchologion*, 1890, p. 288.
[96] While the Address of the first edition of the *Euchologion* is quite different in wording from those of subsequent editions, it gives the same theological emphases.

emphasis upon the mediatorial role of Christ, the redemptive significance of the incarnation, the miraculous exchange, and union with Christ in the Spirit.[97]

The reintroduction of the *Sursum Corda* into the liturgy is to be welcomed,[98] for it highlights the participatory nature of worship and prayer in the *enhypostatic*, or human-Godward, movement of divine grace. Theologically, the lifting of the congregation's hearts in the Eucharist is to be conceived as their being brought by the Spirit to participate in the perfect praise and adoration that Christ the High Priest offers on humanity's behalf.

Whereas the Thanksgiving prayer in Knox's liturgy focuses primarily on Christ's death and its benefits, the *Euchologion*'s Eucharistic Prayer refers also to his incarnation, resurrection and ascension: 'Not as we ought, but as we are able, we bless Thee for His holy incarnation; for His life on earth; for His precious sufferings and death upon the cross; for His resurrection from the dead; and for His glorious ascension to Thy right hand.'[99]

The words which accompany the fraction follow the earliest church liturgies in providing four parallelisms that focus attention on the once and for all priesthood of Christ and the 'wondrous exchange' which stood at the centre of Calvin's doctrine of the Eucharist:[100]

1. 'took bread' is a parallelism for Christ taking human flesh, which refers to the incarnation.
2. 'gave thanks' is a parallelism for Christ's offering of vicarious gratitude on our behalf as the One who is the priest of our humanity and whose ministry is initiated and sanctified by the descent of the Spirit.
3. 'brake it' is a parallelism for Christ going to the cross on our behalf, suffering death in vicarious atonement.
4. 'Take, eat', the words of delivery, constitute a parallelism

---

[97] Cf. *Euchologion*, 1890, pp. 290–2.
[98] The *Sursum Corda* was not included in the first edition of the *Euchologion*.
[99] *Euchologion*, 1890, p. 295.
[100] The existence of these parallelisms has been brought to my attention by Alan Torrance's unpublished notes on Eucharistic liturgies.

for Christ giving himself to us, uniting us with himself so that we might participate in his priesthood.

Prayers for Divine Service

Unlike the *Euchologion* the *Prayers for Divine Service* contains a full Form and Order for the Celebration of Holy Communion, rather than merely adding a communion liturgy on to an ordinary non-eucharistic Order of Divine Service. While its prayer of confession omits the problematic opening reference to 1 John 1:8–9, it does not succeed in overcoming other problems already noted in relation to Reformed prayers of Confession, namely, a failure to acknowledge the ontological as well as the moral dimension of sin, and the tendency to conclude the prayer with a prayer for pardon rather than a declaration of pardon.

The only other point worth noting is the similarity of wording between the *Euchologion* and *Prayers for Divine Service*, which means that the comments made in relation to the individual parts of *Euchologion* order of worship also apply here, and need not be repeated.

Book of Common Order, 1940

Order of worship

> *Liturgy of the Word*
> Call to Worship
> Psalm or hymn, such as Psalm 43:3–5
> Scripture sentence, such as Psalm 116:12–14
> Collect for purity[101]
> Confession
> Prayer for pardon
> Canticle, psalm or hymn
> Lections, interspersed with sung psalm ending with the *Gloria*

---

[101] Taken from the *Book of Common Prayer*.

(Nicene Creed)
Intercessions and Commemoration of Departed
Psalm or hymn
Intimations
Prayer for Illumination
Sermon
Ascription

Liturgy of the Upper Room
Offertory
Invitation with comfortable words
Psalm 24:7–10, Para. 35, psalm or hymn, while elements brought to Table
Nicene Creed
Prayer of approach
Offertory prayer
Words of Institution
Salutation and warrant
Sursum Corda
Eucharistic Prayer, including
   Sanctus and *Benedictus*,
   Thanksgiving and consecration
   Self-oblation
Lord's Prayer
Fraction
Agnus Dei
Delivery
Peace
Post-communion prayer:
   Thanksgiving
   Commemoration of the departed
Psalm 103:1–5, or other psalm or hymn
Benediction

Commentary

The *Book of Common Order*, 1940, provides four Orders for Holy Communion, two of which are designed for such occasions as demand brevity. Our commentary will be confined to the first of the two 'fuller' Orders, which closely approximates in language and arrangement to the service in the *Ordinal for use in the Courts of the Church*, which was issued by authority of the General Assembly in 1931 following the union of the United Free Church of Scotland with the Church of Scotland. It attempts to combine the best features of the *Prayers for Divine Service*, 1923 and 1929, and the *Book of Common Order*, 1928, as does the alternative Order, which is provided 'for Congregations in which the more rigid traditional forms may be felt to be unsuitable'.[102]

Without repeating comments already made in relation to preceding liturgies, we simply note the following recurring features: the Confession does not contain any acknowledgement of the condition into which we are born; the Confession concludes with a prayer for pardon rather than an absolution; Intercessions are made prior to the communion liturgy, perpetuating the unfortunate practice that we noted in relation to the sixth edition of *Euchologion*; the Words of Institution are located outside of the prayer of Thanksgiving; and the words accompanying the fraction follow the same pattern as the *Euchologion*.

Overall, the liturgy reflects the developing richness of the Scottish liturgical tradition. It has a clear structure, is participatory, and is catholic in form and content. In addition, it has two significant features that are worthy of comment. The first is the substitution of an Invitation to the Table[103] for the old 'Calvinist' Exhortation and the *Euchologion*'s Instructional address. This substitution represents a movement away from the tendency towards the overly introspective habit of self-examination that had become so characteristic of the Westminster tradition.

The second feature is the insertion into the Eucharistic Prayer of a phrase that describes the Lord's Supper in terms of 'pleading His eternal sacrifice'.[104] This phrase is

---

[102] *Book of Common Order*, 1940, p. iv.

[103] The Invitation is constituted by the words of Christ: 'Come unto me, all ye that labour'; 'I am the bread of life: he that cometh to Me shall never hunger'; 'Blessed are they which do hunger'.

[104] The relevant section of the prayer reads: 'Wherefore, having in remembrance the work and passion of our Saviour Christ, and *pleading his eternal sacrifice*, we, Thy servants do set forth this memorial, which he hath commanded us to make' (*Book of Common Order*, 1940, p. 119).

found in neither of the precursors to the 1940 *Book of Common Order* – the *Euchologion* and the *Prayers for Divine Service*. Bryan Spinks traces it instead to the United Church of Canada's 1932 liturgy. Interestingly, he notes, W. D. Maxwell was a member of the drafting committee which put the Canadian liturgy together before he moved to Scotland, where he had a hand in preparing the 1940 *Book of Common Order*.[105] Commenting on the phrase in a subsequent report to the World Council of Churches' Theological Commission of Faith and Order, Maxwell said that when we plead Christ's eternal sacrifice

> ... we desire Him to unite our offering and prayers with His,[106] which is eternal, and 'this memorial' in time and space is part of that eternal memorial. His sacrifice is not repeatable, but it is continually renewed; the 'remembering' is not mere recollection in the psychological sense (which, in fact, is never the biblical sense), but a real uniting, possible by grace and through faith, faith which is not mere intellectual assent, but a committal of the whole person to Him. It is, thus, as Calvin declares, a *vera communicatio* with Him.[107]

Although the phrase 'pleading his eternal sacrifice' seems to have had its liturgical origins with the 1932 Canadian *Book of Order*, Spinks attributes its underlying theology to William Milligan and his son George, who both draw attention to the nature of Christ's offering as High Priest in their works, a notion which we discussed at length

---

[105] B. D. Spinks, 'The Ascension and Vicarious Humanity of Christ: The Christology and Soteriology Behind the Church of Scotland's Anamnesis and Epiklesis', in *Time and Community*, ed. J. N. Alexander (Washington: The Pastoral Press, 1990), pp. 186–7. On the subject of Maxwell's influence on liturgical development in Scotland, cf. Forrester's 'Worship since 1929', p. 179.

[106] Consistent with this sense of uniting the Church's offering and prayers with those of Christ is the inclusion in the Eucharistic Prayer of the *self-oblation*. The offering of ourselves fittingly takes place after the remembrance (*anamnesis*) of Christ's self-offering.

[107] W. D. Maxwell, 'Reformed', in *Ways of Worship: The Report of a Theological Commission of Faith and Order*, eds P. Edwall, E. Hayman and W. D. Maxwell (London: SCM Press, 1951), pp. 115–16.

in the previous chapter, especially in relation to the link between William Milligan and John McLeod Campbell.

It was the Milligans' views on the nature of Christ's continuous offering which also led them to describe the activity of prayer in participatory terms and to regard intercessory prayer as participation in the intercessions of Christ through the activity of the Spirit. Of particular significance here is the idea that in prayer the Church does not merely participate in the *benefits* of Christ's work – it participates in the *work* itself.

This is a point emphatically made by another nineteenth-century writer – the South African pastor and evangelist, Andrew Murray. In his book *With Christ in the School of Prayer*, Murray describes Christ's life in heaven in terms of an *ever-praying* life which, when it descends and takes possession of us, does not lose its character, but rather in us too constitutes an *ever-praying* life – a life that without ceasing asks and receives from God. Our faith in the intercession of Jesus, therefore,

> ... must not only be that He prays in our stead, when we do not or cannot pray, but that, as Author of our life and faith, He draws us on to pray in unison with Himself. Our prayer must be a work of faith in this sense too, that as we know that Jesus communicates His whole life in us, He also out of that prayerfulness which is His alone breathes into us our praying.[108]

Murray concludes from this that it is in the work of intercession that the atonement has its true power and glory.

While the distinction between the benefits of Christ's work and the work itself is readily grasped in relation to the activity of prayer, it has not been so readily grasped in relation to the Reformed understanding of the sacraments. The *Larger Catechism*, for example, defines a sacrament as 'a holy ordinance instituted by Christ in His Church, to signify, seal and exhibit to those who are within the

---

[108] A. Murray, *With Christ in the School of Prayer* (Westwood: Spire Books, 1965 reprint), pp. 147–8.

covenant of grace, *the benefits of His mediation'*.[109] Interestingly, this phrase is not to be found in Calvin's definition of a sacrament, nor in his exposition on the Lord's Supper. As we have already seen, Calvin expounds the Lord's Supper in terms of a wondrous exchange, through which believers are drawn into union and communion with the risen and ascended Christ, whose ministry is ongoing. Through the Holy Spirit people are united to Christ, and so are taken up through the eternal Spirit into his sacrifice and his eternal intercession before the Father. In sum, Christians are not merely *beneficiaries* of Christ's work – they are *participants* in it.

It appears, therefore, that the reference in the 1940 *Book of Common Order*'s eucharistic liturgy to Christ's eternal sacrifice is suggestive of a doctrine of the ascension that is highly participatory. In this regard it gives fitting liturgical expression to Calvin's Christology and soteriology in a way that Calvin himself never quite accomplished because of his vehement reaction against the notion of propitiatory sacrifice in the Roman Mass, and his consequent failure to develop the idea of the Eucharist as an offering in a proper way. As we noted in Chapter Two, Calvin assumed too much of a disjunction between Christ's unique sacrifice and the Church's sacrifice of praise and thanksgiving.

Spinks argues that Calvin's eucharistic theology, as developed by the Milligans, is not only Reformed, but also catholic, insofar as it is in harmony with both patristic theology and contemporary eucharistic theology, as expressed in the World Council of Churches' document, *Baptism, Eucharist and Ministry* (*BEM*), paragraph 4 of which reads:

> Christ unites the faithful with himself and includes their prayers within his own intercession so that the faithful are transfigured and their prayers accepted. This sacrifice of praise is possible only through Christ, with him and in him.[110]

[109] *Larger Catechism*, Q.162, (*School of Faith*, p. 224) (italics mine).
[110] *Baptism, Eucharist and Ministry* (Geneva: World Council of Churches, 1982), para. 4, p. 14.

However, in using *BEM* as the basis for defining contemporary catholic eucharistic theology, Spinks fails to see that *BEM*'s notions of intercession, eucharistic sacrifice and eternal offering are themselves underdeveloped. The issue here has been articulated very well by the Roman Catholic Church, in its response to the *BEM* document.

Referring to the above excerpt from *BEM*, the Catholic Church begins by affirming the inclusion of the Church's intercessions in the intercession of Christ. However, the response continues, it is not sufficient to describe the continuity of Christ's saving work only in terms of simple intercession. 'The description of the church's activity in the Eucharist as thanksgiving and intercession needs to be filled out by some reference to the self-offering of the participants of the Eucharist, made in union with the eternal "self-offering" of Christ.'[111] For the Catholic Church this means acknowledging that, 'if Christ "offers himself as a means of sacramental communion to the faithful, it is to allow them to associate themselves with his self-offering to the Father." And, insofar as this happens, and the Church shares in Christ's sacrificial offering, the Eucharist is in itself a real sacrifice, the memorial of the sacrifice of Christ on the cross.'[112]

Interestingly, the Roman Catholic view of eucharistic sacrifice and offering, thus articulated, is remarkably close to that of William Milligan and, more recently, T. F. and J. B. Torrance in the Reformed tradition. Mention should also be made of Scottish theologian Donald Baillie, whose posthumous publication of lectures includes a chapter on the subject of eucharistic offering.[113] In that chapter he acknowledges with regret the 'violence' of the Reforming forefathers' reaction against the medieval doctrine and practice of the sacrifice of the Mass, he pays tribute to the work both of William Milligan and of contemporary

---

[111] *Churches Respond to BEM: Official Responses to the 'Baptism, Eucharist and Ministry' Text*, Vol. VI, ed. M. Thurian (Geneva: World Council of Churches, 1988), p. 21.
[112] *Churches Respond to BEM*, p. 22.
[113] D. M. Baillie, *The Theology of the Sacraments* (London: Faber and Faber, 1957), pp. 108–24.

Catholic divines in expounding the logic of the epistle to the Hebrews, and he issues a plea for the Reformed tradition to give greater recognition to the 'connection between that eternal self-offering of Christ in heaven and what we do in the sacrament of holy communion'.[114] When this happens, he asks, then must not the Reformed tradition understand more fully 'that in the sacrament, Christ Himself being truly present, ... unites us by faith with His eternal sacrifice, that we may plead and receive its benefits and offer ourselves in prayer and praise to God?'

Book of Common Order, 1994

The 1940 *Book of Common Order* (*BCO*) has seen two revisions, the first in 1979 and the second in 1994. While the 1979 edition affirmed very strongly the centrality of the Eucharist, it was not greeted with much enthusiasm, perhaps, suggests Duncan Forrester, because it was the fruit of so many compromises and was a rather bland and pedestrian book, composed of sound, but on the whole unexciting, orders of worship.[115] In relation to the eucharistic liturgy itself, with one exception, the 1979 edition varies only slightly from the 1940 liturgy commented upon above and hence, with two exceptions, does not warrant further comment here.

The first exception relates to the decision to return to the use of the Ante-Communion service on those occasions when the sacrament is not being celebrated. This decision

---

[114] Baillie, *Theology of the Sacraments*, p. 117.
[115] Cf. Forrester, 'Worship since 1929', pp. 185–6. Cf. also, a response by Charles Robertson to Stewart Todd's reaction to the 1994 *BCO* (Todd was the convener of the Committee on Public Worship that produced the 1979 *BCO*), in which he points out that 'when the General Assembly in 1987 instructed the Panel on Worship to proceed with the production of a new *Book of Common Order*, it did so on the clear understanding that the new book should follow the pattern and replicate the provision of the 1940 book and not of the 1979 book. Although no motion was passed to that effect, many speakers in the debate expressed their preference for the 1940 model, regretting that the 1979 book was so slender and so single-minded in its provision' (Robertson, 'Common Order', The Church Service Society, *Record* 28 (1995), p. 24).

has the effect of restoring the Eucharist to the centre of Presbyterian worship and continues the recovery of a proper understanding of the priesthood of Christ in worship. This effect, however, is reversed in the 1994 *BCO*, in which the Orders of Worship for ordinary Morning and Evening non-eucharistic services no longer follow the Ante-Communion pattern of the 1979 *BCO*. This can be attributed to the motion of the General Assembly in 1990 which explicitly said that the new *BCO* should not follow the 'norm' of holy communion. This vacillation of treatment reflects both a reaction against the 'High Church' tenor of the 1979 *BCO*, and continued uncertainty in the Church of Scotland about the place of the Eucharist in worship and the significance of the priesthood of Christ in relation to worship and prayer.

The second comment relates to the inclusion within the 1979 *BCO* of the *Sancta Sanctis* (Holy Things to the Holy) and its subsequent omission from the 1994 *BCO*. Commenting on this inconsistency, Tom Davidson Kelly acknowledges the value placed upon the *Sancta Sanctis* by a number of nineteenth-century Scottish liturgists, 'because it indicates the paradox of the holiness of Christ and the unworthiness of those who come to him in their search for holiness, and because it points to the ecumenical dimension of common witness with the Eastern Orthodox churches'.[116] In Reformed terms, this ancient liturgical formula keeps Calvin's doctrine of the wondrous exchange at the heart of the sacrament. It is only as Christ takes our unrighteousness upon himself and clothes us with his righteousness that we are made worthy to partake of his body and blood. The *Sancta Sanctis'* inclusion in the 1979 *BCO* is to be commended; its omission from the 1994 *BCO* is a matter of regret.

The 1994 liturgy has a number of other changes. It offers five Forms and Orders for Holy Communion, three of

---

[116] '*Common Order* (1994): Pioneering Spirit or Reflective Mode', in *To Glorify God*, eds B. Spynks and I. R. Torrance (Grand Rapids: Eerdmans, 1999), p. 61. Cf. also Davidson Kelly's earlier article 'What Happened to the Sancta Sanctis?', The Church Service Society *Record* 27 (1994), pp. 30–2.

which are designed for shorter services and will not be examined here. Of the two remaining Orders, the principal Order 'follows a more or less classical pattern',[117] while the second Order, though very similar in structure, displays a strong Celtic influence in its wording.

Order of worship

Liturgy of the Word
Introit
Call to Worship
Hymn
Scripture Sentences or Seasonal Sentences
Prayers
   Collect for purity
   Confiteor
   Prayer for pardon or Declaration of pardon
   Collect of the day
Gloria in Excelsis (said or sung)
Lections (interspersed with Psalm, sung or read)
Alleluia or Hymn
Prayer for Illumination
Sermon
Ascription
Nicene Creed
Hymn
Intimations
Prayers of Intercession

Liturgy of the Upper Room
Invitation
Offering
The Great Entrance
The Grace
Unveiling of the Elements
Narrative of the Institution
Taking of the Bread and Wine

[117] *Book of Common Order*, 1994, p. xv.

Prayer of Thanksgiving:
   Sursum Corda
   Thanksgiving
   Sanctus
   Benedictus
   Anamnesis
   Epiclesis
   Self-oblation
Lord's Prayer
Fraction
Agnus Dei
Delivery
The Peace
Post-communion prayer
Hymn
Dismissal and Blessing
Recessional

Commentary

The continuity between the 1940 and 1994 liturgies is evident at many points, but it is the points of departure which are of particular interest here because they highlight the ongoing struggle to give consistent liturgical expression to the doctrine of the priesthood of Christ. The first point worth noting in this regard is that the *Confiteor* still omits any reference to the sinful condition into which people are born, thereby ignoring the fact that the priesthood of Christ involves the healing and sanctification of their human nature as well as the forgiveness of individual sins. This weakness is compounded by the closing words of the *Confiteor*, 'We are truly sorry and turn humbly from our sins', which suggest a rather Pelagian view of repentance as something which *we* do by an act of apology. One slight improvement on the 1940 liturgy is the inclusion of a declaration of pardon, although this improvement is undermined by the fact that the declaration is presented merely as an alternative option that sits alongside the main option of closing the *Confiteor* with a prayer *for* pardon. The second (Celtic) Order's *Confiteor* concludes with a prayer in which divine pardon is implied rather than sought or openly declared.

One of the innovations introduced by the 1979 *Book of Common Order* was the provision of alternative positions for the intercessions – the 1940 Order provided only one location, which was in the Liturgy of the Word rather than in the Eucharistic Prayer. The 1994 Order follows the 1940 rather than the 1979 pattern. As we have already discussed, however, this has the effect of detaching the Church's intercessions from that part of the service in which the eternal offering and intercessions of Christ are most explicitly recognised, thereby casting intercessory prayer in a rather Pelagian mould. It is portrayed as something that the Church does rather than something that Christ the High Priest is eternally doing and in which the Church participates through the activity of the Holy Spirit. In the second (Celtic) Order the intercessions are included within the post-communion prayer. This placement conveys the sense of the Church, having first received Christ in bread and wine, being turned towards, and sent into, the world, but it does not really overcome the theological problem thus stated.

The principal Order offers three Thanksgiving or Eucharistic Prayers, each of which is different in character. The Introduction to the *Book of Common Order* says of them: 'The first follows the classical pattern in structure and language; the second is drawn from our own Reformed tradition, from the *Genevan Service Book*; and the third comes from the world Church (English Liturgical Consultation).'[118]

The second prayer shares the same strengths and weaknesses as the *Genevan Service Book* upon which it is based, and which has already been commented upon. It requires no further comment here. The first prayer is more fully developed, exhibiting the accumulated wisdom of those liturgies which precede it, and upon which we have been commenting throughout this chapter. Of particular significance is the inclusion of the reference to the pleading of Christ's eternal sacrifice, which we discussed in relation

[118] *Book of Common Order*, 1994, p. xv.

to the 1940 *Book of Common Order*. In addition, the Eucharistic Prayer gives more weight to the theme of creation, giving thanks for both the creation of the world and the new creation in Christ. The third prayer and the Eucharistic Prayer in the second (Celtic) Order are very similar to this first prayer in terms of structure and emphasis on the priesthood of Christ, even though they do not refer to Christ's 'eternal sacrifice'.

The ongoing priesthood of Christ is strongly affirmed in the post-communion prayer of the principal Order, with the words, 'Glory to God the Son, who lives to plead our cause at the right hand of God', and the sense of participation is conveyed in the passing of the peace, which is accompanied by the words, 'In the joyful presence of our risen Lord, let us give one another the sign of peace.'

Overall, the 1994 liturgy continues the process by which the doctrine of the priesthood of Christ is being given renewed liturgical emphasis in the Church of Scotland, but the theological legacy of the Westminster tradition continues to be felt, thereby generating a subtle theological tension throughout the liturgy. This tension is felt elsewhere in the *Book of Common Order* too. On the one hand, in the baptismal liturgy the parental and congregational vows are placed *after* the baptism rather than *before* it, thereby giving strong liturgical expression to the unconditional, covenantal nature of God's grace. Baptismal vows do not constitute the conditions of God's love; rather, they constitute a freely given response to God's love, a participatory echo of Christ's response, which has already been made on humankind's behalf in his own person and work.

On the other hand, however, this fine liturgical and theological feature of the baptismal liturgy is somewhat undermined by the Declaration which is made by the officiating minister at the point of baptism. The Declaration is taken from the French Reformed Liturgy, which contains a strong reference to the continuing priesthood of Christ as this relates to the continuing life of the infant, but a crucial phrase from that liturgy has been dropped, presumably as a result of a deliberate decision. Where it declares that Christ has risen in newness of life and, for the child, has

ascended to reign at God's right hand, the French
Reformed Liturgy continues, 'and for you he intercedes,
little child, though you do not know it'. In the light of our
preceding discussion of the eternal nature of Christ's
offering, this omission is significant insofar as it highlights
the uncertainty surrounding the ongoing priesthood of
Christ in Reformed thought and liturgical practice, and a
corresponding ambiguity surrounding the doctrine of the
ascension.

Conclusion

Given the strong link identified by Calvin, Knox, Craig,
McLeod Campbell, Milligan and the Scottish Church
Society between prayer and the Eucharist, and the
importance of the priesthood of Christ in establishing this
link, one would hope to see evidence of a strong presence
of the doctrine of the priesthood of Christ in Reformed
eucharistic liturgies. However, one of the legacies of the
tension between the older Reformed tradition and
the Westminster tradition is a rather underdeveloped and
confused doctrine of the priesthood of Christ, especially in
relation to prayer, and this is evident in the liturgies
themselves, which include the following features:

1. The strong christological focus that is evident
   throughout the liturgies of Calvin and Knox is undermined by their decision to begin worship with a
   reading of the Decalogue and a confession of sins. This
   has the effect of directing one's attention to oneself
   rather than to Christ, conveys the impression that law
   precedes gospel, and opens the door to an *ordo salutis*
   defined in contractual rather than covenantal terms.
2. Most often missing from the post-Reformation liturgies
   is an appreciation of the ontological aspect to both sin
   (it is something into which we are born, not merely
   something that we do) and the atonement (Christ does
   not merely forgive individual sins; rather, in the
   hypostatic union and through his vicarious life of

obedience and faith he has healed and sanctified our sinful human condition).

3. Uncertainty as to whether or not assurance of forgiveness is of the essence of faith is reflected in the vacillation between prayers for pardon and declarations of pardon at the conclusion of the Confession of sins.

4. Liturgies since 1940 refer to the act of 'pleading Christ's eternal sacrifice', thereby acknowledging that what Christ as High Priest offered on the cross, and what he offers now in his ascended glory is nothing less than his *life*. In this simple phrase recognition is given both to the atoning significance of the incarnation and the link between the incarnation and the ascension.

5. The Reformed tradition generally displays an inconsistency in following the earliest Reformed practice of Ante-Communion on those occasions when the sacrament is not celebrated. This inconsistency reflects an uncertainty surrounding the place of the Eucharist in worship and the priesthood of Christ that is such an integral part of eucharistic worship.

6. In conjunction with the preceding point, one of the points of greatest confusion in the liturgies concerns the prayer of Intercession. The words of introduction to the prayer frequently portray Christ as the exemplar of prayer whose example the Church follows rather than the ascended High Priest in whose life of intercession the Church participates by the Spirit. This separation of the Church's intercessions from those of Christ is further emphasised by a general confusion as to where the prayer of Intercession is best situated. Often it is placed very early on in the service, prior to the sermon, and well away from the liturgy of the Eucharist where the priesthood of Christ is given its strongest emphasis, thereby casting intercessory prayer in a rather Pelagian mould.

Overall, our liturgical analysis reveals a centuries-long struggle to recover and give consistent liturgical expression to the doctrine of the priesthood of Christ, understood both retrospectively, in his life, death and resurrection, and prospectively, in his ascension. This struggle was proving difficult enough for Calvin and the early Scottish Reformers, whose own doctrinal inconsistencies and ambiguities were being imported into their liturgies, without the damaging effects of Puritan Calvinism and federal theology. For a two-hundred-year period Reformed worship reached an all-time low, theologically and liturgically. While the last hundred and fifty years have seen a liturgical revival and a heartening recovery of the doctrine of the priesthood of Christ in public worship and prayer, the legacy of the Church of Scotland's Calvinistic past continues to be felt.

Postscript

Resolving the Struggle: The Presbyterian Church (USA)

A year prior to the publication of the *Book of Common Order* (1994) a significant liturgical book of public prayer was published on the other side of the Atlantic by the Presbyterian Church (USA): the *Book of Common Worship*.[119] What I propose to do briefly in this postscript is use the *Book of Common Worship* (*BCW*) as a case study to see if the struggle that has been identified in the Church of Scotland's eucharistic tradition to give adequate recognition to the priesthood of Christ is also evident elsewhere in Presbyterian worship.

The 1993 *BCW* is preceded by four earlier versions in 1906, 1932, 1946 and 1970. The 1906 book constituted a significant stage in the reform of Presbyterian worship in North America because it gave official recognition to the value of liturgical orders and texts in shaping worship. It included orders of morning and evening worship and provided for the celebration of holy communion. The 1932 edition was an expanded version of the 1906 book.

---

[119] *Book of Common Worship* (Louisville, Kentucky: Westminster/John Knox Press, 1993).

A comprehensive revision of the *BCW* resulted in a new edition being published in 1946. Horace Allen notes the influence of the Anglican *Book of Common Prayer*, and says that 'the church had, apparently inadvertently, entered a kind of liturgical schizophrenia between a Puritan/Presbyterian Directory, which was no friend of prayer books, and a quasi-Anglican Prayer Book'.[120] The Church attempted to overcome this liturgical schizophrenia by preparing a new Directory, drafted by Robert McAfee Brown and adopted in 1961, which in turn stimulated a need for a new Confession of Faith, the *Confession of 1967*. In this way the Church was expressing its need and desire to move beyond the *Westminster Confession of Faith* and *Directory of Public Worship*.

In 1970 a new *BCW* was produced. More than a mere revision, it introduced some major changes, including a more contemporary style of language, a revised lectionary and, even more importantly, the presentation of the service of word *and* sacrament as the norm for public worship. In 1972 a collection of 333 hymns was added.

Within a few short years the Church set in motion a process for yet another revision. Horace Allen gives five reasons for this, the most notable, at least for our purposes, being the resistance by the clergy to the 'structural shift in the Service for the Lord's Day from a Puritan Morning Prayer and Sermon to a catholic Word and Sacrament rite, wherein the sermon did not conclude the service but rather was followed by acts of credal confession, intercessory prayer, offering and thanksgiving (eucharistic only occasionally)'.[121]

During the course of the development of a new *BCW*, the reunion in 1983 of the Presbyterian Church in the US and the United Presbyterian Church in the USA to form the Presbyterian Church (USA) occurred, which resulted in the preparation of a new *Directory for Worship* (1989). The

---

[120] Cf. H. Allen, 'Book of Common Worship (1993): The Presbyterian Church (USA), "Origins and Anticipations"', in *To Glorify God: Essays on Modern Reformed Liturgy*, eds B. D. Spinks and I. R. Torrance (Edinburgh: T&T Clark, 1999), p. 16.

[121] Allen, 'Book of Common Worship (1993)', p. 19.

1993 *BCW* is consistent with the provisions in the *Directory*. The Preface to the *BCW* says that the book 'honours the Reformed approach to worship, freedom within order, and thus provides a great variety of options and alternatives'.[122] At the same time, it claims to reflect emerging areas of ecumenical convergence in liturgical developments, paying particular tribute to the impact of the work of the World Council of Churches in *Baptism, Eucharist and Ministry* and its related documents. Moreover, it is claimed that, 'as with the sixteenth century Reformers, the forms in this book are rooted in the earliest liturgical traditions that have characterised Christian worship throughout history. In keeping with the directories for worship, this book, like its 1970 predecessor, sets forth the Service for the Lord's Day as a service of Word and Sacrament. The variety of eucharistic prayers in this book should serve the church well as it moves toward recognising the centrality of the Lord's Supper in its worship.'[123]

The *BCW* provides an impressive description of the Service for the Lord's Day, utilising much of the language and liturgical insights of the directories for worship of the Presbyterian Church (USA) and the Cumberland Presbyterian Church,[124] and translating into liturgical form the basic premise that 'joined in worship to the One who is the source of its life, the church is empowered to serve God in the world'.[125] The service is presented in terms of a fourfold movement: Gathering, Word, Eucharist and Sending. The following points are worthy of note:

1. In describing the Confession of sin as a consequence of our claiming the promises of God sealed in baptism,[126] the *BCW* implicitly makes two commendable theological points:
    (a) It is the gospel rather than the law which prompts confession;

---

[122] *BCW* (1993), p. 8.
[123] *BCW* (1993), p. 9.
[124] *BCW* (1993), pp. 34–45.
[125] *BCW* (1993), p. 1.
[126] *BCW* (1993), p. 35.

(b) Because baptism is an ontological act representing the reconstitution of one's personal being and identity, confession involves more than the mere recital of sins. In bearing witness to the new identity bestowed upon the believer in Christ, there must also be an acknowledgement of the former state of sin into which one was born and from which one has been redeemed.

2. The Confession of sin is most appropriately concluded by an Assurance of pardon, not a prayer for pardon.[127]

3. The rationale for intercessory prayer is that the God who created the world, also cares for it, sent Jesus to die for it, and is working to lead it toward the future intended for it. 'To abide in God's love is to share God's concern for the world.'[128] Intercession is thereby cast in participatory terms, a view reinforced by the actual forms of intercessory prayer, some forms of which acknowledge directly the priority of Christ's intercessions, including the following: 'Gracious God, because we are not strong enough to pray as we should, you provide Christ Jesus and the Holy Spirit to intercede for us in power. In this confidence we ask you to accept our prayers.'[129]

4. In introducing the Eucharist, the *BCW* gives primacy to the concept of 'offering':[130] In worship, God presents people with the costly self-offering of Jesus Christ. This is something to which they respond and in which they participate. The Eucharist is the focal point of this response and participation. Participants do more than remember Christ's sacrificial death and resurrection two thousand years ago; they actively encounter the risen Lord through the bread and the wine. As such, it is appropriate that the Eucharist be celebrated as often as on each Lord's Day, but if that is not possible then at least regularly and frequently enough to make it clear that it is integral to worship, and not an addition to it.

[127] *BCW* (1993), p. 35.
[128] *BCW* (1993), p. 40.
[129] *BCW* (1993), p. 103.
[130] *BCW* (1993), pp. 41–2.

The above points indicate that the *BCW* intends to uphold in liturgical practice the priesthood of Christ, in all its various dimensions. It is to the credit of those who put the book together that on the whole this intention is honoured in the liturgies themselves. In this regard, the *BCW* is more consistent than the Church of Scotland's *Book of Common Order*.

Conclusion

The Significance of the Priesthood of Christ for a Trinitarian Conception of Prayer: A Review

In the British Council of Churches' 1989 Report on trinitarian doctrine, attention is drawn to the fact that 'the passages in the New Testament that distinguish most clearly between the Father, the Son and the Holy Spirit are those that deal with prayer'.[1] Indeed, 'it was when he was thinking about prayer', the Report says, 'that Paul also thought about how in their different ways the Son and the Spirit enable us to approach the Father'.[2] Prayer was thereby conceived in explicitly trinitarian terms: The Church prays to the Father, through the Son, in the Spirit. That prayer is something in which we participate rather than initiate is especially clear in Romans 8, which portrays the work of both Son and Spirit in terms of intercession.

Of central importance to this trinitarian and highly participatory view of prayer is the doctrine of the priesthood of Christ. With this in mind, this book has been devoted to the twofold task of (a) considering the nature of Christ's priestly role in relation to prayer; and (b) considering the effects of a distorted doctrine of Christ's priesthood on the Christian view of prayer.

From the outset we recognised that the doctrines of atonement and prayer are interwoven, biblically and theologically. This means that the way in which the priesthood of Christ is conceived in relation to the former will influence directly the way in which it is conceived in relation to the latter. Conversely, the wording of prayers and doxologies in public worship will convey not only a

---

[1] British Council of Churches, *The Forgotten Trinity: The Report of the BCC Study Commission on Trinitarian Doctrine Today* (London: BCC, Inter-Church House, 1989), Vol. 2, p. 5.
[2] British Council of Churches, *Forgotten Trinity*, p. 5.

particular understanding of the atonement but also a
particular doctrine of God.

In Chapter One we saw this in relation to the impact
of Arianism and Apollinarianism on the worshipping life
of the Church. As the Church responded to the threat
posed by the Arian denial of the deity of Christ, liturgical
prayers and doxologies were increasingly directed to the
Son as well as to the Father. While a trinitarian formula
was thus retained in public prayer it had in fact undergone
a subtle yet profound change. For as the Son was
worshipped and adored along with the Father, his mediatorial role in relation to prayer was obscured, and
substitute figures were found, including the medieval
priesthood, the communion of saints and the Virgin Mary.
These changes were compounded by the subtle influences
of Apollinarianism, which, in its denial of the full
humanity of Christ, encouraged the Church to define
Christ's mediatorial role in divine rather than human
categories. He came to be regarded as the mediator of
divine blessings rather than the mediator of prayer and
worship, and as a distant and exalted Christ who was to be
approached and served with fear rather than the One who
continues to be the sinner's Advocate and Representative
before a loving Father. The medieval Latin Mass reflected
these perceptions.

Having identified the significance of the doctrine of the
priesthood of Christ for a properly trinitarian conception
of prayer, and noted, through our discussion of the impact
of Arianism and Apollinarianism, how that conception was
altered in the fourth century, the bulk of this book has been
devoted to a discussion of the Reformed tradition, and in
particular the Scottish Reformed tradition, which has its
roots in the Genevan Reformation. Following Athanasius
and the Cappadocians, John Calvin and those who transplanted his trinitarian doctrine on to Scottish soil,
including John Knox and John Craig, saw that the doctrine
of the priesthood of Christ was essential to a proper understanding of the atonement and, consequently, of worship
and prayer. It was an insight which Calvin's successor in
Geneva, Theodore Beza, and the federal Calvinism of the

seventeenth century, failed to uphold. As the doctrine of double predestination increasingly provided the framework and starting point for theological discourse, thereby generating a doctrine of limited atonement and recasting it in a contractual mould, so Reformed patterns of worship and prayer underwent a process of change.

Whereas Calvin advocated weekly communion, and the theological position which he shared with Knox and Craig may properly be described as 'eucharistic', the Westminster tradition made the Eucharist peripheral to the life of the Church. Moreover, its internal dynamics underwent considerable change, reflecting a changed perception of the nature of the atonement and of the Christian life. That which for Calvin, Knox and Craig had been a 'converting ordinance' for sinners tended to be regarded as a 'confirming ordinance' for the elect. Eucharistic prayers that in Calvin's and Knox's liturgies conveyed the atonement in terms of an act of God done *ab intra*, from within the depths of the human condition, now conveyed it in terms of an act done *ab extra* upon humankind. All the focus went on the 'merits' and 'benefits' of Christ, which he was deemed to have 'purchased' through his sacrificial death for the elect from the Father. Little was made of the hypostatic union and 'wondrous exchange' which lay at the heart of Calvin's doctrine of the sacraments and which were taken up so strongly by Knox and Craig. The incarnation was portrayed as a means to an end rather than something that had atoning significance in itself. Accordingly, the filial and ontological aspects of the atonement, which featured so strongly in Calvin's theological system, were effectively overwhelmed by the judicial and instrumental.

The effects of this diminished view of the atoning significance of the incarnation were far-reaching. Doctrinally it led to a separation of justification and sanctification, the latter being interpreted in terms of a process that is begun after one has been justified by an act of saving faith, rather than a state of being that arises from the Son's assumption of the fallen human condition which all people share and its healing and sanctification in him. Whereas, for Calvin and the early Scottish Reformers, being united with Christ meant being joined to him by the Spirit in his life of faith, obedience, prayer and worship, and believers were therefore exhorted to look away from their own faith, obedience, prayer and worship to what Christ does for them in their place and on their behalf, under federal Calvinism believers were exhorted to look for the fruits of their election and sanctification in themselves. The Christian life, including the activity of prayer, was increasingly cast in an individualistic, introspective and Pelagian mould, a tendency no doubt fuelled by the pragmatism of seventeenth-century Puritanism, its anti-establishment bias, and its preference for 'free' prayer over against set liturgies. Lengthy exhortations to self-examination, the practice of fencing the Table and the public exercise of ecclesiastical discipline along narrowly moralistic lines became prominent features of the Westminster tradition, which dominated the Reformed ecclesiastical landscape in Scotland for the better part of two hundred years.

The second half of the nineteenth century witnessed a growing spirit of reform. Liturgically, this reform was largely attributable to the efforts of the Church Service Society, whose service book, the *Euchologion*, which first appeared in 1867, was warmly received, passed through several editions, and laid a foundation for twentieth-century liturgical developments in the Church of Scotland. Although the aim of the Church Service Society was liturgical rather than doctrinal reform, a number of its leading figures were convinced that these two aspects of reform in fact constituted two sides of the one coin, and that another Society was needed to concentrate on doctrinal issues. Hence the formation of the Scottish Church Society in 1892. The first President of this Society, and the theologian from whom it took its bearings, was William Milligan.

The works of Milligan, and the publications of the Scottish Church Society and its other leading members, are notable for their emphasis upon the vicarious humanity and priesthood of Christ and their determination to see the Eucharist restored to the centre of church life. The two

issues were not unrelated, for in his exploration of
the inner connection between the incarnation and the
ascension Milligan concluded that Christ's offering of
himself (and all humankind in him) to the Father did not
end at Calvary. It is ongoing, eternal. Accordingly, the
Eucharist must be understood as the divinely ordained
means by which the Church continually feeds upon Christ,
is united with him, and worships the Father through him.
The remembrance meal is also an eschatological banquet
hosted by the One into whose living presence people are
lifted by the Spirit and to whose continual self-offering
they are joined. In this emphasis upon being joined to
Christ's continual self-offering, Milligan and the Scottish
Church Society corrected a flaw in Reformed theology and
liturgy that could be traced back to Calvin.

If there was a resonance of thought between the Scottish
Church Society and its first President, William Milligan, so
too was there a resonance of thought between Milligan and
John McLeod Campbell, whose major work, *The Nature of
the Atonement*, published in 1856, laid the theological
groundwork for subsequent reform. Campbell was highly
critical of federal Calvinism's doctrines of conditional
grace and limited atonement, behind which stood a
doctrine of God that, in its subordination of divine mercy
(for the elect) to divine justice (for all people), represented
mercy and love not as necessary attributes of God, but as
arbitrary. For Campbell, the atonement began not with the
willingness of the Son to suffer and die, but with the prior
resolve of the Father not to let the world slide into the
abyss of destruction. The incarnation is the manifestation
of this filial resolve. In it the incarnate Son has penetrated
the depths of human sin and guilt and, through his life,
culminating in his death on the cross, provided an atoning
response of perfect worship, trust, service, and confession
of sins to the Father on behalf of humanity.

And the atonement does not end there. For it is the
intention of the Father not merely to deal *retrospectively*
with sin and guilt, but to bring people to share actively in
Christ's 'sonship'. Hence for McLeod Campbell the
importance of the *prospective* aspect of the atonement, and

his correspondingly strong emphasis upon the Eucharist as the means by which the Church regularly feeds upon Christ and abides with him, and his portrayal of prayer as an essentially redemptive activity in which the Church participates by the Spirit in the intercessions and ministry of Christ in the world. For Campbell, as for Calvin, Knox and Craig, and indeed Athanasius and the Cappadocians, there is an inextricable link between union with Christ, the atonement, faith, the Eucharist and prayer, and integral to them all is the vicarious humanity and priesthood of Christ.

While McLeod Campbell was deposed from parish ministry for his views, the longer-term effect of his teaching should not be underestimated, especially in relation to liturgical revival in the Church of Scotland. Our comparative analysis of eucharistic liturgies has disclosed a growing, if somewhat persistently inconsistent, appreciation of the priesthood of Christ in relation to prayer, worship and the atonement. This inconsistency is less apparent on the other side of the Atlantic, where the Presbyterian Church (USA) has produced a very useful liturgical resource in the 1993 *Book of Common Worship*.

The Three Aspects of Christ's Mediatorial Role in Prayer: Through Christ, in Christ and with Christ

Having concluded that the mediatorial role of Christ in prayer is crucial to a Reformed understanding of prayer, we are in a position to summarise the three aspects of that mediatorial role. First of all, we noted in Chapter One that the prevailing practice of the early Church was to direct prayers to the Father *through* Christ. When the Church prays in this manner it recognises Christ's role as the leader of its worship and the mediator of its prayer, as he 'takes us where we cannot go ourselves, and he does with us what we as sinful humans cannot do'.[3]

In fulfilling this role Christ is not merely the conduit of prayer, for praying to the Father *through* Christ implies

---

[3]   J. Sankey, '"With, through and in" Christ', in *Atonement Today*, p. 100.

praying *in the Mind of Christ*, as one's mind is joined to his in a reconciling, sanctifying union, and one is brought to share in his life of eternal prayer before the Father. The mediatorial role of Christ in prayer must not be understood in a mechanical way. It is utterly bound up with who Christ is in his person, and the reconciling union by which our fallen human condition, which includes our alienated minds, has been healed and sanctified in and through his vicarious life of faith and prayer, both on earth and in heaven. When the Church prays to the Father *through* Christ, it also prays to the Father *in* Christ.

In biblical language this notion of being in union with Christ is best expressed in the Johannine reference to the believer's *abiding in Christ*. As Andrew Murray has argued in his book *Like Christ*, while the notions of abiding in Christ and walking like Christ are inseparably connected, 'the *abiding in* always precedes the *walking like* him'.[4] In relation to prayer, this means that one cannot pray *like* Christ without first *abiding in* Christ. Prayer is not so much a technique that can be imparted and mastered as the outworking of a relationship as Christ lives in his disciples and they in him.

This point is well-illustrated by reference to the Lord's Prayer. While it was given in response to the disciples' request to be taught how to pray, it cannot be detached from who Jesus is as the One in whom the prayer is truly fulfilled, or from the relationship which his disciples have with him. That the early Church understood the Lord's Prayer in this way is evident from the fact that it was used as part of the preparation for baptism and was a constituent part of the celebration of the Lord's Supper. Commenting upon this fact, renowned New Testament scholar Joachim Jeremias writes: 'Whereas nowadays the Lord's Prayer is understood as the common property of all people, it was otherwise in the earliest times. As one of the holy treasures of the Church, the Lord's Prayer, together with the Lord's Supper, was reserved for full members,

---

[4] A. Murray, *Like Christ* (Springdale: Whitaker House, 1981 reprint), p. 10.

and it was not disclosed to those who stood outside. It was a privilege to be able to pray it.'[5]

As the Church prays to the Father *through* Christ and *in* Christ, there is a very strong sense in which it also prays *with* Christ. Behind this aspect of Christ's mediatorial role lie the doctrines of the ascension and Pentecost, and the belief that the ascended Christ continues to lead humankind (indeed, all of creation) in a life of eternal prayer and worship. As people are joined to him through the outpouring of his Spirit, and he lives in them, so his prayers become theirs. He is not only their Intercessor and Advocate, but also their Brother in prayer.

Thus understood, and as stated repeatedly throughout this book, prayer is not something that the Church does. It is something in which it participates. That which has been stated so strongly by McLeod Campbell is eloquently reiterated by Andrew Murray, who says of Christ: 'He will breathe his own life, which is all prayer into us. As he makes us partakers of his righteousness and his life, he will make us partakers of his intercession too.'[6] That is to say, in prayer we participate not only in the benefits of Christ's work, but in the work itself, as what Christ prays ascends to the Father through his people, and what they pray ascends to the Father through him.[7] Prayer is an essentially redemptive activity.

According to this highly participatory view of prayer, one's union with Christ is not a mere state of being. To be joined to Christ through the Spirit – to *abide in him* – is to *pray with him*, to share in his intercessory work, which renders the ministry of intercession one of the highest forms of Christian ministry.[8] In keeping with this insight, in public worship the prayer of Intercession is most appropriately included in the Eucharistic

---

[5] J. Jeremias, *The Lord's Prayer* (Facet Books Biblical Series: Fortress Press, 1964), p. 4.

[6] Murray, *Like Christ*, p. 14.

[7] Murray, *Like Christ*, p. 195.

[8] Cf. A. Murray, *The Ministry of Intercession* (Fearn, Scotland: Christian Focus Publications, 1996 reprint), p. 7, where Murray argues that 'we have far too little conception of the place that intercession, as distinguished from prayer for ourselves, ought to have in the Church and the Christian life'.

Prayer of Thanksgiving, for it is there that the priesthood of Christ in prayer is given its sharpest liturgical focus.

Prayer as a Trinitarian, Eschatological and Ecclesial Event

A trinitarian event

The main conclusion of this book is that the doctrine of the priesthood of Christ is essential to a Christian doctrine of prayer, especially one that is conceived in trinitarian terms. There is today an increasing recognition of the trinitarian shape of prayer and worship across an ecumenical front, as is reflected in the 1989 publication by the British Council of Churches, *The Forgotten Trinity*. In worship the enduring character of trinitarian prayer is expressed doxologically, in the language of involvement or participation (*koinonia*). This is a point well made by Catherine LaCugna,[9] who says that 'Christian liturgy is sometimes called "the cult of the Trinity" (*le culte de la Trinité*), not for dogmatic reasons but because its symbols, structures, and rhythms disclose the basic pattern of the economy. Everything comes from God through Christ, in the Spirit, and everything returns to God through Christ in the Spirit.'[10]

LaCugna is not the first or only modern theologian to stress the link between doxology and a trinitarian doctrine of God. In the early 1980s Jürgen Moltmann published *The Trinity and the Kingdom of God*, in which he declared that 'the starting point for distinguishing between the economic and immanent Trinity is to be found in *doxology*. The assertions of the immanent Trinity about eternal life and the eternal relationships of the triune God in himself have their *Sitz im Leben*, their situation in life, in the praise and worship of the church: Glory be to the Father and to the Son and to the holy Ghost!'[11]

---

[9] Cf. LaCugna, *God for Us*, chapter 9, and LaCugna and K. McDonnell, 'Returning from the Far Country: Theses for a Contemporary Trinitarian Theology', *Scottish Journal of Theology* 41 (1988), pp. 191–215.
[10] LaCugna, *God for Us*, p. 356.
[11] Moltmann, *Trinity and the Kingdom of God*, p. 152.

Following on from this, Moltmann concludes, 'real theology, which means the knowledge of God, finds expression in thanks, praise and adoration. And it is what finds expression in doxology that is the real theology.'[12]

Moltmann's general point here about the importance of doxology is convincing, but one warning note does need to be sounded. We noted in Chapter One that when the post-Nicene Church reworded its doxologies and prayers so that praise was rendered *to* the Son as well as to the Father, then the mediatorial role of Christ in prayer – the sense of praying *through* the Son – was lost. Thus while worship and prayer retained a trinitarian structure its internal dynamic was significantly altered.

The same might be said of Moltmann's social doctrine of the Trinity. Despite its strong emphasis upon both the *perichoresis* – or mutual indwelling – of Father, Son and Spirit, and the differentiation of the three persons of the Trinity, there is little recognition of the vicarious humanity and priesthood of Christ, either in atonement or in prayer. Much is made of the sacrificial love and suffering of Christ, but little is made of the atoning significance of the hypostatic union, which includes the healing and sanctification of our corrupt human nature in the sanctifying humanity of the Saviour. Similarly, much is made of the exaltation of Christ and the messianic future of creation, but little is made of the intercessions and self-offering of Christ, his role as both Mediator and Leader of the creation's worship, and the link between his mediatorial role in heaven and on earth.

The criticisms made of Moltmann on this subject might equally be made of a number of other modern theologians, including two leading English-speaking theologians, Daniel Hardy and David Ford, whose book, *Jubilate: Theology in Praise*, also tends to detach the acts of praise, prayer and worship from their grounding in the vicarious humanity and priesthood of Christ. While it describes praise as a human (and biblical) activity which enhances one's relationship with God and the world, thereby pointing out

---

[12] Moltmann, *Trinity and the Kingdom of God*, p. 152.

the many practical benefits of praising God, it tends to bypass the Reformation (and New Testament) insight that none of us can pray or praise as we ought. Accordingly, Jesus is portrayed as one who in solidarity and mutuality with us 'embodies the ultimate sacrifice of praise to God'[13] and whose life of praise is vindicated through the resurrection,[14] but little mention is made of the praise which he rendered (and continues to render) *in our place and on our behalf.*

By way of contrast, LaCugna's exposition of the Trinity remains faithful to the early Church's liturgical portrayal of the vicarious humanity and mediatorial role of Christ in prayer,[15] and it displays a proper interrelation between Christology and pneumatology, which in turn ensures a highly participatory view of worship and prayer, which she describes in terms of being 'Christ-mediated and Spirit-empowered'.[16]

An eschatological event

Insofar as Christian prayer is integrally related to the doctrine of the ascension, it must be understood within an eschatological framework. Of the importance of eschatology in Christian doctrine, Moltmann, in his pioneering book of 1967, *Theology of Hope*, declared that 'from first to last, and not merely in the epilogue, Christianity is eschatology, is hope, forward looking and forward moving, and therefore also revolutionising and transforming the present. . . . Hence eschatology cannot really be only a part of Christian doctrine. Rather, the eschatological outlook is characteristic of all Christian proclamation, of every Christian existence and of the whole Church.'[17]

---

[13] D. W. Hardy and D. F. Ford, *Jubilate: Theology in Praise* (London: Darton, Longman and Todd, 1984), p. 136.

[14] Hardy and Ford, *Jubilate*, p. 133.

[15] So too does Geoffrey Wainwright's major book *Doxology: The Praise of God in Worship, Doctrine and Life* (London: Epworth, 1980), which contains a useful historical summary of the notion of Christ as both the Object and Mediator of worship (pp. 44–70).

[16] LaCugna, *God for Us*, p. 363.

[17] J. Moltmann, *Theology of Hope: On the Ground and the Implications of a Christian Eschatology*, trans. J. W. Leitch (London: SCM Press, 1967), p. 16.

To the extent that this applies to prayer as to other aspects of the Christian life, the eschatological dimension must not be forgotten. The kingdom of God about which Jesus taught and for which yearning is expressed in the Lord's Prayer ('Thy kingdom come . . .') is an eschatological concept. It expresses a yearning for the future reign of God, already established in the resurrection and ascension of Christ, to invade and transform the present. It anticipates the future in which 'Christ will be all and in all'.[18] Hans Urs von Balthasar suggests that this means 'we do not build the kingdom of God on earth by our own efforts (however assisted by grace); the most we can do, through genuine prayer, is to make as much room as possible, in ourselves and in the world, for the kingdom of God, so that its energies can go to work'.[19] Thus understood, the time between the incarnation and the parousia – the time of the Church – is not a time for passivity but for prayer. Or, as Christopher Cocksworth puts it:

> It is the time for intercession in which God's people pray for the coming of God's will. And as they pray they discover that their groaning and the groaning of the rest of creation is none less than the groaning of the eschatological Spirit who yearns for manifestation of the new creation and so 'intercedes with sighs too deep for words'.[20]

One of the consequences of prayer being defined as an eschatological rather than a mere religious act, is that such a definition presupposes a certain restlessness and dissatisfaction with the way things are here on earth. The yearning for God's reign is accompanied by pessimism toward human potentialities and progress in themselves, for the Church derives its commitment to prayer and its yearning for the kingdom of God, not from political or scientific or

[18] Cf. LaCugna, *God for Us*, pp. 343–4.
[19] H. U. von Balthasar, *Prayer*, trans. G. Harrison (San Francisco: Ignatius Press, 1986), p. 105.
[20] C. Cocksworth, *Holy, Holy, Holy: Worshipping the Trinitarian God* (London: Darton, Longman and Todd, 1997), pp. 35–6.

economic processes, but rather from what Christ has done and continues to do as creation moves toward its ultimate *telos* in him. We might even go so far as to say that, in this regard, prayer should be regarded as a *subversive* activity. That is to say, insofar as it takes its bearings not from the processes of history, but rather from the kingdom of God, it must be regarded as being subversive of the status quo and the tendency to acquiesce either to so-called natural 'orders of creation' or to some kind of historicism or determinism.

The refusal to acquiesce to the status quo has been one of the distinguishing features of liberation theology in recent decades. One of the founders of liberation theology, Gustavo Gutiérrez, has coined the term 'paschal joy' to refer to that joy which is grounded in the gratuitous, suffering love of God, and which is deeply transformative of situations of suffering and death. Paschal joy is an agent of transformation in an unjust world. It constitutes a stubborn refusal to accept things as they currently are, and is therefore subversive of deterministic thinking. As Stephen May describes it, in responding to Gutiérrez, 'Joy overturns the pattern of the world, as in the Magnificat. It is thus deeply subversive and ... threatening to the powers that be. It signifies their overthrow.' [21]

If the Western Church had understood this more fully then it might have been better placed to offer more substantial and consistent resistance to the policy of racial segregation in the Southern United States, the 'cultural Protestantism' of Nazi Germany, the sectarianism of Northern Ireland, the policy of apartheid in South Africa, and the ethnic cleansing in Bosnia, not to mention the prevailing economic ideology of the Western world.

An ecclesial (and eucharistic) event

A trinitarian doctrine of God and theology of prayer compels us to affirm that prayer is an ecclesial rather than

---

[21] S. May, 'Response to Gutiérrez's paper entitled, "Joy in the Midst of Suffering"', in *Christ and Context*, eds H. Regan and A. Torrance, (Edinburgh: T&T Clark, 1993), p. 99.

a private event. Against the Enlightenment tendency to make the individual the measure of prayer,[22] the biblical tradition locates prayer firmly in the activity of the triune God and in the particular ecclesial community instituted by Christ and constituted by the Holy Spirit. The opening word of the Lord's Prayer (*Our* Father . . .) suggests, first, the public nature of Christian prayer and, second, the existence of a particular ecclesial community without, and apart from, which the prayer is rendered nonsensical.

If prayer is acknowledged as a function not merely of individual Christians but of the Church as the body of Christ, then further acknowledgement must be given to the inner connection between prayer and worship, and in particular between prayer and the Eucharist. Ironically, the strongly eucharistic theology of Calvin and Knox, which was discussed in Chapter Two, has been undermined by the Westminster tradition, resulting in a profound failure to appreciate the centrality of the Eucharist in Calvinist ecclesiology. Despite significant efforts to rectify this failure over the last one hundred and fifty years, there is much still to be learned from our earlier Reformed heritage, the ecumenical movement, and in particular the Roman Catholic and the Greek Orthodox Church traditions, for which the Eucharist stands at the centre of the Church's life and being.

In this regard, one theologian who, in recent years, has made a significant contribution to raising ecumenical awareness of the importance of the Eucharist is John Zizioulas, writing from within the Orthodox tradition. In his seminal work, *Being as Communion*, he detects in Greek patristic thought (and in scripture) an inextricable link

---

[22] In his book *Religion Within the Limits of Reason Alone* (trans. T. M. Greene and H. H. Hudson (New York: Hudson and Row, 1960), p. 181), Immanuel Kant argued that prayer is a private observance of religious duty intended to 'establish the morally good in ourselves and to awaken the disposition of goodness in the heart'. Since we cannot know whether God actually listens to prayer or not, we must consider prayer to be a conversation of the self with the self, reminding ourselves of our resolution to be morally worthy persons. Prayer which claims more for itself than this, said Kant, is a 'superstitious illusion' that the performance of a certain act or ritual will bring about certain results.

between the truth of being and the truth of communion, so that the latter is regarded not as distinct from and subsequent to the former but as utterly bound up with the former. Communion is thus defined ontologically. Just as Christ himself does not exist first as truth and then as communion,[23] neither does the Church, for through the Spirit Christ is actively present, not *in abstracto* or as an individual, but in and through a *community*.[24] 'This community', Zizioulas suggests, 'is formed from out of ordinary existence, through a radical conversion from individualism to personhood in baptism. As death and resurrection in Christ, baptism signifies the decisive passing of our existence from the "truth" of individualized being into the truth of personal being.'[25]

If baptism is that event which constitutes a radical conversion from the biological to ecclesial mode of existence, from the 'truth' of individualised being into the truth of personal being, the Eucharist is that gathering in and through which the latter is continually realised and sustained. It is thus claimed to have ontological significance. Zizioulas' views here are well summed up by Paul McPartlan, who says that the Eucharist for Zizioulas 'is not something which takes place within a certain gathering or in the context of communion; rather it is this gathering and communion themselves. Further, the eucharistic gathering is not just something which the Church, having her definition elsewhere, does; it itself is what defines the Church and is where the Church *is* the Church.'[26]

Thus understood, the title of McPartlan's book serves as an apt summary of Zizioulas' position: 'the Eucharist makes the Church'. While this strong eucharistic affirmation might at first seem at odds with the Reformed emphasis upon the preaching of the word, in fact it resonates both with our observation in Chapter Two that

---

[23] J. Zizioulas, *Being as Communion: Studies in Personhood and the Church* (London: Darton, Longman and Todd, 1985), p. 111.
[24] Zizioulas, *Being as Communion*, p. 113.
[25] Zizioulas, *Being as Communion*, p. 113.
[26] P. McPartlan, *The Eucharist Makes the Church: Henri de Lubac and John Zizioulas in Dialogue* (Edinburgh: T&T Clark, 1993), p. 133.

Calvin considered union with Christ as quite unthinkable apart from the sacrament, and with James McEwen's observation, noted in Chapter Five, that for Knox there was no question of waiting for the establishment of an organised church before administering the sacrament. In the Eucharist Christ, through the Spirit, not only brings his once and for all earthly ministry to our remembrance. He also lifts up our hearts and minds in the *Sursum Corda* into his communion with the Father, to make us participants of the new humanity in him.[27] The vicarious humanity and priesthood of Christ, which lie at the heart of a Christian understanding both of the atonement and of prayer, are brought to their sharpest focus in the eucharistic gathering. The triple formula 'through', 'with', 'in' applies equally to the Eucharist as it does to prayer.[28]

Concluding Note

This book began with a critical comment by J. B. Torrance that most worship today 'is in practice unitarian, has no doctrine of the mediator or sole priesthood of Christ, has no proper doctrine of the Holy Spirit, is too often non-sacramental, and can engender weariness'. To the extent that this description is accurate, in relation to both worship and prayer, it constitutes the antithesis of that which we noted in relation to Athanasius and Cyril in the patristic period, Calvin, Knox and Craig in the seventeenth century, and McLeod Campbell and Milligan in the nineteenth century.

It is the basic contention of this book that when the vicarious humanity and mediatorial role of Christ are obscured, then the affirmation that stood at the centre of the Reformation, *sola gratia*, is radically undermined, and prayer and worship (as with other aspects of Christian life and thought) are inevitably recast in a Pelagian mould.

[27] Cf. Torrance, *Worship, Community and the Triune God of Grace*, p. 87.
[28] Cf. H. U. von Balthasar, 'Toward a Theology of Christian Prayer', *Communio* 12 (1985), p. 256.

That is to say, the emphasis falls on what *we must do* to pray, rather than on what *Christ has done* for us, once and for all, in his self-offering to the Father, in his life and death on the cross, on what he is *continuing to do* for us in the presence of the Father and in his mission from the Father to the world, and on *our participation* in this work.[29]

Moreover, when the mediatorial role of Christ in prayer is obscured then, as we saw in relation to both the Church in the fourth century and the Westminster tradition in the seventeenth century, the dynamics of worship tend to change. Thus the Church can uphold the doctrine of the Trinity and the principle of *sola gratia* on a doctrinal level, and yet be unitarian and Pelagian in its worship. The question raised by this book is whether this is precisely the situation in which Church finds itself today. Despite a strong resurgence in trinitarian theology in recent years, is the absence of a proper doctrine of the priesthood of Christ, in relation to both the atonement and prayer, resulting in a gap, or perhaps even a contradiction, between what is being affirmed doctrinally and what is being reflected in Christian worship?

If the Church's worship is unitarian and Pelagian, so too will be the model of prayer that it imparts to its members. One of the most popular yet alarming images of prayer that exists in churches today is that of the telephone. Prayer, we are often told, is about communication with God, and may be likened to a conversation over the telephone. Children are encouraged to chat to God in much the same way as they would chat to a close friend. The emphasis here is on regularity, spontaneity and familiarity. Just as we have to work at our communication with friends, so we are exhorted to work at our communication with God. Books and lessons abound with practical advice on the techniques of a successful prayer life.

This model of prayer is doing considerable harm to the worshipping life of the Church and leading to an impover-ished conception and experience of prayer. The stronger the exhortation to maintain a good line of communication

---

[29] Cf. Torrance, *Worship, Community and the Triune God of Grace*, p. 21.

with God and the greater the emphasis on technique, the greater the sense of guilt and failure when one's prayer life falls short of the ideal, and the more desperate and/or despondent one becomes. Moreover, the stronger the emphasis on spontaneity and familiarity, the more worship is dependent upon the talents and personality of the so-called worship leader,[30] and the more narcissistic, banal and trivial prayer and worship (and music) become. Sadly, one does not have to look far to see proof of this. Too often youth ministry and youth-oriented worship are dependent upon the personal charisma of the youth leader. And the same is increasingly true of the Church at large in relation to its ordained ministers.[31]

This is the case right across the theological spectrum. While one church is exhorting its members to work hard at maintaining their prayer life, a neighbouring church will be exhorting its members to develop their own spirituality. Either way, one comes face to face with a model of the

[30] Where it appears, the title of 'worship leader' should be critiqued, for it suggests a model of worship in which Christ has been displaced from his rightful place. In the Middle Ages it was the priest, now it is the worship leader. Christ's displacement is accentuated by the focus, either implicitly or explicitly, on the leader's personality, charisma and gifts. In this regard, it is noticeable how the leader's casual greeting has replaced the traditional call to worship in many services. It is almost as though the worship leader is the host, welcoming people as he/she would to his/her home. Also interesting to observe is the role of the 'worship team', usually consisting of a music group, whose task it is to open worship with a 'worship time'. This consists of a bracket of worship choruses, interspersed with the leader's exhortations, humorous asides and extempore prayers. A lot of effort goes into creating the right atmosphere. Music has come to assume a kind of priestly role in much worship, insofar as it is regarded almost as the primary vehicle by which people enter the presence of God.

[31] Forty years ago, T. F. Torrance coined the phrase 'Protestant sacerdotalism' to describe the displacement of the humanity of Christ by the humanity of the minister, and the obscuring of the person of Christ by the personality of the minister. 'How frequently', he says, 'the minister's prayers are so crammed with his own personality (with all its boring idiosyncrasies!) that the worshipper cannot get past him in order to worship God in the name of Christ – but is forced to worship God in the name of the minister! . . . And how frequently the whole life of the congregation is so built up on the personality of the minister that when he goes the congregation all but collapses or dwindles away' (*Theology in Reconstruction*, pp. 167–8).

Christian life that is inherently individualistic, unitarian and Pelagian.

To the extent that much prayer today is in practice unitarian, this book maintains the urgency of recovering a trinitarian conception of prayer and worship. To the extent that much prayer today is Pelagian, this book maintains that the human priesthood of Christ is intrinsic to a trinitarian conception of prayer and worship. To the extent that much prayer today is regarded as little more than a means of communicating with God, this book maintains that prayer is essentially a redemptive activity, in and through which the Church participates in the Son's communion with the Father and in his mission to the world. To the extent that much prayer today is described as a Christian duty, this book maintains that prayer, through the Spirit, is essentially an eschatological event. To the extent that much prayer today is believed to be a private and individualistic affair, this book maintains that, first and foremost, prayer is a corporate, ecclesial event. It is eucharistic.

While these conclusions have been reached via a critical examination of the Reformed tradition, especially as it has manifested itself in the Church of Scotland, the conclusions themselves can surely also be seen to be catholic and apostolic.

Select Bibliography

Allmen, J. J. von, *Worship: Its Theology and Practice* (London: Lutterworth Press, 1965)

Arianism After Arius: Essays on the Development of the Fourth Century Trinitarian Conflicts, eds M. R. Barnes and D. H. Williams (Edinburgh: T&T Clark, 1993)

Athanasius: *Select Works and Letters*, in *Nicene and Post-Nicene Fathers* (Second Series, Vol. 4), eds P. Schaff and H. Wace (Massachusetts: Hendrickson Publishers Inc., 1892)

Atonement Today, ed. J. Goldingay (London: SPCK, 1995)

Baillie, D. M., *The Theology of the Sacraments* (London: Faber and Faber, 1957)

Balthasar, H. U. von, *Prayer*, trans. G. Harrison (San Francisco: Ignatius Press, 1986)

— 'Toward a Theology of Christian Prayer', trans. P. Verhalen, *Communio* (1985), pp. 12, 245–57

Baptism, Eucharist and Ministry (Geneva: World Council of Churches, 1982)

Barclay, A., *The Protestant Doctrine of the Lord's Supper: A Study in the Eucharistic Teaching of Luther, Zwingli and Calvin* (Glasgow: Jackson, Wylie and Co., 1927)

Barkley, J. M., *The Worship of the Reformed Church: An Exposition and Critical Analysis of the Eucharistic, Baptismal, and Confirmation Rites in the Scottish, English–Welsh and Irish Liturgies* (London: Lutterworth Press, 1966)

Barth, K., 'The Election of God', in *Church Dogmatics* (Vol. II, Part 2): *The Doctrine of God*, eds G. W. Bromiley and T. F. Torrance, trans. Bromiley, Campbell, Wilson, McNab, Knight and Stewart (Edinburgh: T&T Clark, 1957), pp. 3–506

— 'The Justification of Man', in *Church Dogmatics* (Vol. IV, Part 1): *The Doctrine of Reconciliation*, eds G. W. Bromiley and T. F. Torrance, trans. Bromiley, Campbell, Wilson, McNab, Knight and Stewart (Edinburgh: T&T Clark, 1957), pp. 514–642

— *The Knowledge of God and the Service of God According to the Teaching of the Reformation: Recalling the Scottish*

Confession of 1560, trans. J. L. M. Haire and I. Henderson (London: Hodder and Stoughton, 1938)
— *Prayer and Preaching* (London: SCM Press, 1964)
— 'Very God and Very Man', in *Church Dogmatics* (Vol. II, Part 1): *The Doctrine of the Word of God*, eds G. W. Bromiley and T. F. Torrance, trans. G. T. Thomson and H. Knight (Edinburgh: T&T Clark, 1956), pp. 132–71
Bartlett, J. V., 'Christian Worship as Reflected in Ancient Liturgies', in *Christian Worship: Studies in its History and Meaning*, ed. N. Micklem (Oxford: Clarendon Press, 1936), pp. 83–99
Basil, *Letters and Select Works*, in *Nicene and Post-Nicene Fathers* (Second Series, Vol. 8), eds P. Schaff and H. Wace (Massachusetts: Hendrickson Publishers Inc., 1892)
Bell, M. C., 'Calvin and the Extent of the Atonement', *Evangelical Quarterly* 55 (1983), pp. 115–23
— *Calvin and Scottish Theology: The Doctrine of Assurance* (Edinburgh: Handsel Press, 1985)
— 'Was Calvin a Calvinist?', *Scottish Journal of Theology* 36 (1983), pp. 535–40
Boff, L., *Trinity and Society*, trans. P. Burns (New York: Orbis, 1988)
Book of Common Order (Edinburgh: St Andrew Press, 1979)
The Book of Common Order of the Church of Scotland, commonly known as John Knox's Liturgy, and The Directory for the Public Worship of God, agreed upon by the Assembly of Divines at Westminster, eds G. W. Sprott and T. Leishman (Edinburgh and London: William Blackwood and Sons, 1868)
Book of Common Order of the Church of Scotland (London: Oxford University Press, 1940)
Book of Common Order of the Church of Scotland (Edinburgh: St Andrew Press, 1994)
Brilioth, Y., *Eucharistic Faith and Practice Evangelical and Catholic*, trans. A. G. Hebert (London: SPCK, 1956)
British Council of Churches, *The Forgotten Trinity: The Report of the BCC Study Commission on Trinitarian Doctrine Today*, Vol. 2 (London: BCC, Inter-Church House, 1989)
Bürki, B., 'The Celebration of the Eucharist in *Common Order* (1994) and in the Continental Reformed Liturgies',

in *To Glorify God: Essays on Modern Reformed Liturgy*, eds
B. D. Spinks and I. R. Torrance (Grand Rapids, Michigan:
Eerdmans, 1999), pp. 241–54

Burnet, G.B., *The Holy Communion in the Reformed Church of Scotland, 1560–1960* (Edinburgh and London: Oliver and Boyd, 1960)

Calvin, J., *Commentaries on the Epistle of Paul the Apostle to the Hebrews*, trans. J. Owen (Edinburgh: Calvin Translation Society, 1853)

— *Concerning the Eternal Predestination of God*, Geneva, 1552, trans. J. K. S. Reid (London: James Clarke and Co., 1961)

— *Institutes of the Christian Religion*, Geneva, 1559, ed. J. T. McNeill, trans. F. L. Battles (Philadelphia: Westminster Press, 1960)

Campbell, J. McLeod, *Christ the Bread of Life: An Attempt to Give a Profitable Direction to the Present Occupation of Thought with Romanism*, second edn (London: Macmillan and Co., 1869)

— *Memorials of John McLeod Campbell: Being Selections from his Correspondence*, ed. D. Campbell, Vols 1 and 2 (London: Macmillan and Co., 1877)

— *The Nature of the Atonement*, 1856 (Edinburgh: Handsel Press, 1996)

— *Notes of Sermons by the Rev. J. McL. Campbell*, Vol. 1 (Greenock: R. B. Lusk), 1831

— *Reminiscences and Reflections: Referring to his Early Ministry in the Parish of Row, 1825–31*, ed. D. Campbell (London: Macmillan and Co., 1873)

— *Sermons and Lectures by the Rev. J. McL. Campbell*, Vol. 2 (Greenock: R. B. Lusk, 1832)

The Canons and Decrees of the Council of Trent, trans. T.A. Buckley (London: George Routledge and Co., 1851)

Christ in our Place: The Humanity of God in Christ for the Reconciliation of the World, eds T. A. Hart and D. P. Thimell (Exeter: Paternoster Press, 1989)

The Christian Faith in the Doctrinal Documents of the Catholic Church, fourth edn, eds J. Neuner and J. Dupuis (London: Collins Liturgical Publications, 1982)

Christian Worship: Studies in its History and Meaning, ed. N. Micklem (Oxford: Clarendon Press, 1936)

The Church at Prayer: An Introduction to the Liturgy (Vol. 1): *Principles of the Liturgy*, ed. A. G. Martimort, trans. M. J. O'Connell (London: Geoffrey Chapman, 1987)

Church Service Society, *The Book of Common Order of the Church of Scotland (Commonly known as John Knox's Liturgy)*, ed. G. W. Sprott (Edinburgh and London: William Blackwood and Sons, 1868)

— *Euchologion, a Book of Common Order*, sixth edn (Edinburgh and London: William Blackwood and Sons, 1890)

— *Euchologion, a Book of Common Order*, eighth edn (Edinburgh and London: William Blackwood and Sons, 1905)

Churches Respond to BEM: Official Responses to the 'Baptism, Eucharist and Ministry' Text, Vol. VI, ed. M. Thurian (Geneva: World Council of Churches, 1988)

Clark, F., *Eucharistic Sacrifice and the Reformation*, second edn (Oxford: Basil Blackwell, 1967)

Clarke, F. S., 'Christocentric Developments in the Reformed Doctrine of Predestination', *Churchman* 98.3 (1984), pp. 229–45

Cocksworth, C., 'The Cross, our Worship and our Living', in *Atonement Today*, ed. J. Goldingay (London: SPCK, 1995), pp. 111–27

— *Holy, Holy, Holy: Worshipping the Trinitarian God* (London: Darton, Longman and Todd, 1997)

Collinson, P., *The Elizabethan Puritan Movement* (London: Jonathan Cape, 1967)

Cowan, I. B., *The Scottish Reformation: Church and Society in Sixteenth-century Scotland* (London: Weidenfeld and Nicolson, 1982)

Davidson Kelly, T., 'Common Order (1994): Pioneering Spirit or Reflective Mode?', in *To Glorify God: Essays on Modern Reformed Liturgy*, eds B. D. Spinks and I. R. Torrance (Grand Rapids, Michigan: Eerdmans, 1999), pp. 55–68

Davies, H., *The Worship of the English Puritans* (Westminster: Dacre Press, 1948)

Dix, G., *The Shape of the Liturgy* (Westminster: Dacre Press, 1945)

Donaldson, G., 'Covenant to Revolution', in *Studies in the History of Worship in Scotland*, second edn, eds D. Forrester and D. Murray (Edinburgh: T&T Clark, 1996), pp. 59–72

— *Scottish Church History* (Edinburgh: Scottish Academic Press, 1985)

— *The Scottish Reformation* (Cambridge: Cambridge University Press, 1960)

Dragas, G. D., 'The Eternal Son (An Essay on Christology in the Early Church with Particular Reference to St Athanasius the Great)', in *The Incarnation*, ed. T. F. Torrance (Edinburgh: Handsel Press, 1981), pp. 16–57

— 'St Athanasius on Christ's Sacrifice', in *Sacrifice and Redemption: Durham Essays in Theology*, ed. S. W. Sykes (Cambridge: Cambridge University Press, 1991), pp. 73–100

Duba, A. D., 'The *Book of Common Worship* – the Book of *Common Order*: What Do they Say and what Do they Assume About Christ?', in *To Glorify God: Essays on Modern Reformed Liturgy*, eds B. D. Spinks and I. R. Torrance (Grand Rapids, Michigan: Eerdmans, 1999), pp. 115–42

Eucharistic Worship in Ecumenical Contexts: The Lima Liturgy – and Beyond, eds T. F. Best and D. Heller (Geneva: World Council of Churches, 1998)

Ferguson, S. B., 'The Teaching of the Confession', in *The Westminster Confession in the Church Today*, ed. A. I. C. Heron (Edinburgh: St Andrew Press, 1982), pp. 31–9

Fergusson, D. A. S., 'Predestination: A Scottish Perspective', *Scottish Journal of Theology* 46 (1993), pp. 457–78

Forrester, D., 'Worship since 1929', in *Studies in the History of Worship in Scotland*, second edn, eds D. Forrester and D. Murray (Edinburgh: T&T Clark, 1996), pp. 177–95

Forsyth, P. T., *The Soul of Prayer*, second edn (London: Independent Press, 1949)

— *The Work of Christ* (London: Independent Press, 1938)

Gerhards, A., 'Zu Wem Beten? *Liturgisches Jahrbuch* 32 (1982), pp. 219–30

Gerrish, B. A., *Grace and Gratitude: The Eucharistic Theology of John Calvin* (Edinburgh: T&T Clark, 1993)

— *The Old Protestantism and the New: Essays on the Reformation Heritage* (Edinburgh: T&T Clark, 1982)

Goodloe, J. C., 'John McLeod Campbell: Redeeming the Past by Reproducing the Atonement', *Scottish Journal of Theology* 45 (1992), pp. 185–208

Greene-McCreight, K., 'What's the Story? The Doctrine of God in *Common Order* and in the *Book of Common Worship*', in *To Glorify God: Essays on Modern Reformed Liturgy*, eds B. D. Spinks and I. R. Torrance (Grand Rapids, Michigan: Eerdmans, 1999), pp. 99–114

Grillmeier, A., *Christ in Christian Tradition* (Vol. 1): *From the Apostolic Age to Chalcedon (AD 451)*, second edn, trans. J. Bowden (London: Mowbrays, 1975)

Gunton, C., *The Actuality of Atonement: A Study of Metaphor, Rationality and the Christian Tradition* (Edinburgh: T&T Clark, 1988)

— 'Karl Barth's Doctrine of Election as Part of his Doctrine of God', *Journal of Theological Studies* 25 (1974), pp. 381–92

— *The Promise of Trinitarian Theology* (Edinburgh: T&T Clark, 1991)

Gutiérrez, G., 'Joy in the Midst of Suffering', in *Christ and Context*, eds H. Regan and A. Torrance (Edinburgh: T&T Clark, 1993), pp. 78–91

Hageman, H. G., *Pulpit and Table* (London: SCM Press, 1962)

Hall, B., 'Calvin Against the Calvinists', in *John Calvin*, ed. G. E. Duffield (London: Sutton Courtenay Press, 1966), pp. 19–37

Hanson, R. P. C., *The Search for the Christian Doctrine of God: The Arian Controversy 318– 381* (Edinburgh: T&T Clark, 1988)

Hardy, D. W. and Ford, D. F., *Jubilate: Theology in Praise* (London: Darton, Longman and Todd, 1984)

Hart, T., 'Anselm of Canterbury and John McLeod Campbell: Where Opposites Meet?', *Evangelical Quarterly* 62 (1990), pp. 311–33

— 'Atonement and Worship', *Anvil* 11.3 (1994), pp. 203–14

— 'Humankind in Christ and Christ in Humankind: Salvation as Participation in our Substitute in the Theology of John Calvin', *Scottish Journal of Theology* 42 (1989), pp. 67–84

— 'Irenaeus, Recapitulation and Physical Redemption', in *Christ in our Place: The Humanity of God in Christ for the Reconciliation of the World*, eds T. A. Hart and D. P. Thimell (Exeter: Paternoster Press, 1989), pp. 152–81

— 'Universalism: Two Distinct Types', in *Universalism and the Doctrine of Hell: Papers Presented at the Fourth Edinburgh Conference on Christian Dogmatics, 1991*, ed. N. M. de S. Cameron (Grand Rapids: Baker Book House, 1992), pp. 1–34

Hazlett, I., 'Eucharistic Communion: Impulses and Directions in Martin Bucer's Thought', in *Martin Bucer: Reforming Church and Community*, ed. D. F. Wright (Cambridge: Cambridge University Press, 1994), pp. 72–82

Hazlett, W., 'The Scots Confession, 1560: Context, Complexion, and Critique', *Archiv für Reformationsgeschichte* 78 (1987), pp. 287–320

Helm, P., 'Are they few that Be Saved?', in *Universalism and the Doctrine of Hell: Papers Presented at the Fourth Edinburgh Conference on Christian Dogmatics, 1991*, ed. N. M. de S. Cameron (Grand Rapids: Baker Book House, 1992), pp. 257–81

— *Calvin and the Calvinists* (Edinburgh: Banner of Truth Trust, 1982)

— 'Calvin and the Covenant: Unity and Continuity', *Evangelical Quarterly* 55 (1983), pp. 65–81

— 'Calvin, English Calvinism and the Logic of Doctrinal Development', *Scottish Journal of Theology* 34 (1981), pp. 179–85

— 'The Logic of Limited Atonement', *Scottish Bulletin of Evangelical Theology* 3 (1985), pp. 47–54

— 'Was Calvin a Federalist?', *Reformed Theological Journal* 10 (1994), pp. 47-59

Henderson, G. D., 'The Idea of Covenant in Scotland', *Evangelical Quarterly* 27 (1955), pp. 2–14

— *Scots Confession, 1560, and Negative Confession, 1581* (Church of Scotland Committee on Publications, 1937)

Hendry, G. S., *The Westminster Confession for Today* (London: SCM Press, 1960)

Heron, A., *Table and Tradition: Towards an Ecumenical Understanding of the Eucharist* (Edinburgh: The Handsel Press, 1983)

Hicks, F. C. N., *The Fullness of Sacrifice: An Essay in Reconciliation* (London: Macmillan and Co., 1930)

Holifield, E. B., *The Covenant Sealed: The Development of Puritan Sacramental Theology in Old and New England, 1570–1720* (New Haven and London: Yale University Press, 1974)

Hughes, K. G., 'Holy Communion in the Church of Scotland in the Nineteenth Century', PhD Thesis, University of Glasgow, 1987

Jedin, H., *A History of the Council of Trent*, Vol. 2, trans. E. Graf (Edinburgh: Thomas Nelson and Sons, 1961)

Jeremias, J., *The Lord's Prayer* (Facet Books Biblical Series: Fortress Press, 1964)

Jinkins, M., *A Comparative Study in the Theology of Atonement in Jonathan Edwards and John McLeod Campell: Atonement and the Character of God* (San Francisco: Mellen Research University Press, 1993)

— *Love is of the Essence: An Introduction to the Theology of John McLeod Campbell* (Edinburgh: St Andrew Press, 1993)

— 'Theodore Beza: Continuity and Regression in the Reformed Tradition', *Evangelical Quarterly* 64 (1992), pp. 131–54

John Calvin, ed. G.E. Duffield (London: Sutton Courtenay Press, 1966)

Jungmann, J. A., *The Early Liturgy: To the Time of Gregory the Great*, trans. F.A. Brunner (London: Darton, Longman and Todd, 1959)

— 'Liturgy on the Eve of the Reformation', *Worship* 33 (1959), pp. 505–15

— *Pastoral Liturgy* (London: Challoner Publications, 1962)

— *The Place of Christ in Liturgical Prayer*, second English edn, trans. A. Peeler (London: Geoffrey Chapman, 1989)

— *Public Worship*, trans. C. Howell (London: Challoner Publications, 1957)

Kendall, R. T., *Calvin and English Calvinism to 1649* (Oxford: Oxford University Press, 1979)

Kettler, C. D., 'The Atonement as the Life of God in the Ministry of the Church', in *Incarnational Ministry: The Presence of Christ in Church, Society, and Family*, eds

C. D. Kettler and T. H. Speidell (Colorado Springs: Helmers and Howard, 1990), pp. 58–78

Klauser, T., *A Short History of the Western Liturgy: An Account and Some Reflections*, second edn, trans. J. Halliburton (Oxford: Oxford University Press, 1979)

Klempa, W., 'The Concept of Covenant in Sixteenth- and Seventeenth-Century Continental and British Reformed Theology', in *Major Themes in the Reformed Tradition*, ed. D. K. McKim (Grand Rapids, Michigan: Eerdmans, 1992), pp. 94–107

Knight, G. A. F., *A Christian Theology of the Old Testament* (London: SCM Press, 1959)

Knox, J, *The Works of John Knox*, collected and ed. by D. Laing (Edinburgh: Woodrow Society), Vol. 1, 1846; Vol. 2, 1848; Vol. 3, 1854; Vol. 4, 1855; Vol. 5, 1858; Vol. 6, 1864

Küng, H., *Justification: The Doctrine of Karl Barth and a Catholic Reflection* (London: Burns and Oates, 1964)

LaCugna, C. M., *God for Us: The Trinity and Christian Life* (San Francisco: Harper, 1991)

LaCugna, C. M. and McDonnell, K., 'Returning from the Far Country: Theses for a Contemporary Trinitarian Theology', *Scottish Journal of Theology* 41 (1988), pp. 191–215

Lehne, S., *The New Covenant in Hebrews*, JSNT Supplementary Series 44 (Sheffield: JSOT Press, 1990)

Letham, R., 'Theodore Beza: A Reassessment', *Scottish Journal of Theology* 40 (1987), pp. 25–40

Liturgies of the Western Church, ed. B. Thompson (Philadelphia: Fortress Press, 1980)

McDonnell, K., *John Calvin, the Church, and the Eucharist* (Princeton: Princeton University Press, 1967)

— 'A Trinitarian Theology of the Holy Spirit?', *Theological Studies* 46 (1985), pp. 191–227

McEwen, J. S., *The Faith of John Knox* (London: Lutterworth Press, 1961)

— 'How the Confession Came to be Written', in *The Westminster Confession in the Church Today*, ed. A. I. C. Heron (Edinburgh: St Andrew Press, 1982), pp. 6–16

McGiffert, M., 'Grace and Works: The Rise and Division of Covenant Divinity in Elizabethan Puritanism', *Harvard Theological Review* 75 (1982), pp. 463–502

— 'The Perkinsian Moment of Federal Theology', *Calvin Theological Journal* 29 (1994), pp. 117–48

McGrath, A. E., *Iustitia Dei, A History of the Christian Doctrine of Justification* (Vol. II): *From 1500 to the Present Day* (Cambridge: Cambridge University Press, 1986)

McGuckin, J. A., *St Cyril of Alexandria: The Christological Controversy* (Leiden: E. J. Brill, 1994)

McHugh, J. F., 'The Sacrifice of the Mass at the Council of Trent', in *Sacrifice and Redemption: Durham Essays in Theology*, ed. S. W. Sykes (Cambridge: Cambridge University Press, 1991), pp. 157–81

McKim, L. H., 'Reflections on Liturgy and Worship in the Reformed Tradition', in *Major Themes in the Reformed Tradition*, ed. D. K. McKim (Grand Rapids, Michigan: Eerdmans, 1992), pp. 305–10

Macleod, D., 'Covenant Theology', in *Dictionary of Scottish Church History and Theology*, eds N. M. de S. Cameron, D. F. Wright, D. C. Lochman, D. E. Meek (Downers Grove, Illinois: Intervarsity Press, 1993), pp. 214–18

MacLeod, D. J. 'The Doctrinal Center of the Book of Hebrews', *Bibliotheca Sacra* 146 (1989), pp. 291–300

MacLeod, D. J. 'The Present Work of Christ in Hebrews', *Bibliotheca Sacra* 148 (1991), pp. 184–200

McNeill, J. T., *The History and Character of Calvinism* (New York: Oxford University Press, 1954)

McPartlan, P., *The Eucharist Makes the Church: Henri de Lubac and John Zizioulas in Dialogue* (Edinburgh: T&T Clark, 1993)

MacPherson, J., *The Confession of Faith* (Edinburgh: T&T Clark, 1881)

Major Themes in the Reformed Tradition, ed. D. K. McKim (Grand Rapids, Michigan: Eerdmans, 1992)

Manson, T. W., *Ministry and Priesthood: Christ's and Ours* (London: Epworth Press, 1958)

Martin Bucer: Reforming Church and Community, ed. D. F. Wright (Cambridge: Cambridge University Press, 1994)

Matthews, A. G., 'The Puritans', in *Christian Worship: Studies in its History and Meaning*, ed. N. Micklem (Oxford: Clarendon Press, 1936), pp. 172–88

Maxwell, W. D., *Concerning Worship* (London: Oxford University Press, 1948)

— *A History of Worship in the Church of Scotland* (London: Oxford University Press, 1955)

— *The Liturgical Portions of the Genevan Service Book*, (Westminster: Faith Press, 1931)

— 'Reformed', in *Ways of Worship: The Report of a Theological Commission of Faith and Order*, eds P. Edwall, E. Hayman and W. D. Maxwell (London: SCM Press, 1951), pp. 111–24

— *An Outline of Christian Worship: Its Development and Forms* (London: Oxford University Press, 1936)

Milligan, G., *The Theology of the Epistle to the Hebrews* (Edinburgh: T&T Clark, 1899)

Milligan, W., *The Ascension and Heavenly Priesthood of our Lord* (London: MacMillan and Co., 1892)

— *The Present Position and Duty of the Church of Scotland: Being the Closing Address of the Moderator of the General Assembly of 1882* (Edinburgh: William Blackwood and Sons, 1882)

— *The Resurrection of our Lord* (London: Macmillan and Co., 1890)

— *The Scottish Church Society: Some Account of its Aims* (Edinburgh: J. Gardner Hitt, 1893)

Moloney, R., *The Eucharist* (London: Geoffrey Chapman, 1995)

Moltmann, J., *Theology of Hope: On the Ground and the Implications of a Christian Eschatology*, trans. J. W. Leitch (London: SCM Press, 1967)

— *The Trinity and the Kingdom of God*, trans. M. Kohl (London: SCM Press, 1981)

Muller, R. A., 'Calvin and the "Calvinists": Assessing Continuities and Discontinuities Between the Reformation and Orthodoxy' (Part 1), *Calvin Theological Journal* 30 (1995), pp. 345–75

— 'Calvin and the "Calvinists": Assessing Continuities and Discontinuities Between the Reformation and Orthodoxy' (Part 2), *Calvin Theological Journal* 31 (1996), pp. 125–60

— *Christ and the Decree: Christology and Predestination in Reformed Theology from Calvin to Perkins* (Grand Rapids: Baker Book House, 1986)

Murray, A., *The Holiest of All: An Exposition of the Epistle to the Hebrews* (Springdale: Whitaker House, 1996 reprint)
— *Like Christ* (Springdale: Whitaker House, 1981 reprint)
— *The Lord's Table: A Help to the Right Observance of the Holy Supper* (London: James Nisbet and Co. Ltd, 1897)
— *The Ministry of Intercession* (Fearn, Scotland: Christian Focus Publications, 1996 reprint)
— *With Christ in the School of Prayer* (Westwood: Spire Books, 1965 reprint)
Murray, D. M., 'Disruption to Union', in *Studies in the History of Worship in Scotland*, second edn, eds D. Forrester and D. Murray (Edinburgh: T&T Clark, 1996), pp. 87–105
— *Freedom to Reform: The 'Articles Declaratory' of the Church of Scotland 1921* (Edinburgh: T&T Clark, 1993)
— 'The Scottish Church Society, 1892–1914: A Study of the High Church Movement in the Church of Scotland', PhD Thesis, Cambridge University, 1975
Niesel, W., *Reformed Symbolics: A Comparison of Catholicism, Orthodoxy, and Protestantism*, trans. D. Lewis (Edinburgh: Oliver and Boyd, 1962)
— *The Theology of Calvin*, trans. H. Knight (London: Lutterworth Press, 1956)
Nuttall, G. F., *The Holy Spirit in Puritan Faith and Experience* (Oxford: Blackwell, 1946)
Paul, R. S., *The Atonement and the Sacraments: The Relation of the Atonement to the Sacraments of Baptism and the Lord's Supper* (London: Hodder and Stoughton, 1961)
Perry, W., *The Scottish Liturgy: Its Value and History* (London: Mowbray and Co., n.d.)
Pettersen, A., *Athanasius* (London: Geoffrey Chapman, 1995)
— 'The Courage of Christ in the Theology of Athanasius', *Scottish Journal of Theology* 40 (1987), pp. 363–77
— 'Did Athanasius Deny Christ's Fear?', *Scottish Journal of Theology* 39 (1986), pp. 327–40
Prayers for Divine Service, second edn, issued by the Committee on Aids to Devotion by authority of the General Assembly of the Church of Scotland (Edinburgh and London: William Blackwood and Sons, 1929)

Prayers of the Eucharist: Early and Reformed, trans. and ed. R. C. D. Jasper and G. J. Cuming (London: Collins, 1975)

Quasten, J., *Patrology* (Vol. III): *The Golden Age of Greek Patristic Literature from the Council of Nicaea to the Council of Chalcedon* (Antwerp: Spectrum Publishers, 1960)

Reid, J. K. S., 'The Office of Christ in Predestination', *Scottish Journal of Theology* 1 (1948), pp. 5–19, 166–83

Sacrifice and Redemption: Durham Essays in Theology, ed. S. W. Sykes (Cambridge: Cambridge University Press, 1991)

Sankey, J., '"With, through, and in" Christ: A Eucharistic Approach to Atonement', in *Atonement Today*, ed. J. Goldingay (London: SPCK, 1995), pp. 93–110

The Scottish Book of Common Prayer (Edinburgh: Cambridge University Press, 1929)

The Scottish Church Society, *The Catholic Faith*, Occasional Papers III (Edinburgh: Andrew Elliot, 1926)

— *The Common Cup in the Sacrament of Holy Communion: A Statement and Appeal*, Occasional Papers II (Edinburgh: Andrew Elliot, 1926)

— *Conferences, First Series* (Edinburgh: J. Gardner Hitt, 1894)

— *Conferences, Second Series*, Vols 1 and 2 (Edinburgh: J. Gardner Hitt, 1895)

— *The Cup of Blessing* (Coatbridge: Alex Pettigrew Ltd, 1931)

— *Its Work, 1892–1925, and its Claims*, Occasional Papers I (Edinburgh: Andrew Elliot, 1925)

— *Presbyterian Orders*, Occasional Papers IV (Edinburgh: Andrew Elliot, 1926)

Sellers, R. V., *Two Ancient Christologies: A Study in the Christological Thought of the Schools of Alexandria and Antioch in the Early History of Christian Doctrine* (London: SPCK, 1954)

Simon, Archbishop of Ryazan and Kasimov, 'The Trinity and Prayer', in *Theological Dialogue Between Orthodox and Reformed Churches*, Vol. 2, ed. T. F. Torrance (Edinburgh: Scottish Academic Press, 1993), pp. 193–210

Smail, T., 'Can one Man Die for the People?', in *Atonement Today*, ed. J. Goldingay (London: SPCK, 1995), pp. 73–92

— *The Forgotten Father* (London: Hodder and Stoughton, 1980)

— *The Giving Gift: The Holy Spirit in Person* (London: Hodder and Stoughton, 1988)

Spijker, W. van't, 'Bucer's Influence on Calvin: Church and Community', in *Martin Bucer: Reforming Church and Community*, ed. D. F. Wright (Cambridge: Cambridge University Press, 1994), pp. 32–44

Spinks, B. D., 'The Ascension and Vicarious Humanity of Christ: The Christology and Soteriology Behind the Church of Scotland's Anamnesis and Epiklesis', in *Time and Community*, ed. J. N. Alexander (Washington: The Pastoral Press, 1990), pp. 185–201

Sprott, G. W., *The Worship and Offices of the Church of Scotland* (Edinburgh and London: William Blackwood and Sons, 1882)

Stephens, W. P., *The Holy Spirit in the Theology of Martin Bucer* (Cambridge: Cambridge University Press, 1970)

— *The Theology of Huldrych Zwingli* (Oxford: Clarendon Press, 1986)

Stevenson, K., *Eucharist and Offering* (New York: Pueblo Publishing Co., 1986)

Studies in the History of Worship in Scotland, second edn, eds D. Forrester and D. Murray (Edinburgh: T&T Clark, 1996)

The Study of Liturgy, revised edn, eds C. Jones, G. Wainwright, E. Yarnold and P. Bradshaw (London: SPCK, 1978)

Theological Dialogue Between Orthodox and Reformed Churches, Vol. 2, ed. T. F. Torrance (Edinburgh: Scottish Academic Press, 1993)

Thimell, D. P., 'Christ in our Place in the Theology of John McLeod Campbell', in *Christ in our Place: The Humanity of God in Christ for the Reconciliation of the World*, eds T. A. Hart and D. P. Thimell (Exeter: Paternoster Press, 1989), pp. 182–206

Thompson, J., *Modern Trinitarian Perspectives* (Oxford: Oxford University Press, 1994)

Time and Community, ed. J. N. Alexander (Washington: The Pastoral Press, 1990)

To Glorify God: Essays on Modern Reformed Liturgy, eds B. D. Spinks and I. R. Torrance (Grand Rapids, Michigan: Eerdmans, 1999)

Toon, P., *Justification and Sanctification* (London: Marshall, Morgan and Scott, 1983)

Torrance, I., 'Patrick Hamilton and John Knox: A Study in the Doctrine of Justification by Grace', *Archiv für Reformationsgeschichte* 65 (1974), pp. 171–84

Torrance, J. B., 'Calvin and Puritanism in England and Scotland – Some Basic Concepts in the Development of "Federal Theology"', in *Calvinus Reformator: His Contribution to Theology, Church and Society* (Potchefstroom: Potchefstroom University for Christian Higher Education, 1982), pp. 264–86

— 'The Concept of Federal Theology – Was Calvin a Federal Theologian?', in *Calvinus Sacrae Scripturae Professor (Calvin as Confessor of Holy Scripture)*, ed. W. H. Neuser (Grand Rapids, Michigan: Eerdmans, 1994), pp. 15–40

— 'The Contribution of McLeod Campbell to Scottish Theology', *Scottish Journal of Theology* 26 (1973), pp. 295–310

— 'Covenant or Contract? A Study of the Theological Background of Worship in Seventeenth-Century Scotland', *Scottish Journal of Theology* 23 (1970), pp. 51–76

— 'The Incarnation and "Limited Atonement"', *Evangelical Quarterly* 55 (1983), pp. 83–94

— 'Interpreting the Word by the Light of Christ or the Light of Nature? Calvin, Calvinism, and Barth', in *Calviniana: Ideas and Influence of Jean Calvin* (Sixteenth- Century Essays and Studies, Vol. 10), ed. R. V. Schnucker (Missouri: Sixteenth-Century Journal Publishers, 1988), pp. 255–67

— 'Introduction' to John McLeod Campbell's *The Nature of the Atonement* (Edinburgh: Handsel Press, 1996), pp. 1–16

— 'The Ministry of Reconciliation Today: The Realism of Grace', in *Incarnational Ministry: The Presence of Christ in Church, Society, and Family*, eds C. D. Kettler and T. H. Speidell (Colorado Springs: Helmers and Howard, 1990), pp. 130–9

— 'The Place of Jesus Christ in Worship', in *Theological Foundations for Ministry: Selected Readings for a Theology of the Church in Ministry*, ed. R. S. Anderson (Grand Rapids, Michigan: Eerdmans, 1979), pp. 348–69

316 PRAYER AND THE PRIESTHOOD OF CHRIST

— *Prayer and the Triune God of Grace* (Set of four tapes, 1997)
— 'The Priesthood of Jesus', in *Essays in Christology for Karl Barth*, ed. T. H. L. Parker (London: Lutterworth Press, 1956), pp. 153–73
— 'Strengths and Weaknesses of the Westminster Theology', in *The Westminster Confession in the Church Today*, ed. A. I. C. Heron (Edinburgh: St Andrew Press, 1982), pp. 40–53
— 'The Vicarious Humanity of Christ', in *The Incarnation*, ed. T. F. Torrance (Edinburgh: Handsel Press, 1981), pp. 127–47
— 'The Vicarious Humanity and Priesthood of Christ in the Theology of John Calvin', in *Calvinus Ecclesiae Doctor*, ed. W. H. Neuser, (Kampen, Netherlands: Uitgevers-maatschappij J. H. Koh, n.d.), pp. 69–84
— *Worship, Community and the Triune God of Grace* (Downers Grove, Illinois: InterVarsity Press, 1996)
Torrance, T. F., 'The Atonement. The Singularity of Christ and the Finality of the Cross: The Atonement and the Moral Order', in *Universalism and the Doctrine of Hell: Papers Presented at the Fourth Edinburgh Conference on Christian Dogmatics, 1991*, ed. N. M. de S. Cameron (Grand Rapids: Baker Book House, 1992), pp. 225–6
— 'The Atoning Obedience of Christ', *Moravian Theological Seminary Bulletin* (Fall 1959), pp. 65–81
— 'The Biblical Conception of "Faith"' *Expository Times* 68, (1957), pp. 221–2
— *Calvin's Doctrine of Man* (London: Lutterworth Press, 1949)
— *Conflict and Agreement in the Church*, Vol. 1: *Order and Disorder* (London: Lutterworth Press, 1959), Vol. 2: *The Ministry and the Sacraments of the Gospel* (London: Lutterworth Press, 1960
— 'The Distinctive Character of the Reformed Tradition', in *Incarnational Ministry: The Presence of Christ in Church, Society, and Family*, eds C. D. Kettler and T. H. Speidell (Colorado Springs: Helmers and Howard, 1990), pp. 2–15
— 'Eschatology and the Eucharist', in *Intercommunion: The Report of the Theological Commission Appointed by the*

Continuation Committee of the World Conference on Faith and Order, Together with a Selection from the Material Presented to the Commission, eds D. Baillie and J. Marsh (London: SCM Press, 1952), pp. 303–50

— *The Hermeneutics of John Calvin* (Edinburgh: Scottish Academic Press, 1988)

— *Karl Barth: Biblical and Evangelical Theologian* (Edinburgh: T&T Clark, 1990)

— 'Legal and Evangelical Priests: the Holy Ministry as Reflected in Calvin's Prayers', unpublished notes.

— *The Mediation of Christ* (Exeter: Paternoster Press, 1983)

— 'One Aspect of the Biblical Conception of Faith', *Expository Times* 68 (1957), pp. 111–14

— 'The Place of the Humanity of Christ in the Sacramental Life of the Church', *Church Service Society Annual* 26 (1956), pp. 3–10

— 'Predestination in Christ', *Evangelical Quarterly* 13 (1941), pp. 108–41

— 'Review of *Concerning the Eternal Predestination of God*' by John Calvin, translated with an introduction by J. K. S. Reid (London: James Clarke and Co., 1961), *Scottish Journal of Theology* 15 (1962), pp. 108–10

— 'The Roman Doctrine of Grace from the Point of View of Reformed Theology', *Eastern Churches' Quarterly* 16 (1964), pp. 290–312

— *Royal Priesthood: A Theology of Ordained Ministry*, second edn (Edinburgh: T&T Clark, 1993)

— *The School of Faith: The Catechisms of the Reformed Church* (London: James Clarke and Co., 1959)

— *Scottish Theology: From John Knox to John McLeod Campbell* (Edinburgh: T&T Clark, 1996)

— *Space, Time and Incarnation* (Oxford: Oxford University Press, 1969)

— *Space, Time and Resurrection* (Edinburgh: Handsel Press, 1976)

— *Theology in Reconciliation: Essays Towards Evangelical and Catholic Unity in East and West* (Grand Rapids, Michigan: Eerdmans, 1975)

— *Theology in Reconstruction* (London: SCM Press, 1965)

— *The Trinitarian Faith* (Edinburgh: T&T Clark, 1988)

— 'Universalism or Election?', *Scottish Journal of Theology* 2 (1949), pp. 310–18

Trinity, Incarnation, and Atonement: Philosophical and Theological Essays, eds R. J. Feenstra and C. Plantinga, Jr (Notre Dame, Indiana: University of Notre Dame Press, 1989)

Tripp, D. H., 'Protestantism and the Eucharist', in *The Study of Liturgy*, revised edn, eds C. Jones, G. Wainwright, E. Yarnold and P. Bradshaw (London: SPCK, 1978), pp. 294–308

Tuttle, G. M., *So Rich a Soil: John McLeod Campbell on Christian Atonement* (Edinburgh: Handsel Press, 1986)

Twombly, C. C., 'The Nature of Christ's Humanity: A Study in Athanasius', *Patristic and Byzantine Review* 8.3 (1989), pp. 227–41

Underhill, E., *Worship* (London: Nisbet and Co., 1937)

Van Dyk, L., *The Desire of Divine Love: John McLeod Campbell's Doctrine of the Atonement* (New York: Peter Lang Publishing, 1995)

Wainwright, G., *Doxology: The Praise of God in Worship, Doctrine and Life* (London: Epworth Press, 1980)

— *Eucharist and Eschatology* (London: Epworth Press, 1971)

— *For our Salvation: Two Approaches to the Work of Christ* (Grand Rapids, Michigan: Eerdmans, 1997)

— *Worship with One Accord: Where Liturgy and Ecumenism Embrace* (New York and Oxford: Oxford University Press, 1997)

Wakefield, G. S., *Puritan Devotion: Its Place in the Development of Christian Piety* (London: Epworth Press, 1957)

Wallace, R. S., *The Atoning Death of Christ* (London: Marshall, Morgan and Scott, 1981)

— *Calvin, Geneva and the Reformation* (Edinburgh: Scottish Academic Press, 1988)

— *Calvin's Doctrine of the Christian Life* (London: Oliver and Boyd, 1959)

Wallis, I. G., *The Faith of Jesus Christ in Early Christian Traditions* (Cambridge: Cambridge University Press, 1995)

— 'Jesus, Human Being and the Praxis of Intercession', *Scottish Journal of Theology* 48 (1995), pp. 225–51

Wand, J. W. C., *The Four Great Heresies* (London: Mowbray, 1955)

Watson, D. S., 'In Union with Christ: Calvin', in *Open to God: Discovering New Ways to Pray*, ed. R. Pryor (Melbourne: Uniting Church Press, 1991), pp. 102–7

Ways of Worship: The Report of a Theological Commission of Faith and Order, eds P. Edwall, E. Hayman and W. D. Maxwell (London: SCM Press, 1951)

Weber, O., *Foundations of Dogmatics*, trans. D.L. Guder (Michigan: Eerdmans, Vol. 1 (1981), Vol. 2 (1983))

Weir, D. A., *The Origins of the Federal Theology in Sixteenth-Century Reformation Thought* (Oxford: Clarendon Press, 1990)

Wendel, F., *Calvin: The Origins and Development of his Religious Thought*, trans. P. Mairet (New York: Harper and Row, 1963)

The Westminster Confession in the Church Today, ed. A. I. C. Heron (Edinburgh: St Andrew Press, 1982)

Widdicombe, P., 'Attitudes to Arius in the Arian Controversy', in *Arianism After Arius: Essays on the Development of the Fourth Century Trinitarian Conflicts*, eds M. R. Barnes and D. H. Williams (Edinburgh: T&T Clark, 1993), pp. 31–43

Wiles, M., *Archetypal Heresy: Arianism through the Centuries* (Oxford: Clarendon Press, 1996)

— *The Making of Christian Doctrine: A Study in the Principles of Early Doctrinal Development* (Cambridge: Cambridge University Press, 1967)

— 'The Nature of the Early Debate about Christ's Human Soul', *Journal of Ecclesiastical History* 16 (1965), pp. 139–51

Williams, R., *Arius: Heresy and Tradition* (London: Darton, Longman and Todd, 1987)

Wolterstorff, N., 'The Reformed Liturgy', in *Major Themes in the Reformed Tradition*, ed. D. K. McKim (Grand Rapids, Michigan: Eerdmans, 1992), pp. 273–304

The Work of William Perkins, ed. I. Breward (Abingdon, Berks: Sutton Courtenay Press, 1970)

Wotherspoon, H. J., *Religious Values in the Sacraments* (Edinburgh: T&T Clark, 1928)

Wotherspoon, H. J. and Kirkpatrick, J. M., *A Manual of*

320   PRAYER AND THE PRIESTHOOD OF CHRIST

Church Doctrine According to the Church of Scotland,
revised and enlarged by T. F. Torrance and R. S. Wright
(London: Oxford University Press, 1960)
Yancey, H. L., 'The Development of the Theology of
William Milligan (1821–1893)', PhD Thesis, University of
Edinburgh, 1970
Zizioulas, J., *Being as Communion: Studies in Personhood and
the Church* (London: Darton, Longman and Todd, 1985)

Index of Names

Twombly, Charles C. 26 n32, 32,
34, 42

United Church of Canada 263
United Free Church of Scotland
253, 262
United Presbyterian Church in the
USA 276
United Presbyterian Devotional
Service Association 253 n87
Ursinus, Zacharias 149 n36,
151 n40

Valentinus 39
Van Dyk, Leanne 192 n12, 207
Vaughan, D. J. 206
Voisin, G. 28

Wainwright, Geoffrey 291 n15
Wakefield, Gordon S. 183, 252 n83
Wallis, Ian G. 39, 45–6

Watson, Duncan S. 83
Weber, Otto 76 n8, 77
Weir, David A. 91 n61, 142, 149
n36, 150 n37
Wendel, F. 92–3, 96
Wiles, Maurice 15–17, 26–8, 32–3,
40–1, 44
Wolterstorff, Nicholas 62–4,
87 n50
World Council of Churches 265,
277
World Council of Churches
Theological Commission of
Faith and Order 263
Wotherspoon, Henry J. 210

Yancey, Hogan L. 211 n80, 218

Zizioulas, John 1, 294–5
Zwingli 142, 236–7, 242